FROM SCIENCE TO ACTION? 100 YEARS LATER – ALCOHOL POLICIES REVISITED

From Science to Action? 100 Years Later – Alcohol Policies Revisited

Edited by

Richard Müller

Swiss Institute for the Prevention of Alcohol and Other Drug Problems, Lausanne, Switzerland

and

Harald Klingemann

University of Applied Sciences, School of Social Work, Bern, Switzerland

KLUWER ACADEMIC PUBLISHERS
DORDRECHT / BOSTON / LONDON

A C.I.P. Catalogue record for this book is available from the Library of Congress.

ISBN 1-4020-1801-0

Published by Kluwer Academic Publishers,
P.O. Box 17, 3300 AA Dordrecht, The Netherlands.

Sold and distributed in North, Central and South America
by Kluwer Academic Publishers,
101 Philip Drive, Norwell, MA 02061, U.S.A.

In all other countries, sold and distributed
by Kluwer Academic Publishers,
P.O. Box 322, 3300 AH Dordrecht, The Netherlands.

Printed on acid-free paper

Printed in the Netherlands.

Generous support and sponsorship has been assured by a number of national as well as international agencies, societies and public authorities:

- The Regional Office for Europe of the World Health Organization
- The Kettil Bruun Society for Social and Epidemiological Research on Alcohol
- IVO (Instituut voor Onderzoek naar Leefwijzen & Verslaving)
- Addiction Research Institute, Rotterdam
- The Swiss Federal Office of Public Health
- The Swiss Alcohol Board
- The Swiss National Science Foundation
- The Swiss Academy of Medical Sciences
- The Swiss Foundation for Alcohol Research

TABLE OF CONTENTS

ETHICS AND POLITICS OF POLICIES

100 YEARS SWISS ALCOHOL POLICY

R. MÜLLER

INTRODUCTION

100 Years Later – Alcohol Policies Revisited

Alcohol has been central to social, religious and personal use throughout history. Alcohol drinking goes back almost as far as the human race does. A hundred years, therefore, may be seen as only a flash. The past century, however, has witnessed a fundamental change in dealing with alcohol problems. Hence, to give an overview of a hundred years of alcohol policies is a rather ambitious task and the contributions to this book shed only some light on the ways in which alcohol policy issues have changed in this period.

Alcohol control peaked in the politics of prohibition in many countries in the first half of the 20th century, and has decreased in the last 50 years in Europe and North America. Alcohol control measures directed at alcohol availability and supply have lost ground, mainly, it is thought, because of the orientation towards a free market and the growth of consumerism. Many control measures concerned with production, import, export and wholesale monopolies ended in new, liberal regulations on licensing of retail sale outlets and were finally abolished. Every applicant fulfilling some basic requirements could obtain a licence. Consumers are no longer willing to be guided by governments. Restrictions of the days and hours of retail sale of alcoholic beverages were increasingly criticized, therefore, and have been abolished. The legal-age limits for buying alcoholic beverages have, however, been retained and even been made stricter in recent years. At the same time, alcohol policy has shifted gradually from control of supply to reduction of demand. Numerous alcohol-education programmes were developed and implemented in many parts of the world. It has to be admitted, however, that prevention and education programmes have proven less than effective. One lesson of alcohol policy over the last 50 years appears clear, therefore: the more restrictive countries still show lower alcohol consumption and lower rates of alcohol problems than the less restrictive.

Through the lens of economic theory, the effectiveness of any control system depends upon the extent to which the control system is empowered to interrupt the mutual stimulation of supply and demand. With the liberalization of the markets during the last 30 years this power has decreased remarkably. An exception to the liberal trend is the harsher alcohol-control measures directed nowadays at drunken driving. Many countries have adopted lower limits of blood alcohol concentration (BAC), reflecting growing concern about traffic accidents but also the development of technical devices that can measure BAC quickly and reliably.

R. Müller and H. Klingemann (eds.),
From Science to Action? 100 Years Later - Alcohol Policies Revisited, 1–3.

As the years have passed, with the alcohol industry steadily whittling away the powers initially legislated for the licensing agencies, the public has gradually come to the view that alcohol control measures are mere revenue-collecting devices, devoid of any public health objective. The practice of directing alcohol-tax revenues to a general fund has the disadvantage of creating a conflict of interest between revenue generation and the public-health purpose of alcohol control. The alcohol industry exploits this conflict of interest by mobilizing friendly constituencies to weaken the legislative shackles in order to allow more sales and increase government revenue, and ultimately to maximize its own profits.

The most striking points of concern about alcohol policy today are that the production of alcoholic beverages and the trade are increasingly in the hands of multinational corporations that operate worldwide, and that beer, wine and spirits are considered as common goods, irrespective of their intoxicating and addictive properties. Marketing strategies on a global level will help to embed the industrial beverage products in the daily life of the global population. An alcohol industry thus creates new markets in developing countries. At the same time "beverage designers" create new products, such as Alcopops, for special target groups (youth, women). For every lifestyle the appropriate drink is produced and promoted on the market. The prevention of alcohol-related problems has to be on the top of these global developments. The change and the meaning of drinking patterns have to be understood in order to prevent negative consequences of alcohol consumption, Obviously, innovative approaches are most needed in that direction.

A new harm-reduction approach – inspired by the prevention of illicit-drug use – has recently been adapted to alcohol problems. The basic idea is to minimize alcohol-related problems without reducing the individual or collective amount of drinking. Thus the "world of problematic drinking and drunkenness" would be safer. Night-bus systems or pick-up services for drunk drivers, and unbreakable glasses and conflict management for bar brawls, are examples of this harm-reduction approach to alcohol problems. In a globalized world of alcohol marketing with minimal state intervention, this form of alcohol prevention without reduction in general consumption is an additional option.

Increasingly, the beverage-alcohol industry aims to create an image of a socially concerned and responsible business and engages in efforts to reduce alcohol-related problems. For the producers and distributors, education is the key to tackling alcohol abuse; the message is the demand for "responsible drinking", especially at young ages. The industry, therefore, implements and funds programmes, including educational programmes at school, to support young people in their understanding of responsible lifestyles. In the search for legitimacy the industry seeks partnership with governmental and non-governmental organizations.

The ethical base of such cooperation is controversial and conflicts of interest are inevitable. The partners do not start from a common base. The industry claims that alcohol does not have the characteristics of a drug and that the benefits of drinking outweigh its negative effects. Since it is known that the prevalence of alcohol-related problems is related not only to average per capita consumption, but also to problematic drinking patterns, policy-makers are persuaded to shift their focus to the elimination of negative patterns of drinking and to the promotion of beneficial patterns. A partnership between the drinks industry and governmental and non-governmental organizations can compromise the independence of public health; this risks damaging the public good and impairing the trust of civil society in its public institutions. Non-governmental organizations may find it appealing to cooperate with the beverage-alcohol industry, but the industry has invested enormously in the promotion of new alcoholic drinks for youth; hence all cooperation remains questionable and should be carefully assessed.

In our fun-oriented consumer society the trend toward the consumption of all kinds of drugs will prevail and alcohol will continue to be the drug of choice of a large part of the population worldwide. Janus, the god of two faces, will point his noses in two directions. Humans can derive enjoyment and benefits from the responsible use of alcohol but many suffer the negative consequences of drinking. Prevention in the form of individual or collective intervention is needed to minimize alcohol-related harm. A hundred years from now our activities will be judged as to whether we have advanced one step further in living with alcohol without producing harm.

S. AHLSTRÖM, T. KARLSSON & E. ÖSTERBERG

ALCOHOL POLICY ON THE AGENDA OF THE EUROPEAN UNION

Key words: alcohol, alcohol policy, prevention, European Union, Europe

Abstract. Preventive alcohol policy has gained in importance in many European Union member states as well as at the European Union level especially during the last decade. However, the European Union is still basically an economic union and its mandate to affect alcohol consumption, drinking habits, or alcohol-related problems is very restricted. Still today the European Union cannot harmonise any public health laws or regulations of its member states. Therefore, for instance, there are no directives affecting or guiding preventive alcohol control measures in the member states. Still, one may find some European Union-induced activity in member states concerning the control of alcohol advertising, drunk driving and drinking by adolescents in particular. There are also desires at the European Union-level to develop a comprehensive community strategy aimed at reducing alcohol-related harm.

1. EUROPEAN UNION'S INTEREST WITH REGARD TO ALCOHOL

The European Union (EU) is founded on the European Communities (EC) supplemented by new forms of co-operation agreed by the member states in Maastricht in 1993, and amended in the Amsterdam Treaty in 1999 and in the Treaty of Nice ratified in 2003. Presently the EU consists of three pillars. The first pillar is the EC level co-operation laid down in the Community law and in the treaties establishing the European Coal and Steel Community, the European Economic Community (EEC) and the European Atomic Energy Community. The second pillar consists of a common foreign and security policy governed by the provisions of title V in the Treaty on European Union. It differs from the traditional Community co-operation by its inter-governmental nature and the decision-making procedures. The third pillar consists of police and judicial co-operation in criminal matters (Österberg & Karlsson, 2002a).

According to Klaus Mäkelä and Matti Viikari (1977), the state has four different basic interests and tasks with regard to alcoholic beverages. They are the fiscal interest, the economic development interest, the interest in maintaining public order and safety, and the interest in maintaining reproduction and health of the population (Mäkelä & Viikari, 1977). These tasks and interests concerning alcoholic beverages are often split between different departments and levels of government. Neither the EU nor the EC is a state or a federal state. Therefore, at the Community level, the interests with regard to alcoholic beverages are not the same as those in the individual member states.

The EC has always been an economic community. This was clearly stated in the Treaty of Rome, and it is also clearly stated in the second article of the Treaty establishing the European Community, according to which "The Community shall have as its task, by establishing a common market and an economic and monetary

R. Müller and H. Klingemann (eds.),
From Science to Action? 100 Years Later - Alcohol Policies Revisited, 5–14.

union and by implementing common policies or activities referred to in Articles 3 and 4, to promote throughout the Community a harmonious, balanced and sustainable development of economic activities, a high level of employment and of social protection, equality between men and women, sustainable and non-inflationary growth, a high degree of competitiveness and convergence of economic performance, a high level of protection and improvement of the quality of the environment, the raising of the standard of living and quality of life, and economic and social cohesion and solidarity among Member States" (Consolidated version of the Treaty establishing the European Community, article 2).

As the EU is first and foremost an economic union, also the primary role of alcoholic beverages in the Community is an economic one. Consequently, the EU has an economic development interest with regard to alcoholic beverages. In practice, this has concerned alcohol especially as an agricultural product in the EU's common agricultural policy (CAP). It has also concerned the production and trade of alcoholic beverages when the EU in general or in specific cases has removed different kinds of barriers to the trade. The Community has not directly collected any taxes on alcoholic beverages and, therefore, the EU does not have any special direct fiscal interests with regard to alcoholic beverages. However, special taxation of alcoholic beverages has interested the EU as part of the attempts to harmonise value added taxes and all excise duties in the Community area for the sake of the undisturbed functioning of the common market (Österberg & Karlsson, 2002a).

2. ALCOHOL IN THE EU

Former as well as current alcohol policies at the EU level can be said to have dealt with four different questions. The most important one has dealt with wine as an agricultural product. The second question has concerned different kinds of barriers to the trade in alcoholic beverages. Alcoholic beverages have also received special attention in attempts to harmonise excise duties and value added taxes in the Community area. Along its development, the Community has also become more interested in alcohol in the contexts of social policy and public health (Österberg & Karlsson, 2002a).

As an integrated part of the CAP the common wine policy of the EU has certainly affected the member states and their citizens in many ways. It is mostly felt in the everyday life of wine farmers, in their possibilities to earn their living and to continue earning their living by growing grapes and making wine. It is also reflected in the volume of wine production and in the acreage under viticulture as well as in the price and quality of the wines produced, which again is felt in the everyday life of many EU citizens as consumers. It is important to bear in mind that in many countries a good number of the population regards alcoholic beverages mostly as ordinary consumer goods or as their source of livelihood. All this, of course, affects their attitudes towards preventive alcohol policy (Österberg & Karlsson, 2002a, 47-49).

The building up of an integrated common European market has meant that the EU has in many ways acted for lifting up different kinds of barriers to trade. As a consequence, it is nowadays a must to treat domestic products and products coming from another EU member state alike. This has not been the case earlier. For instance, it was a common practice in many, if not in all, EU member states to favour domestic beverages at the expense of imported products especially in taxation policy. As the cases in the Court of Justice of the European Communities have shown, this is no longer possible. Furthermore, other court cases had led to the general practice that a beverage lawfully marketed in some EU Member State could be lawfully marketed also in the other EU member states (Österberg & Karlsson, 2002a, 50-56).

The interpretation of article 31 (ex article 37) of the EC Treaty dealing with the adjustment of commercial state monopolies in order to abandon all discrimination with regard to production and marketing has affected alcohol control policy especially in the Nordic countries. In practice, this has meant that Finland and Sweden were forced to give up their state monopolies on the production, import, export and wholesale of alcoholic beverages on January 1, 1995. On the other hand, the so called Franzén case dealing with the Swedish off-premise alcohol retail monopolies has led to the conclusion that these kinds of arrangements are not in conflict with the Community law (Holder et al., 1998; Ugland, 2002).

The harmonisation of alcohol excise duties has been an important element in the overall strategy to harmonise indirect taxation in creating the common European market. Thus far, the EU has been successful only in harmonising tax structures. This has had its effects in many countries with regard to the level of excise duties of different alcohol labels inside a certain beverage category. The very low EC minimum excise duty rates for alcoholic beverages have also forced some member states to increase their excise duty level of alcoholic beverages. In broad terms, however, the low minimum rates for all alcoholic beverage categories and the target rate only for distilled spirits mean that the EU member states have been, in practice, almost free to set their own excise duty rates for all alcoholic beverages or at least for beer, wine and intermediate products. On the other hand, the single European market with free flow of goods combined with small possibilities to restrict cross-border trade has affected and will affect the level of alcohol excise duties in many member states (Österberg & Karlsson, 2002a, 58-61).

At the time the Community was created, the member states did not give the Community any direct role with regard to controlling alcohol's effects on social order or public health. In the preamble of the Treaty of Rome, the founders of the EEC only mentioned, in addition to the need to guarantee economic development, the need to guarantee social development. Neither was a direct mandate for public health included in the Single European Act of 1986, although it did stress that the Commission should seek a high level of protection of health and safety, environmental issues and consumer protection in relation to the founding of the common European market.

The adoption of the Maastricht Treaty in 1993 gave the EU some competence to act in the area of public health through Article 129. This competence was, however, limited to promoting health and encouraging inter-state co-operation as the Maastricht Treaty explicitly excluded the harmonisation of national laws or regulations regarding public health. Community activity on the public health area was to be directed at preventing illnesses, including drug addiction, through research, health information, and education.

The Amsterdam Treaty of May 1, 1999, expanded the scope of EU activities for improving public health. Article 152 (previous article 129) of the EC Treaty is viewed as the first legislative instrument to be given to public health policy makers since it provides a basis for introducing a public health impact assessment of policy proposed for other areas in the EU. As article 152 states: "A high level of human protection shall be ensured in the definition and implementation of all Community policies and activities. Community action, which shall complement national policies, shall be directed towards improving public health, preventing human illness and diseases, and obviating sources of danger to human health. Such action shall cover the fight against the major health scourges, by promoting research into their causes, their transmission and their prevention, as well as health information and education." (Consolidated version of the Treaty establishing the European Community, article 152). On the other hand, the Amsterdam Treaty still excludes any harmonisation of public health laws and regulations of the EU member states by stating that "Community action in the field of public health shall fully respect the responsibilities of the Member States for the organisation and delivery of health services and medical care". (Consolidated version of the Treaty establishing the European Community, article 152). In a strict sense, public health activities at the Community level still lack a real legal base.

3. ON THE WAY TO COMMUNITY ALCOHOL POLICY

Even today the EU has no practice of any coherent preventive alcohol policy. Given that a public health mandate was not explicit until 1993, it is not surprising that one does not find a trace of preventive alcohol policy development before the 1990s. One can, however, locate other frames of reference to the harmful effects of alcohol consumption even earlier (Sutton & Nylander, 1999).

Before the 1980s, alcoholic beverages were regarded at the EU level as normal commodities without any considerations of their public health consequences, and alcohol was mostly discussed from the perspective of the common agricultural policy or as a tax harmonisation issue (Sulkunen, 1981; Tigerstedt, 1990; Österberg, 1993; van Iwaarden, 1994). The first time alcohol was treated as a potential target of regulation motivated by public health aims was in 1981 in a Council resolution that adopted the second programme of the EEC for consumer protection and information (Sutton & Nylander, 1999, 78).

Alcohol abuse was referred to in its own right for the first time in a Council resolution in 1986, which stated that the increase in alcohol abuse is causing serious concern for public health and social welfare (Official Journal C 184/02, 29.05.1986). On the other hand, this resolution also highlighted the economic importance of alcoholic beverages and concluded that a joint initiative is advisable in the field of prevention of alcohol abuse.

Beyond the Council resolution, in the 1980s, attempts were made to establish a unified blood alcohol concentration (BAC) limit for drunk driving under the auspices of traffic safety policy. The resolution and call for action sought a common BAC limit, and a Commission proposal for a Council directive was presented in 1988, but it was stalemated in the Council (Sutton & Nylander, 1999, 79).

Alcohol-related problems were also dealt with within the context of the Europe against Cancer programme initiated in 1987. In a ten-point code, it was noted that certain cancers might be avoided by moderating one's alcohol consumption. Even if the role of alcohol in the cancer programme was not given a high priority, it is important to note that in this programme alcohol was for the first time discussed squarely within a public health framework (Sutton & Nylander, 1999, 79).

One indicator of public health expansion during the late 1980s was the establishment of a public health unit within the Commission. However, its work in the area of public health could not be justified for its own sake, but strictly in terms of economic considerations related to the single European market (Sutton & Nylander, 1999).

In addition to political actions, the trend towards a greater recognition of alcohol-related problems after the Maastricht Treaty in 1993 included increased attention to producing information about alcohol and alcohol-related problems. The programme for community action on health promotion, information, education and training for the 1996-2000 period included the promotion of the examination, assessment and exchange of experience and the support for actions concerning measures to prevent alcohol abuse and related social and health problems. In 1996, the Commission also established a working group on alcohol as a forum for sharing experiences on alcohol-related problems and preventive alcohol policy (Sutton & Nylander, 1999, 79).

Until the late 1990s, public health policy was addressed within Directorate-General (DG) V of the Commission, dealing with employment, industrial relations and social affairs. The public health unit of the EU was located here, and this unit, Public Health and Safety at Work, was a sub-directorate containing five units. Alcohol was largely handled within the unit of health promotion, health monitoring and injury prevention. In 1999, in the newly created DG Health and Consumer Protection (SANCO), alcohol is mostly handled in Unit G 3 Health promotion, health monitoring and injury prevention.

EU policies are not simply the outcome of bargaining between member states. The EU institutions themselves play an important part in shaping the type and content of policy. The nature of policy intervention of the EU is determined in part through the legal basis for action as well as earlier precedents in the same area. Health and public health interventions fall almost exclusively under inter-state co-operation. It can further be observed that SANCO, and DG V before it, has been engaged almost exclusively in the production of recommendations, and its opinions set goals in relation to issues but they are not binding in any way. Although the legal basis for making public health policy set out in the treaties is largely restricted to encouraging trans-state co-operation, the Commission's public health sector has identified alternative venues for political action. Caroline Sutton and Sven Nylander (1999) identified four venues that are common within the public health sector when constructing of European phenomena, namely supporting the accumulation of

European knowledge, the support to developing interest groups, the building of public opinion, and the construction of practical competence.

4. ALCOHOL POLICY AS A PART OF THE EU'S PUBLIC HEALTH POLICY

The first case of alcohol policy being processed as public health policy in the EU was the case of so-called 'alcopops', or designer drinks, as they are also called. In the summer of 1995 these types of beverages hit the market in the UK, and shortly thereafter found their way into other European markets. The fact that these very sweet drinks with curious names and fancy labels seemed to be aimed at a very youthful market resulted in demands for action at the European level by interest organisations and the European Parliament, and the alcopops issue was also raised within the Council (Sutton & Nylander, 1999).

A declaration by the European Parliament called upon the Commission to introduce European-wide guidelines for the promotion, marketing and retailing of alcopops and designer drinks, to enforce regulatory control of the promotion, marketing and retailing of these products, and to examine ways of taxing such drinks at the same rate as distilled spirits.

During the process, the subject of discussion shifted away from alcopops towards alcohol consumption by youth and children, and later on even the concepts of alcopops and designer drinks disappeared from the draft of the Council recommendation. The final Council recommendation, accepted on June 5, 2001, dealt with the drinking of alcohol by young people, in particular children and adolescents, and encouraged member states to foster a multi-sectoral approach to educate young people about alcohol and to increase young people's involvement in health-related policies and actions (Council Recommendation 2001/458/EC). It was also recommended that should action be taken against the illegal sale of alcohol to minors and that proof of age should be required. It furthermore included codes of conduct for the alcohol industry and trade with the recommendation not to target alcoholic beverages in marketing, advertising and sponsoring specifically on children and adolescents.

On the same day the above mentioned Council recommendation was accepted, the Council also made a Conclusion on a Community Strategy to reduce alcohol-related harm (Council Conclusion 2001/C 175/01). In this conclusion the Council "underlines the desirability of developing a comprehensive Community strategy aimed at reducing alcohol-related harm comprising, in particular, the following elements:

- Further development of comparative and comprehensive information together with relevant high-quality research, and an effective monitoring system of alcohol consumption, alcohol-related harm, and policy measures and their effects in the European Community.
- A co-ordinated range of Community activities in all relevant policy areas; a high level of health protection shall be ensured in the definition and implementation of Community activities, in fields such as research, consumer protection, transport, advertising, marketing, sponsoring, excise duties and

other internal market issues, while fully respecting Member States' competencies.
- Strengthened co-operation and exchange of knowledge between Member States.
- International co-operation, in particular with and within the World Health Organization" (Council Conclusion 2001/C 175/01).

In 2002 the European Parliament and the Council adopted a programme of community action in the field of public health for the years 2003-2008. The programme shall complement national policies and aim to protect human health and improve public health. The general objectives of the programme are
- to improve information and knowledge for the development of public health,
- to enhance the capability of responding rapidly and in a coordinated fashion to health treats, and
- to promote health and prevent disease through addressing health determinant across all policies and activities.

For information and guidance, the following areas of work have been identified as priority areas for 2003: cross-cutting themes, health information, health treats and health determinants. Under health determinants alcohol, alongside with tobacco and drugs has been mentioned. With regard to alcohol the work plan for 2003 will establish a network of expert organisations to support the implementation of the Council Recommendation on the drinking of alcohol by young people and to contribute to further development of a Community strategy to reduce alcohol-related harm. Also a conference on alcohol, health and society is to be held in 2005.

5. EUROPEAN MONITORING CENTRE FOR DRUGS AND DRUG ADDICTION

The Lisbon-based European Monitoring Centre for Drugs and Drug Addiction (EMCDDA), one of 12 decentralised European Community agencies, was set up in 1993 in response to the escalating drug problem in Europe and to demands for an accurate picture of the phenomenon throughout the European Union. The Centre became fully operational in 1995.

The EMCDDA is responsible for collecting information on the drug situation in all the EU member states so as to support decision-making in the drug field. The EMCDDA is organised as a network among all member states, and it also has the status of an agency within the EU. Its action must therefore be based on the working principles of the EU. A main objective of the Centre is to produce objective, reliable and comparable data about the drug situation and to analyse the responses to this situation in different countries. This comparability will contribute to the construction of a common understanding of the European drug problem. The agency also plays a key role in implementing the EU joint action on new synthetic drugs as well as monitoring national and Community strategies and policies and their impact on the drug situation.

Under the terms of the enhanced pre-accession strategy preparing for adhesion to the EU, the European Council decided to allow the candidate countries to participate in selected Community programmes and European agencies. Priority was given to the EMCDDA and the Copenhagen-based European Environment Agency. To this end, a modification to the founding regulation of the EMCDDA, allowing the Centre to provide technical assistance to the candidate countries and to the countries eligible for the Phare programme, was adopted by the Council of the European Union and approved by the European Parliament in 2000.

Alcohol was not included in the EMCDDA's founding regulation. In some European countries, alcohol and drug strategies are separate, in others, they form an integrated strategy. The EU enlargement calls for reviewing the founding regulation. In this context, it is possible that the scope of the Centre's activities will be discussed as well.

6. SUMMARY AND DISCUSSION

Preventive alcohol policy has gained in importance at the EU level especially during the last decade. However, the EU is still basically an economic union and its mandate to affect alcohol consumption, alcohol abuse, drinking habits, or alcohol-related problems is very restricted. There are, for instance, no directives affecting or guiding preventive alcohol control measures in the member states. Still, one may find some EU-induced activity in member states concerning the control of alcohol advertising, drunk driving and drinking by adolescents in particular.

Alcohol policies are nowadays more similar in the EU member states than they used to be in the early 1950s. This overall converging trend consists of two kinds of developments. On the one hand, measures affecting alcohol availability are nowadays applied to a much lesser extent than fifty years ago. In other words, countries which in the 1950s practised strict alcohol control policies targeted on alcohol availability and supply have dismantled them, while countries that have begun to be interested in alcohol policies have not focused on controlling the availability of alcohol. On the other hand, alcohol control measures targeting on certain alcohol-related problems or aiming to affect the demand for alcoholic beverages have become more common in all EU member states (Österberg & Karlsson, 2002b). It could be argued that EU member states have at the same time abolished alcohol control measures affecting alcohol availability and known to be effective, and introduced control measures aiming to affect alcohol demand even if they are known to be much less effective, at least in the short run.

The basic explanation for the decreasing control of alcohol availability is that guaranteeing free movement of capital, goods, services and labour has been the leading principle in organising the world economy in recent decades. Therefore, many alcohol control measures affecting alcohol supply have been seen as obstacles to free trade in alcoholic beverages, and they have been abolished. It is difficult to see that this trend would be discontinued or turned even if public health and social policy considerations have gained increased importance in the EU during the last decade. Consequently, many of the remaining control measures on alcohol availability will most certainly be challenged in the future. In any case, it seems to be impossible that structures like the comprehensive alcohol monopoly system could be rebuilt in any EU member state.

7. REFERENCES

Holder, H. D., Kühlhorn, E., Nordlund, S., Österberg, E., Romelsjö, A. & Ugland, T. (1998). *European Integration and Nordic Alcohol Policies. Changes in Alcohol Controls and Consequences in Finland, Norway and Sweden, 1980-1997.* Aldershot: Ashgate.

Mäkelä, K. & Viikari, M. (1977). Notes on alcohol and the state. *Acta Sociologica,* 20, 155-179.

Österberg, E. (1993). European integration and its consequences for Nordic alcohol monopolies, in: Kolstad, H. (Ed.) *Nordic Alcohol Control Policy. Description and Assessment of Alcohol Political Measures in Denmark, Finland, Iceland, Norway and Sweden*, 87-101. Oslo: The Norwegian Temperance Alliance.

Österberg, E. & Karlsson, T. (2002a). Alcohol policies at the European Union level, in: Österberg, E. & Karlsson, T. (Eds) *Alcohol policies in EU member states and Norway. A collection of country reports.* Helsinki: National Research and Development Centre for Welfare and Health.

Österberg, E. & Karlsson, T. (2002b). Alcohol policies in EU member states and Norway in the second half of the twentieth century, in: Österberg, E. & Karlsson, T. (Eds) *Alcohol policies in EU member states and Norway. A collection of country reports.* Helsinki: National Research and Development Centre for Welfare and Health.

Sulkunen, P. (1981). Economic integration and the availability of alcohol: the case of the European Economic Community. *Contemporary Drug Problems*, 8, 75-102.

Sutton, C. & Nylander, J. (1999). Alcohol policy strategies and public health policy at an EU-level. The case of alcopops. *Nordic Studies on Alcohol and Drugs*, 16 (English Supplement), 74-91.

Tigerstedt, C. (1990). The European Community and the alcohol policy dimension, *Contemporary Drug Problems,* 17, 461-479.

Ugland, T. (2002). *Policy re-organization and integration. Europeanization of Nordic alcohol control policies.* ARENA report No 3/2002 & SIRUS report No 1/2002. Oslo: ARENA & SIRUS.

van Iwaarden, M. J. (1994). En alkoholpolitik inom Europeiska unionen? (An alcohol policy in the European Union?) *Nordisk Alkoholtidskrift*, 11, 264-267.

8. AFFILIATIONS

Salme Ahlström, Research Professor: Alcohol and Drug Research, the National Research and Development Centre for Welfare and Health (STAKES), P.O. Box 220, FIN-00531 Helsinki, Finland. E-mail: salme.ahlstrom@stakes.fi

Thomas Karlsson, Researcher: Alcohol and Drug Research, the National Research and Development Centre for Welfare and Health (STAKES), P.O. Box 220, FIN-00531 Helsinki, Finland. E-mail: thomas.karlsson@stakes.fi

Esa Österberg, Senior Researcher: Alcohol and Drug Research, the National Research and Development Centre for Welfare and Health (STAKES), P.O. Box 220, FIN-00531 Helsinki, Finland. E-mail:esa.osterberg@stakes.fi

P. SULKUNEN

FROM "*ALCOHOL, SOCIETY AND THE STATE*" TO "*BROKEN SPIRITS*" TO…

Key words: alcohol, control, epidemiology, population, total consumption, welfare state

The alcohol policy doctrine that emerged during the era when modern welfare states were consolidated resulted from a battle between two options: the medical model and the epidemiological total consumption framework. This development was described and analysed in Alcohol, Society and the State. It saw the medical model as an alternative to and a competitor with alcohol control, meaning Aany government measure to the purchase, production, or trade of alcoholic beverages@. Alcohol control as an instrument of prevention was grounded in what I here call the population argument - a public health theory that sets priority on rates of problems in a population rather than their individual determination. It further argues that rates of problems depend on rates of exposure, i.e. availability and consumption. Even if the practical implications of the population argument have nowhere been fully implemented, the argumentation became dominant among experts. This paper discusses the reasons why the epidemiological approach is compatible with welfare state thinking, and why its legitimacy depends on the social philosophy that underlies it, rather than technical or evidence-based considerations. This connection between the epidemiological approach and welfare state thinking is discussed in the context the changing Nordic ideas and power structures in Broken Spirits. The conclusion is that the epidemiological approach is experiencing difficulties to the extent to which the legitimacy of the welfare state is weakened.

1. INTRODUCTION

> We are dependent on very many things: sexual contacts, coffee or tobacco, but the occurrence of these states does not as such inform us about their effects. This term is often used so that s assumptions on dependency are made on the basis of effects, which means that we have no independent indicators of dependency itself. Often alcoholism is used to label people who are wanted under control and who are suspected of using alcohol unconventionally. Therefore alcoholism becomes a concept with a variable content and that reflects the environment=s reactions against drinking itself rather than its consequences. (Bruun, 1971a, p. 102, my translation)

The title of my article refers to two collective books in which I have been one of the authors *Alcohol, Society and the State* by Klaus Mäkelä, Robin Room, Eric Single, Pekka Sulkunen and Brendan Walsh (1981), and *Broken Spirits. Power and Ideas in Nordic Alcohol Control* by Pekka Sulkunen, Caroline Sutton, Christoffer Tigerstedt and Katariina Warpenius (2000).The first book was a sequel to Alcohol Control Policies in Public health Perspective by Kettil Bruun and ten other authors

R. Müller and H. Klingemann (eds.),
From Science to Action? 100 Years Later - Alcohol Policies Revisited, 15–28.

(Bruun et al.,1975). This volume had been a systematic comparative review of evidence that supports the so-called total consumption theory and its implications in alcohol control policy. The theory is also known as availability theory or the single distribution theory. The book recommended that this theory be taken as the starting point for public health oriented alcohol policy.

In the following I am going to reflect on this policy doctrine, which binds these three volumes together and forms the nucleus of the research they report. It is the idea that alcohol-related harm in society can (best) be minimised by measures that reduce the average quantity of alcohol consumed among the whole population. This idea is still today debated, challenged and defended among experts, albeit rarely implemented in practice and even when it is flagged as the policy theory, the practical significance of the measures it is used to justify are often in serious doubt. Yet it is probably the most consistent and also the most evidence-based policy theory in the public health field in the second half of the twentieth century, and deserves attention beyond the limited alcohol policy context. The argument I am making here is that the doctrine has in fact been much more than a technical policy theory. It incorporates a social philosophy that expounds major moral issues raised by late modernity and exposes key difficulties in our understandings of the role of the state in late modern society. When we discuss alcohol policy and attempt to identify its viable options in the contemporary situation, we do better in trying to diagnose the underlying social philosophies in each of them rather than set them against each other only on technical and evidence basis.

The two books referred to in my title belong to the genre of comparative historical policy analysis. They bear on the social preconditions of alcohol policy in modern societies, and have both theoretical ambitions and practical policy implications. Policy discourses never come and go only because they either work or do not work, or because they are based on firm evidence, or because such evidence proves them wrong. In our contemporary expert culture such a technocratic fallacy is a cunning illusion:

> AOur exploration begins with alcohol consumption, production and trade. To the classical causal-explanation mode of thinking, this is to begin with the middle. >The degree of control affects the level of consumption which, in turn, affects the rate of problems= would be a formulation attractive to many alcohol and drug policy analysts and a paradigm into which much previous work would fit@ (Mäkelä et al., 1982, p. 5).

However, the authors found that Athere was no single direction of causality among the domains [control, consumption, problems], but that all were caught up in a complicated network of interactions that also involved more general cultural processes beyond the three domains."

Alcohol, Society and the State was an analysis of alcohol control policies as they actually had developed during the post-war period, from about 1950 to about 1975, in seven countries: California, Ontario, Ireland, Norway, Holland, Poland and Finland. This was the time when the modern welfare states were consolidated, and alcohol policy also became in many countries one of the professional fields of state-centred policy- making. The field consisted of expert systems including research and education, of voluntary organisations and of specialised public and administrative organisations. The break-through of the Atotal consumption theory@ was taking place in many countries, competing with alternative theoretical approaches to alcohol addiction and its control. The authors observed that growing popularity of the medical model - the disease concept of addiction and increased responsibility of the medical institutions and professions for alcohol problems - was challenging not only traditional punitive and selective controls of alcoholics but also the availability and price regulations recommended by the total consumption approach. This challenge was partly a reaction to a change in the problem profile from social disruption to health disorders related to alcohol use. Another change was the increasing accuracy with which alcohol could be identified as an etiological factor in a growing number of diseases. However, the authors concluded that the medical rhetoric did not seem to imply improved medical services to alcoholics also in the future, given the cost-burden it incurs in state budgets. Instead, it might turn attention again to deviant drinking and away from the beverage as the locus of alcohol problems. Government interventions in the alcohol markets have in fact reinforced the vested interests, and they exert a constraining influence on the possibilities of preventing alcohol problems. (Mäkelä et al., 1980, pp. 104-105, 109-110).

The total consumption framework was invented in France by the demographer Sully Ledermann in the 1950s, and it has continually been one of the dominant policy doctrines in French alchol policy (Sulkunen and Ugland, forthcoming). Research on the epidemiological foundation of the policy has been conducted in many countries and the policy recommended to governments in general under the auspices of the World Health Organization (Edwards et al., 1994). However, in the Nordic countries with their state alcohol monopolies the availability theory was established maybe more firmly as the dominant policy doctrine than elsewhere in the world. Even there it began to be challenged increasingly severely - and mostly for the very reasons that Alcohol, Society and the State warned about, albeit on a scale and in a context that could not be foreseen in the late 1970s. *Broken Spirits* analysed these challenges in the context where Finland, Norway and Sweden were integrated to the European Union and its free market policy. This integration coincided with mounting neo-liberal criticism of the Nordic welfare states. The major conclusion of the book was that adjustment to the changes in the external pressures was only a minor factor in the tide of more liberal alcohol policy that started already in the middle of the 1980s. The more profound changes stem from the role of the welfare state in advanced capitalist society. The differences in reacting to the same external impulse reflected the differences in the position of the welfare state in these societies, Finland being much weaker in this respect than Norway or Sweden. The future of the Nordic alcohol control systems seem to us much more dependent on general ideological factors than on the merits of the system itself, or on the gravity of the alcohol problem. In any case, the foundation on which the system today stands is fragile and hardly sustainable on the basis of public health concerns alone.

2. ALCOHOL CONTROL AND MODERNITY

Alcohol policy is a powerful indicator of key issues in the area of lifestyle regulation in modern and late modern society for two reasons. First, alcohol itself has many meanings, use-values, functions and dysfunctions in different types of social contexts. As Selden Bacon (1945 and 1962) pointed out in his seminal article *"Alcohol in Complex Society"*, in modern societies the ambivalence of drinking is pronounced. Drinking depresses inhibitions and anxieties and thus serves as a social lubricant in societies which place high value on social interaction between strangers. On the other hand, intoxication reduces accuracy, coordination and sense of responsibility, and these are competences whose value and functionality are also pronounced in modern society. In late nineteenth and early twentieth century, temperance movements constructed a utopia of rational and intoxication-free modern society, but only a few decades later temperance itself, rather than drinking, became an icon of conservative traditionalism. The secular rise of alcohol consumption levels throughout the industrialised world that accompanied the economic growth and cultural change during the "glorious three decades" after the Second World War can reasonably be interpreted as an indication of the post-traditional consumer society.

Secondly, alcohol policy operates in the precarious zone between the private, the public and the political in democratic and pluralistic society. Modernity means individualism in three ways. *Economically,* as wage earners we are all masters of our own budgets. Even highly developed welfare states with their income maintenance programmes and public services are not an exception to but a complement and the midwife of the pecuniary individualism of the individualistic consumer society in which we now live. *Socially* the civilising process of modernity produced the distinct sphere of privacy in which the intimate bodily functions and pleasures were enclosed. The regulation of body contact, hygiene and emotions separate individuals and place high requirements of self-control on everyone. *Politically,* modern societies consist of citizens with legally defined rights and duties, which are legally defined and supervised by the state.

As Norbert Elias (1978) has shown, the civilising process of individualisation had been going on in European societies for two hundred years before the rise of nationalism and the construction of the nation states, a process in which the temperance movements played a not insignificant role. The short twentieth century, as Eric Hobsbawm (1994) calls it, from 1914 to 1989, saw a massive democratisation of this process. The democratisation has not happened all by itself. It has been the outcome of a complex process of historical action where contradicting, nonlinear and heterogeneous economic, social and political interests have partly overlapped, pointed approximately in the same direction and compromised in a way that has resulted in three great social ideals in which also lifestyle regulation has fitted: progress, universal individual citizenship and the nation.

Progress means an idea of a future that can be influenced by rational planning and that is worth a sacrifice and work here and now. Universal individual citizenship means that persons should be treated equally and according to their achieved merits rather than ascribed properties both economically, socially and as citizens. This implies that inter-generational mobility has been considered not only acceptable but a social virtue, and educational systems have been built to make this possible. Nation means that the social bond constituted by belonging to one national society has been stronger than the divisions caused by class, age, gender and even religion or ethnicity. Nation has provided a higher cause for which even extreme sacrifices have been made in the world war in two acts, superseding both personal and group identities with a force that has made the short twentieth century probably the most violent period in human history but also bestowed the national state with a moral authority to regulate lifestyles in a way and to an extent that less than one hundred years later already seems drastic and strange to us.

The population argument

This was the context in which alcohol control policy has evolved as we now know it, and in this context also the argument that was developed in "Alcohol Control Policies in Public Health Perspective" should be understood, especially in the Nordic countries. The sociological idea and the policy recommendations that were based on the argument reflected not only a technical theory, nor only an epidemiological regularity of the statistical distribution of alcohol consumption, and certainly not simply a negative attitude towards drinking itself. The argument of the book has sometimes been labelled as "prohibitionist", as an obsolete prolongation of the anti-alcohol movement of the early twentieth century into a pluralistic consumer society. This misrepresents the underlying social philosophy of the approach in such a way that makes it impossible not only to assess its practicability but also to identify correctly the real predicament that alcohol policy has become, and which indeed is one of public health generally in so far as it depends on lifestyle regulation.

The total consumption approach was never developed into a coherent and unambiguous policy, not even in Sweden where its legitimacy has been and still is more uncontested than in any other country. Therefore I prefer not to use the term "model" about the approach but rather refer to it as the population argument or the total consumption framework. Also terms like single distribution theory or availability theory insufficiently reflect the social philosophy that connects the approach to the ideological reality of late modernity and its relationship to the modern context that I described above. The central idea of the approach is that the focus and target of alcohol policy, like any other policy with social goals, should be the population - not the individual. Therefore we should be interested in rates and not in individual variations, however explained, and if the distributions are fairly regular as they seem to be in alcohol consumption and its harmful consequences, so much the better.

Bio-politics and the life of the population

In this way the population argument is a continuation *not* of the anti-alcohol attitude of the temperance movements *but* of what Michel Foucault (Foucault, 1976, p.183-191; Foucault, 1991) called bio-politics to describe how the control of life of the population became the object of state politics in modern societies. Until the French revolution, the political function of controlling life was merely punitive and its function was to assure the loyalty of the monarch's subjects, to maintain the "King's peace". Towards the beginning of the twentieth century the focus of the politics on life turned from deviant or rebellious individuals to the size of the population, its health, hygiene, sexuality, mental fitness; and increasingly also its manners and ways of thinking were conceived as products of good government. The populations of national societies were not only the *objects* of national states; they were also the *source* of the states' sovereignty. The people, le peuple, das Volk, folket, kansa, was thought to act on itself through the institutions of parliamentary politics that were expected to reflect not only the people's needs but also its common will.

The total consumption framework in alcohol policy represents one version of this discourse on the relationship between the government and the population. However, there is an important rupture between the concern for the population in the early twentieth century and the concern articulated in the population argument on alcohol policy in the 1970s and after. It is well known what kind of selective and discriminating policies developed out of the combination of the Apeople's@ sovereignty and the scientific management of life for the purposes of "improving the quality of the population", as Alva and Gunnar Myrdal (1935), the founding theorists of the Swedish welfare state, formulated the goals of their solution to the "population question". Certainly, eugenics, cost-benefit calculations and general civilization policies were not uncontested, and there were many conflicting opinions on them throughout the early twentieth century. What was not in question however, was the idea of the norm itself. As Michel Foucault wrote, the kind of power that has life as its object "will need continuous, regulating and corrective mechanisms... It has to qualify, to measure, to appreciate, to stratify... It operates distributions around the norm." (Foucault, 1976, p.189-190) What from our contemporary perspective is so strange, and shocking, in the early twentieth century bio-politics, is precisely its normative nature in the control and sometimes repress the *kind of life*; both of life that was accorded the right to be born and also of life already existing.

The temperance movements they were successful in implementing the norm of abstinence as law in many countries, either in the form of prohibition or of strictly regulated market for alcoholic beverages. There is an apparent contradiction between their state-centred control policy and their individualistic stress on self-control and free will. There are three interrelated ways to understand this contradiction. First, the idea of the sovereignty of the people, supported by the democratic institutions of parliamentary politics, lent itself to the service of their populism that was common in the era of nationalism before the First World War (Hobsbawm, 1992, pp. 43-65). Secondly, they based their norm on the new bioscientific views on the possibilities to manipulate also human populations genetically; and temperance leaders in Switzerland, Austria and Germany were indeed also eugenicists (Sulkunen & Warpenius, 2000). Thirdly, the temperance ideologists had inherited from the Enlightenment the principle of the naturally good desires that should not be violated by desires that are

> "...palpably fallacious and ruinous. The world has seen too much of the destructive effects of such indulgences to believe that they come within the scope of the wise Creator's plans. The true philosopher discriminates between acquired desires and appetites, or vitiated, perverse, and inordinate impulses, and those which are normal, necessary, and beneficent." (Dorchester 1883, 2)

Intoxication is a disastrous desire because it is a deviation from the natural order of things, and therefore leads to the loss of free will - the most valued aspect of human beings as compared to animals. (Sulkunen and Warpenius 2000)

As Norbert Elias has shown, the modern conception of the state involved the sovereign government's duty to civilize the population by education, by disciplinary technologies and, in the last resort, legal force. The will was therefore not completely free to make choices between desires and to construct the good life as each individual saw fit. It was free only in so far as it served the public good of the national population.

> "...from the late nineteenth to the mid twentieth centuries, a common vocabulary was formed that sought a general codification of these problems as issues entailing the whole of society. This vocabulary sought to discover the means of translating the particular, the personal and the private into the general, the public and the social. It sought to locate the law, and the juridical subject of right and responsibility, as but one region within the wider, concrete and more fundamental evolution of society" (Dean 1999, 129).

But the vocabulary, and the practices that this vocabulary justified, operated also in the other direction: translating the wider concerns of the public whole to solutions concerning the private and singular. Eugenics and selective disciplinary practices such as vagrancy laws or involuntary incarceration or sterilisation of the mentally ill, addicts and orphans, sought to combat what was seen as a threat of degeneration caused by the modern population law: the poor bred more children than the well-educated, with the result that the proportion of the poorly equipped population increased at the cost of the more qualified breed. The overall population growth was considered too slow; therefore rational family planning, selective fertility and family policy were key instruments in assuring progress for the nation.

Thus the normative idea of naturally good desires was not limited to eugenics and the temperance ideology. It was carried over to controlling sexuality, organising the family, looking after and educating the children, eating and drinking, taking exercise, appreciating nature, maintaining social relationships and educating oneself in the arts and literature. Like in eugenics, cost-benefit calculations were not excluded from the argumentation, but the benefit of society was only one among the grounds on which social policy should educate people:

> "The positive task in social policy is to make clear what practical measures a person should rationally desire in terms of his own values, if he had improved knowledge@. And: ABad habits must be straightened out. The unwise must be enlightened. The irresponsible must be aroused. There is plenty of room for a comprehensive, socially organised education of the entire nation and for propaganda action, which, if it is going to be of use where it is most needed, must be intensive and insistent, and must make an effort to utilize all channels to parents who otherwise perhaps have only cramped connections with the social world outside@ (Kris i befolkningsfrågan, cited in Hirdman ,1997, p. 66).

3. THE PUBLIC HEALTH PERSPECTIVE

The population argument in alcohol policy might appear to be a direct consequence of the normative bio-politics of the early twentieth century. Its implementation leads to the infringement of the free market in the interest of making the population to drink, smoke or eat less or in a healthier way. It also infringes with the free choice of consumers to satisfy their desires, on the basis of scientific knowledge on what desires are worthy of satisfaction. And finally, it introduces the force of law to impose this rationality on everyone in the name of the public good that also is designated as the good of everyone.

On closer investigation, however, the epidemiological mode of addiction is very distant from the idea of the norm in the modern bio-politics as analysed by Michel Foucault and as exemplified by the early twentieth century temperance politics. Let us first take a closer look at what the population argument actually is.

The universal citizen

Alcohol Control Policy was written in a situation where alcohol consumption had been increasing in almost all advanced capitalist countries since the war, and this growth continued until the 1980s. This rise was related to the improved opportunities for consumption made possible by material and technical progress. In cultural conceptions, new cosmopolitan ways of using alcohol, adopted from ancient European civilisations or from North American mass media, was a sign of 'modernity' (Sulkunen 1983). New ways of using alcoholic beverages became a sign of distinction in the cultural battle for competence and style (Bourdieu 1986).

In one sense, then, the population argument was a rational reaction to increasing rates of drinking-related problems. However, it entailed a sea change from the form of individualism that was embedded in the bio-political climate of the preceding decades. The epidemiological vocabulary marked a shift from the national duty to exercise free will to the benefit of the public good to a new kind of universalism and moral neutrality. This was a change that influenced all areas of control policy, ranging from understandings of crime and mental health to addiction. As we show in *The Broken Spirits*, the Nordic state monopoly systems in particular had been based on principles of social discrimination, which intended to exclude women, young people and the working class from the world of drink (Bruun 1985; Järvinen 1991). As late as the 1970s, there were still traces of discriminatory alcohol policy also in many other countries. In Belgian legislation, for example, strong drinks could not be served in public places and they were sold in retail only in vessels of two litres or more. The main purpose was to prevent workers from buying spirits. The well-known British rules on opening hours of public houses were also originally aimed at disciplining the working class (Harrison 1971), and they have been relaxed only very recently. French working class cafes have been subjected to similar restrictions, but here the motivation was even more explicitly political: cafes and other public drinking places have been important scenes of political agitation since the eighteenth century (Brennan 1989), even more obviously so after the Commune (Barrows 1991). The dry history of Swedish restaurants has a very similar background (Magnusson 1985).

For the radical generation of the 1960s the issue of equal universal citizenship was far more important than the romantic ideal of "emancipating the self", especially in the Nordic countries. The most important policy issue concerned the handling of alcoholics and other deviants. Involuntary treatment of alcoholics in institutions was specifically criticised by legal experts and social scientists. Kettil Bruun was influential among them in the whole Nordic context. He showed in an important article (Bruun,1971b) that the reason why Finland applies a "non-medical model" to addictions is that legislation puts the responsibility in the hands of the police and the social workers. In 1960 about 1000 persons were hospitalised for alcoholism but about six times as many were sentenced to jails or given involuntary treatment in farms for alcohol-related reasons (unpaid drunkenness fines, drunkenness arrests, violence, social irresponsibility and violations of the alcohol legislation). The penal measures were selectively targeted to the poor and marginalised population. Bruun welcomed the trend towards interpreting drinking problems as a disease rather than a crime for its humanitarian implications, but given the low priority of alcoholism treatment in the medical institutions (and the low rate of success) he feared that this may lead to another mechanism of labelling. Doctors should treat the drinkers' diseases but leave their alcoholism alone.

The social scientists criticism of the injustices in the handling of deprived alcoholics and petty criminals led to the organisation of The November Movement (Marraskuun liike) in 1967, with similar aims and purposes as KRUM in Sweden and KROM in Norway. This Nordic protest movement led in due course to both legislative reforms and changes in the treatment structures themselves (Hauge 1998, 228-232; Nycander 1996, 245-272; Stenius 1999, 84-101).

Although civilisation and the constitution of self-controlling individual citizenship with equality of rights and duties was an important part also in the radical discourse of the 1960s, its content was the opposite to the earlier regime of the civilising welfare state. Now the Enlightenment idea of natural desires had disappeared from the public policy agenda. The welfare state - and equally the alcohol control policy - was said not to 'promote the good life but to prevent bad circumstances' (Allardt, 1998). Bad circumstances would be poverty and exclusion, ill health and lack of necessary social and medical services.

In alcohol policy this implied focussing not on individuals, and not on drinking at all but on its consequences. In the article mentioned above Kettil Bruun objected strongly to definitions of alcoholism in terms of intoxication and to treatment approaches that focus on the underlying causes or determinants of drinking. For him these attitudes involved too strong a risk of selective discrimination against drinking by poor people. The target should only be the consequences of bad drinking, not intoxication. The same rationalism about consequences was characteristic of the whole Nordic alcohol policy liberalism in the 1960s. Even the medium beer reform of the 1960s - making beer available in grocery stores - was almost never justified in terms of the pleasures of drinking. Its declared intentions were, first, to assure equal access to alcohol to everyone, and secondly, to replace vodka with milder beer and in this way make drinking less violent and harmful. (Sulkunen et al., 2000)

Alcohol control and the welfare state

The population argument therefore was the first universalistic, truly modern response to the alcohol question in the welfare state in three respects. First, it was an expert-driven concept of addiction, even more than its alternatives, since only population-based statistical studies allow the generalisations on which it is founded. Secondly, it is a liberal view in the sense that it respects individual freedom universally, especially supporting the weak:

> "Strategies which single out individuals - whether for correction, treatment, or rehabilitation - tend to involve large and continuing costs of state-funded agencies and professional personnel. The labelling of individuals also carries social costs in that it tend to be applied to those with least resources to protect themselves@ (Bruun et al. 1975, p. 67)

Thirdly, contrary to what the "prohibitionist" label attached to the population argument indicates, it is not and never was intended as a position on the value of drinking or any specific drinking pattern. As Kettil Bruun wrote in the opening quotation of this paper, the selective concept of alcoholism tends to turn into a reaction against drinking itself instead of its consequences, and this is what the population-based approach was intended to change. This intention was enveloped in a wider change in the moral relationship between society, the individual and the state that consisted in the break-up of the theory of naturally good desires. Its consequence could be called *normative neutralisation*, a strategy that has been extensively used in health policy. The new public health movement starts from the premise that public health work can no longer be limited to preventing specific diseases. Risks related to lifestyle must be included in the objectives of public health work but it should not, according to this line of thinking, set norms on what is healthy life. It should only inform citizens about risks but the choices people make in taking them are individuals' own responsibility. (Lupton, 1994) The change of focus from specific risks to consequences is reflected in organisational changes in public administration. In many countries departments of health education, research and policy-making that earlier were organised in specialised units (tobacco, alcohol, cancer, traffic safety etc.) have been regrouped under one general heading of public health.

In alcohol policy the population argument is in a similar way morally neutral: the value of drinking as such is not commented on; only consequences matter. The authors of *Alcohol Control Policy* admitted that social and anthropological aspects may bear on social control, but for policy purposes it is more useful to concentrate not on individual self-control or consumers' choices but on more "manipulable aspects of control", i.e. the availability and the prices of alcoholic beverages (Bruun et al., 1975, p.12). Even the specific kinds of risks related to drinking were not a legitimate focus of public policy. For Kettil Bruun it was ethically dubious, politically ineffective, and economically unprofitable to define, identify, calculate and prevent, in every detail, the endless row of risks (Tigerstedt, 2001, p.123).

4. AND TO...?

The new value of life

The worries that characterised Alcohol, Society and the State are both understandable and paradoxical. They are understandable in that the neo-liberal tide had already begun its work to relax the regulations of alcohol markets, although the authors stated that protectionist interests continued to influence the production side. On the other hand, the fear of the medical model now appears paradoxical, because the advances of medical technology have been an integral part of the modern project and the welfare state has been an indispensable instrument in their support. Progress in this area has in twenty years significantly changed the problematic of treatment and prevention so that we now should talk about life-regulating technology rather than treatment and prevention separately. It has translated the state=s responsibility for the life of the population into a precarious question of the rights and responsibilities for the life of the individual. Given the enormously growing discrepancy between what medical technology can do and what the state, insurance companies or individuals can afford to have cured and cared for, how should responsibility be divided between individuals, professionals, the market and the state? This question is especially burning in the context of lifestyle risks but concerns the role of life-regulating technology as a whole. In a way, medical technology has marginalised itself by its very success: expensive treatments are of little use unless the patient cooperates in maintaining the improved condition. The same dilemma concerns the regulation of life that is not yet born. Who is responsible for the birth of a child known to have a high risk of serious genetically transmitted defects? The medical professions have been shown to be very reluctant to take the charge beyond technical advice, and costs-benefit calculations are strongly criticized for re-introducing eugenics to public health policy (Bosk, 1995). It appears as if every innocent life is too valuable to allow a death sentence by experts and public officials on the basis of the burden it presents to others. Individuals and their near ones themselves must decide.

Broken Spirits concluded that in the welfare state modernity appears to have achieved its ideals of progress and universal individualism to such an extent that even the morally neutral focus on consequences rather than intoxication, which the total consumption framework represents, does not seem to enjoy the confidence of consumers and citizens. At the same time it is quite obvious that the medical model is no solution; on the contrary, the advances in medical technology make health promotion and disease prevention even more important and in fact inseparable from treatment. This is the public health predicament of advanced consumer societies, and no obvious paths forward seem to offer themselves to avoid the uncomfortable and morally impossible selection of those who will be given help from those who will be left on their own because they fail to collaborate in promoting their own health and preventing the burden for others.

In his foreword to Alcohol, Society and the State Nils Christie sympathised with the pessimism of the authors and asked what other alternatives might there be to controlling the supply of alcohol, besides the medical model and more extensive treatment. He took up two – one which he saw as likely but not acceptable, and another that he saw as unlikely but which he recommended. The first was to bring back law and order to alcohol control. This would renew the punitive and discriminating approaches that the total consumption framework had tried to replace with its universalism. The second was a communitarian solution, to create a Gemeinschaft structure, to replace the consumer society with one that is more conductive to self-control and mutual support. To some extent both have taken place, but his remarks on the population argument is as valid as it was twenty years ago:

> "The more realistically alcohol is seen in relation to other drugs, the better are the chances of state controls over this substance. We are very much aware of the problems involved in controlling both the pharmaceutical industry and the tobacco industry. The difficulties of controlling the alcohol industry are no les f
>
> ormidable. But, in itself, this is not an argument against renewed attempts, particularly since the alternative development seems so grim".

5. REFERENCES

Allardt, E. (1998): Det goda samhället. Välfärd, livsstil och medborgardygder (The public good. Welfare, livestyle and civil virtues). *Tidskrift för Velferdsforskning 1* (3), 123-133.

Bacon, S.D.(1945): Alcohol and complex society. In *Alcohol, Science and Society. Journal of Studies on Alcohol.* New Haven. (Revised in: Pittman, D.J. and Snyder, E. (Eds.)(1962): *Society, Culture and Drinking Patterns.* New York: Wiley).

Barrows, S. (1991). Parliaments of the People. The Political Culture of Cafés in the Early Third Republic. In Barrows, S. & Room, R. (eds.). *Drinking Behaviour and Belief in Modern History.* Berkeley: University of California Press.

Bosk, C. (1995). All God's Mistakes. Genetic Couseling in a Pediatric Hospital. Chicago: The University of Chicago Press.

Bourdieu, P. (1986): *Distinction.* London: Routledge.

Brennan, T. (1989). *Public Drinking and Popular Culture in Eighteenth Century Paris.* (New Jersey, Princeton University Press).

Bruun, K. (1971a). *Alkoholi: käyttö, vaikutukset, kontrolli* (Alcohol: use, effects, control). Helsinki: Tammi.

Bruun, K., (1971b). Finland: The non-medical approach. In Kiloh, L.G. & Bell, D.S. (Eds.), Proceedings of the 29th International Congress on Alcoholism & Drug Dependence. Butterworths, Australia: Chatswood.

Bruun, K. (1985): Maktens centru,m - centraladministrationen. (The centre of power - the central administration). In Bruun & Frånberg (eds): Den svenska supen. En historia om brännvin, Bratt och byråkrati (Swedish drink. A story of voozing, Bratt and bureaucracy). Stockholm: Prisma.

Bruun, K., Edwards, G., Lumio, M., Mäkelä, K., Pan, L., Popham, R. E., Room, R., Schmidt, W., Skog, O.-J., Sulkunen, P., & _Österberg, Esa: *Alcohol control policies in public health perspective.* Helsinki, The Finnish Foundation for Alcohol Studies, 1975, Vol. 25.

Dean, M. (1999): *Governmentality.* London: Sage.

Dorchester, D. (1884). *The Liquor Problem in All Ages.* New York: Phillips Hunt.

Edwards, G., Anderson, P., Babor, T. F., & et al. (1994). *Alcohol Policy and the Public Good.* Oxford: Oxford University Press.

Elias, N. (1978). *The History of Manners.* New York: Pantheon.

Foucault, M. (1976). *Histoire de la sexualité 1. La volonté de savoir.* Paris: Gallimard.
Foucault, M. (1991). Governmentality. In Burchell, Gordon and Miller (eds): *The Foucault Effect.* Chicago: University of Chicago Press.

Harrison, B. (1971). *Drink and the Victorians. The Temperance Question in England 1815-1872.* (London, Faber).

Hauge, R. (1998). *Norsk alkohollovgivning gjennom 1000 år* (Nordic alkohol legislation throughout 1000 years).Oslo: Rusmideelsdirektoratet.

Hobsbawm, E. (1992). *Nations and Nationalism.* Cambridge: Cambridge University Press.

Hobsbawm, E. (1994): *The Age of Extremes. The Short Twentieth Century*. London: Abacus.

Hirdman, Y. (1997). Social planning and rational control. Social engineering in Sweden in the 1 ' 930s and 1940s. In: Kettunen, P. & Eskola, H. (eds) *Models, Modernity and the Myrdals*. Helsinki: The Renvall Institute.

Järvinen, M.(1991). Kontrollerade kontrollörer - kvinnor, män och alkohol (Controlled controllers - women, men and alcohol). *Nordisk alkoholtidskrift. Vol. 8*, pp. 143-152.

Lupton, D. (1994). *The Imperative of Health*. London: Sage.
Magnusson, L. (1985). Orsaker till det förindustriella drickandet. Supandet i hautverkets Eskilstuna (Causes of pre-industrial drinking). *Alkoholpolitik*, 2(1), 23-29.

Mäkelä, Klaus & Room, Robin & Single, Eric & Sulkunen, Pekka & Walsh, Brendan: *Alcohol, society, and the state 1*. Toronto,Addiction Research Foundation of Ontario, 1981.

Myrdal, A. and Myrdal, G. (1935) AKris i befolkningsfrågan@ (Crisis in the population question). Stockholm 1: Bonniers.

Nycander, S. (1996). Svenskarna och spriten. Alkoholpolitik 1855-1995. (Swedes and spirits 1855-1995). Malmö: Sober.

Sulkunen, P. (1983). Alcohol consumption and the transformation of living conditions. A comparative study. In Smart & Glaser & Israel & Kalant & Popham & Schmidt (eds). *Research advances in alcohol and drug problems,, Vol. 7*, p. 247 - 297, London, Plenum.

Sulkunen, P. & Warpenius,K. (2000). Reforming the self and the other: the temperance movement and the duality of modern subjectivity. Critical Public Health, Vol. 10, No.4, pp. 423-438.

Stenius, K. (1999). *Privat och offentligt i svensk alkoholistvård.* (Private and public in Swedish alcoholism treatment). Lund: Arkiv.

Tigerstedt, C. (2001). *The Dissolution of Nordic Alcohol Control.* Helsinki: Department of Social Policy, University of Helsinki.

Sulkunen, Pekka & Tigerstedt, Christoffer & Suton, Caroline & Warpenius, Katariina: *Broken Spirits. Power and Ideology in Nordic Alcohol Control.* NAD Publications, Helösinki 2002.

Sulkunen, P. and Ugland, T. (forthcoming). The Public Health Cycle. The Total Consumption Framework in French Alcohol Policy and the Evin Law.

6. AFFILIATION

Department of Sociology
P.O. Box 18, 00014 University of Helsinki, Finland
+358-9-19123975, e-mail: Pekka.Sulkunen@Helsinki.fi

T.F. BABOR AND THE ALCOHOL AND PUBLIC POLICY GROUP[1]

ALCOHOL POLICY AND THE PUBLIC GOOD: AS SIMPLE AS ONE, TWO, THREE?

Abstract. This chapter summarizes recent advances in alcohol policy research within the tradition of three integrative literature reviews sponsored by the World Health Organization since 1975. The first review (*Alcohol Control Policies in Public Health Perspective*) introduced the idea of population approaches to the prevention of alcohol-related problems, and suggested that alcohol control policies should focus on the reduction of average alcohol consumption in a society. The second book (*Alcohol Policy and the Public Good*) expanded that perspective to include a wider variety of individual and population level interventions. The third study (*Alcohol: No Ordinary Commodity*) indicates that there is now a wide range of evidence-based policy options that should be considered at the local, national and international levels. These options have different strengths, weaknesses and costs, which need to be considered in the development of the optimal mix of alcohol policies to fit the needs of a given community or society. The differences among countries in per capita consumption, patterns of drinking and alcohol-related problems suggest that alcohol policies may have to be tailored to fit the needs of each society. Key Words: alcohol, policy, prevention, alcohol-related problems.

1. INTRODUCTION

Public policy measures designed to prevent, control and manage alcohol-related problems have had a long history, but the scientific study of alcohol policy as a public health strategy has had a much more abbreviated past. The growing interest in the scientific study of alcohol policy is part of a maturation process that is illustrated by the publication of a seminal monograph entitled: *Alcohol Control Policies in Public Health Perspective* (Bruun et al., 1975). Sponsored by the World Health Organization (WHO), the monograph drew attention to the preventable nature of alcohol problems throughout the world, and to the role of national governments and international agencies in the formulation of rational and effective alcohol policies. Despite the relative obscurity of the authors, *Alcohol Control Policies* stimulated a heated international debate about the nature of alcohol-related problems and their prevention, not just among academics, but also among policymakers. The most controversial aspect of the book was its main argument that the average amount of alcohol consumption in a society has a direct relationship to the prevalence of problems experienced by that society. It followed that the best way to prevent alcohol-related problems is through policies directed at the reduction of average alcohol consumption, such as taxation and limits on the availability of alcohol.

Two decades later a similar book was commissioned by WHO. Its purpose was to review the world literature pertaining to alcohol policy. The new study

R. Müller and H. Klingemann (eds.),
From Science to Action? 100 Years Later - Alcohol Policies Revisited, 29–47.

produced *Alcohol Policy and the Public Good* (Edwards et al., 1994) and a set of more detailed literature reviews (Holder & Edwards, 1995). The book reviewed the epidemiological evidence on alcohol consumption and alcohol-related problems throughout the world as a prelude to a critical analysis of six different policy approaches to alcohol-related problems: taxation of alcohol, environmental measures, drink driving countermeasures, school-based education, community action programs, and treatment interventions. The international group of authors concluded that public health policies on alcohol had come of age because of the strong body of scientific research that has grown in breadth and sophistication since 1975. They argued that the research establishes beyond doubt that public health measures of proven effectiveness are available to serve the public good. Moving beyond the emphasis of Bruun et al. (1975) on the total amount of alcohol consumed in a society, they proposed a dual approach that included measures to reduce the average amount of drinking in a society as well as those targeted at specific contexts and behaviors.

Within this tradition of collaborative ventures between WHO and international alcohol researchers, a third study was published in 2003 (Babor et al., 2003). This study was commissioned because of new epidemiological research on the way alcohol affects the health of populations in different parts of the world, particularly in the emerging states of the former Soviet Union and in the countries of the developing world. In the remainder of this chapter, we summarize the findings and conclusions of *Alcohol: No Ordinary Commodity*. Our goal is to suggest that despite the advances in alcohol research and theory, one should never suggest that the answer to effective alcohol policy is "as simple as one, two, three." Whereas the first major review of alcohol policy research in 1975 suggested a relatively simple approach to the prevention of alcohol-related problems, the most recent integrative review indicates that a wide range of evidence-based policy options must be considered at the local, national and international levels in order to prevent and manage alcohol-related problems.

2. SETTING THE POLICY AGENDA

Alcohol policies have been implemented throughout history to minimize the effects of alcohol on the health and safety of the population. The purpose of *Alcohol: No Ordinary Commodity - Research and Public Policy* (Babor et al., 2003) is to describe recent advances in alcohol research that have direct relevance to alcohol policy on the local, national, and international levels. Alcohol policies serve the interests of public health through their impact on drinking patterns, the drinking environment, and the health services available to treat problem drinkers. Public health concepts provide an important vehicle to manage the health of populations in relation to the use and misuse of beverage alcohol by helping communities and nation states to design better preventative and curative services.

3. NO ORDINARY COMMODITY

In many countries, the production and sale of alcoholic beverages generates profits for farmers, manufacturers, advertisers, and investors. Alcohol provides employment for people in bars and restaurants, brings in foreign currency for exported beverages, and generates tax revenues for the government. Alcoholic beverages are, by any reckoning, an important, economically embedded commodity. But the benefits connected with the production, sale, and use of this commodity come at an enormous cost to society. Three important mechanisms explain alcohol's ability to cause medical, psychological, and social harm: 1) physical toxicity, 2) intoxication, and 3) dependence.

Alcohol is a toxic substance in terms of its direct and indirect effects on a wide range of body organs and systems. But the main cause of alcohol-related harm in the general population is alcohol intoxication, rather than its toxic effects. The link between intoxication and adverse consequences is strong, especially for violence, traffic casualties, and other injuries. Alcohol dependence has many different contributory causes including genetic vulnerability, but it is a condition that is contracted by repeated exposure to alcohol: the heavier the drinking, the greater the risk.

As illustrated in Figure 1, the mechanisms of toxicity, intoxication and dependence are closely related to the ways in which people consume alcohol, called 'patterns of drinking'. Drinking patterns that lead to rapidly elevated blood alcohol levels result in problems associated with acute intoxication, such as accidents, injuries, and violence. Similarly, drinking patterns that promote frequent and heavy alcohol consumption are associated with chronic health problems such as liver cirrhosis, cardiovascular disease, and depression. Finally, sustained drinking may result in alcohol dependence. Once dependence is present, it impairs a person's ability to control the frequency and amount of drinking. For these reasons, alcohol is not a run-of-the-mill consumer substance. Public health responses must be matched to this complex vision of the dangers of alcohol as they seek better ways to respond to population-level harms.

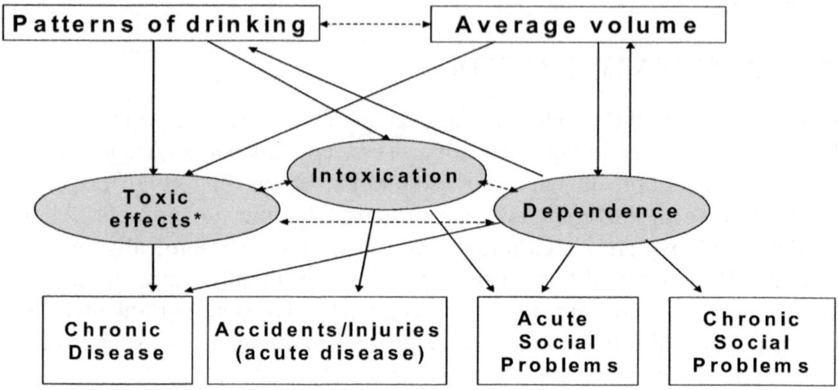

Figure 1. Why alcohol is no ordinary commodity. Relationships among alcohol consumption, mediating factors and alcohol-related consequences (Reprinted with permission from Babor et al., 2003).

4. ALCOHOL CONSUMPTION TRENDS AND PATTERNS OF DRINKING

Alcohol consumption varies enormously, not only among countries, but also over time and between different population groups, especially according to gender and age. Variations in these drinking patterns affect rates of alcohol-related problems, and have implications for the choice of alcohol policy measures. Two aspects of alcohol consumption are of particular importance for comparisons across populations and across time. First, total alcohol consumption in a population is an important indicator of the number of individuals who are exposed to high amounts of alcohol. Adult per capita alcohol consumption is, to a considerable extent, related to the prevalence of heavy use, which in turn is associated with the occurrence of negative effects. Second, the relationship between total alcohol consumption and harm is modified by the number of drinkers in a population and by the way in which alcohol is consumed.

Recorded alcohol consumption is highest in the economically developed regions of the world (e.g., Europe, North America). In contrast, recorded consumption is generally lower in Africa and parts of Asia, and is particularly low in Moslem states and the Indian subcontinent. Western Europe, Russia and other non-Moslem parts of the former Soviet Union now have the highest per capita consumption levels, but Latin American levels are not far behind (WHO, 1999).

Sales data from established market economies show a slight overall decrease in alcohol consumption in recent years, as well as converging trends in traditional high consumption and low consumption countries. This is particularly the case in the wine-producing countries in Europe, such as France, Italy, and Portugal, where the decrease is mostly due to reductions in wine consumption (Gual and Colom, 1997). Of particular concern, however, is the increasing consumption in some of the emerging economies of the developing world, such as China, given that the drinking appears to be concentrated in a smaller fraction of the population in these countries (WHO, 1999, 2000).

Regarding population group differences, there are striking gender differences in whether a person drinks, with men more likely to be drinkers and women abstainers. Among drinkers, men drink 'heavily' (i.e., to intoxication, or large quantities per occasion) much more often than women (e.g., Dawson, 2000; Mäkelä et al., 1999; Mohan & Sharma, 1995). Regarding age differences, abstinence and infrequent drinking are more prevalent in older age groups, and frequent intoxication is more prevalent among young adults (e.g., Demers 1997; Dawson 1998; Mäkelä et al., 1999).

Most of the alcohol in a society is consumed by a relatively small minority of drinkers (e.g., Greenfield & Rogers, 1999; Lemmens, 1991). When alcohol consumption levels increase in a country, there tends to be an increase in the prevalence of heavy drinkers (Skog, 1985, 2001).

Countries and population groups vary in the extent to which drinking to intoxication is a characteristic of the drinking pattern. They also differ in how intoxicated people get, and how people behave while intoxicated. In the southern European countries, approximately one out of ten drinking occasions lead to a state of intoxication among adolescents, whereas the majority of drinking occasions in the most northern European countries result in intoxication (Hibell et al., 1997, 2000).

5. THE GLOBAL BURDEN OF ALCOHOL CONSUMPTION

According to the World Health Organization, in the year 2000, alcohol-related death and disability accounted for 4.0% of the global burden of disease, quantified according to the impact of premature deaths and disability in a population (Murray & Lopez, 1996; Ezzati et al., 2002). Ranking as the fifth most detrimental risk factor of 26 examined, alcohol accounted for about the same amount of disease as tobacco (Ezzati et al., 2002). In developed countries, alcohol was the third most detrimental risk factor, accounting for 9.2% of all burden of disease. In emerging economies like China, alcohol was the most detrimental risk factor. Overall, injuries accounted for the largest portion of alcohol-attributable disease burden, which ranged from close to zero among females in the predominantly Moslem Eastern Mediterranean regions to more than 20% for males in Eastern Europe (Ezzati et al., 2002).

The relation between disease and alcohol consumption is complex. The volume of drinking is linked to most disease outcomes through specific dose-response relationships. These relationships can be linear at the individual level (as in the case of breast cancer or suicide), accelerating (as in the case of liver cirrhosis or motor vehicle accidents), or J-shaped (as in the case of heart disease or all-cause mortality) (Rehm, 2000; Rehm et al., 2001a, 2001b). Patterns of drinking also play an important role in the disease burden, and are variously linked to coronary heart disease, motor vehicle accidents, suicide, and breast cancer.

Moderate drinking has positive as well as negative health effects. Although it has been linked to an increased risk of cancer and other disease conditions, studies indicate a cardioprotective effect of regular, light, and moderate alcohol consumption at the level of the individual drinker (Murray & Lopez, 1996). This effect applies mainly to the age group of 40 years and older, where the overwhelming majority of coronary heart disease occurs (Rehm and Sempos 1995a, 1995b). This effect explains the lower death rate of light drinkers relative to abstainers. However, studies suggest that there may be no net protective effect at the population level from an increase in alcohol consumption, and even a detrimental effect in societies with heavy episodic drinking patterns.

Although public discussion has often concentrated on alcohol-related problems connected with disease and other medical conditions, alcohol is also linked to consequences in the social realm, which has been called 'the forgotten dimension.' Clearly, alcohol is related to many social problems, especially violence.

In summary, alcohol accounts for a significant disease burden worldwide and is related to many negative social consequences. While there may be some offsetting psychological and cardio-protective benefits from drinking, the lower the consumption, the better.

6. STRATEGIES AND INTERVENTIONS TO REDUCE ALCOHOL-RELATED HARM

Alcohol policy is broadly defined as any purposeful effort or authoritative decision on the part of governments or non-government groups to minimize or prevent alcohol-related consequences. Policies may involve the implementation of a specific strategy with regard to alcohol problems (e.g., increase alcohol taxes), or the allocation of resources that reflect priorities with regard to prevention or treatment efforts. Policies that unintentionally increase harm should also be examined, in order to provide insight into the public health risks associated with ill-advised policy decisions.

6.1. Pricing and Taxation

Evidence suggests that alcohol prices have an effect on the level of alcohol consumption (Pindyck & Rubinfeld, 1989). Consumers of alcoholic beverages increase their drinking when prices are lowered, and decrease their consumption when prices rise. Heavy or problem drinkers appear to be no exception to this rule. Moreover, economic studies demonstrate that increased alcoholic beverage taxes and prices are related to reductions in alcohol-related problems.

Despite these findings, the real price of alcoholic beverages has decreased in many countries over the last 50 years, even as many other alcohol control measures have been liberalized or abandoned completely (Cook, 1981). A major reason for the price decline has been the failure of governments to increase tax levels in accordance with inflation. Alcohol taxes are thus an attractive instrument of alcohol policy because they can be used both to generate direct revenue and to reduce alcohol-related harm. The most important downside to raising alcohol taxes is the possibility of smuggling or illegal in-country alcohol production. The net effects of taxation and price increases, however, are to reduce alcohol use and related problems.

6.2. Regulating the Physical Availability of Alcohol

The physical availability of alcoholic beverages refers to the accessibility or convenience of obtaining and consuming these products. Most countries have restrictions on who may buy and sell alcohol, primarily because of social concerns about health, safety, and public order. Experience has shown that extreme restrictions on alcohol availability, such as the banning of all alcohol sales (i.e., total prohibition), can lower drinking and reduce alcohol problems. Yet these restrictions often have adverse side effects, such as the criminality associated with illicit markets (Room et al., 2002; Levine, 1985).

Research on limiting alcohol availability demonstrates that reductions in the hours and days of sale, numbers of alcohol outlets, and restrictions on access to alcohol are associated with reductions in both alcohol use and alcohol-related problems. Laws that raise the minimum legal purchasing age reduce alcohol sales and problems among young drinkers (Wagenaar et al., 1998). Regulations directed toward commercial vendors of alcohol who sell to minors and ignore other restrictions can also be effective, provided the system has the power to suspend or revoke a license in the case of selling infractions. The evidence suggests that making available and promoting beverages of low alcohol content may be an effective strategy because it has the potential to reduce the level of absolute alcohol consumed and associated intoxication and impairment (e.g., Skog, 1988).

One means to regulate alcohol availability in a comprehensive way is through government-owned alcohol outlets. There is strong evidence that off-premise monopoly systems limit alcohol consumption and alcohol-related problems, and that elimination of government off-premise monopolies can increase total alcohol consumption (Wagenaar and Holder, 1995).

In general, changes in availability can have large effects in nations or communities where there is popular support for these measures. The cost of restricting physical availability of alcohol is cheap relative to the costs of health consequences related to drinking, especially heavy drinking. The most notable adverse effects of availability restrictions include increases in informal market activities (e.g., home production, illegal imports). Nevertheless, informal market activities are generally not sufficient to replace formal production and have not produced equivalent levels of alcohol-related problems (Rossow, 2000).

6.3. Modifying the Drinking Context

Many prevention measures seek to limit drinking in the contexts or environments where alcohol is typically sold and consumed (e.g., bars and restaurants). The most effective options involve enforcement of serving regulations and the legal liability of bar staff and owners for the actions of those they serve. Responsible Beverage Service (RBS) programs focus on attitudes, knowledge, skills, and practices of persons involved in serving alcoholic beverages on licensed premises (see Carvolth, 1995; Toomey et al., 1998). If supported by actual changes in the serving policies of licensed establishments and reinforced by local police, RBS training can reduce heavy consumption and high risk drinking (Howard-Pitney et al., 1991; Lang et al., 1998).

Community mobilization has been used to raise public awareness of problems associated with on-premise drinking in licensed establishments, develop specific solutions to problems, and pressure owners to recognize that they have a responsibility to the community in terms of such bar-related issues as noise level and patron behavior (Hauritz et al., 1998a, 1998b; Homel et al., 1992; Putnam et al., 1993). Community mobilization can be highly successful at reducing aggression and other problems related to drinking in licensed premises, but the long-term sustainability of these efforts remains to be demonstrated.

Other approaches include general safety measures that have particular relevance to intoxicated persons and modifying the potential behavior of bystanders or victims. Research shows that the adoption and enforcement of policies to make licensed premises safer are associated with lower levels of intoxication and problems. A number of communities, most notably in Australia, have implemented voluntary codes of practice among local bar owners to limit the major risk factors for violence and other alcohol-related problems. This approach has had mixed results.

6.4. Drinking-Driving Countermeasures

Traditionally, law enforcement directed at drinking-driving has been designed to catch offenders, on the assumption that such practices will prevent or deter people from driving after drinking. Punishment for a drinking-driving conviction has typically been increased either by changing the maximum penalties or by introducing mandatory minimum penalties. There is limited evidence to support the positive impact of these laws. 'Celerity', or swiftness of punishment, is related to the proximity of punishment to the drinking-driving event. The one punishment that seems to have a consistent impact on drinking-driving offenses is administrative license suspension, or revocation for drinking-driving (McKnight & Voas, 2001; Homel, 1981). License loss can be effective for both alcohol-involved and non-alcohol-involved accidents.

One strategy for increasing certainty of apprehension and punishment is to increase the frequency and visibility of drinking-driving enforcement. The traditional way of producing a higher perceived probability of apprehension is simply to intensify police enforcement through such measures as sobriety or selective checkpoints. A more effective approach is through Random Breath Testing (RBT) or Compulsory Breath Testing (Shults et al., 2001; Henstridge et al., 1997). Motorists are stopped at random by police and required to take a preliminary breath test, even if they are in no way suspected of having committed an offence or been involved in an accident. The evidence is quite strong that highly visible, non-selective testing can have a sustained effect in reducing drinking-driving and the associated crashes, injuries, and deaths (Stewart & Conway, 1999).

In addition, when combined with enforcement, national and state laws lowering the legal limit of the driver's blood alcohol concentration (BAC) have been a successful way to reduce drinking-driving. The evidence indicates that setting a reasonably low level of BAC (e.g., .08) significantly reduces alcohol-related driving fatalities (Shults et al., 2001).

Treatment programs have also been used in many countries to provide a therapeutic or educational alternative to punishment. Evidence from some countries supports the effectiveness of comprehensive treatment including counseling or therapy plus license suspension in reducing recidivism. Successful programs are well structured, go beyond information provision to address alcohol abuse, are conducted for more than ten weeks, and have rules of attendance enforced by a court (Wells-Parker 2000).

Another approach for high-risk repeat offenders is to use ignition interlock devices that prevent a vehicle from being started until the driver passes a breath test. These devices have been very effective for many alcohol-impaired drivers, but have not been widely tested in countries other than the US (McKnight & Voas, 2001).

In general, young drivers (adolescents aged between 16-20 years) are at higher risk for traffic accidents, especially alcohol-involved crashes, as a result of their limited driving experience and their tendency to experiment with heavy or binge drinking. Traditional countermeasures such as driver training and school-based education programs are either ineffective or have yielded mixed results. One effective measure is the use of graduated licensing for novice drivers, which limits the time and other conditions of driving during the first few years of licensing (Begg et al., 2000; Mayhew, 2000; Ulmer et al., 2000).

In summary, the evidence suggests that drinking-driving countermeasures consistently produce long-term problem reductions of between 5% and 30%. Deterrence-based approaches, using innovations such as Random Breath Testing, yield few arrests but substantial accident reductions. The persistent delinquency of some impaired drivers and their consistent contribution to the fatality statistics should not detract from the enormous achievements of recent decades.

6.5. Regulating alcohol promotion

The marketing of alcohol is a global industry. Alcohol brands are advertised through television, radio, print, point-of-sale promotions, and the Internet. Exposure to repeated high-level alcohol promotion inculcates pro-drinking attitudes and increases the likelihood of heavier drinking. Alcohol advertising predisposes minors to drinking well before legal age of purchase. Indeed, advertising has been found to promote and reinforce perceptions of drinking as positive, glamorous, and relatively risk-free.

Legislation restricting alcohol advertising is a well-established precaution used by governments throughout the world, despite opposition from the alcoholic beverage industry. Some bans are partial, applying only to spirits, to certain hours of television viewing, or to state-owned media. These bans often operate alongside codes of self-regulation that govern permitted forms of alcohol advertising. Although many countries have restricted alcohol advertising to various degrees, the evaluation findings suggest that while the restrictions have not achieved a major reduction in drinking and related harms in the short-term, countries with greater restrictions on advertising have less drinking and fewer alcohol-related problems (Saffer, 1991).

Despite industry claims that they adhere to codes of responsible advertising, the detrimental influences of marketing practices are not adequately addressed by industry self-regulation. Self-regulation tends to be fragile and largely ineffective (Baggott, 1989; Campbell, 1999). These codes may work best where the media, advertising, and alcohol industries are all involved, and an independent body has powers to approve or veto advertisements, rule on complaints, and impose sanctions. Few countries currently have all these components.

6.6. Education and Persuasion Strategies

School-based alcohol education programs have been found to increase knowledge and change attitudes toward alcohol and other substances, but actual substance use remains unaffected (Botvin et al., 1995; Hansen, 1994; Tobler, 1992). Approaches that address values clarification, self-esteem, general social skills, and “alternatives” approaches that provide activities inconsistent with alcohol use (e.g., sports) are equally ineffective (Moskowitz, 1989). Many contemporary school-based programs include both resistance skills training and normative education, which attempts to correct adolescents’ tendency to overestimate the number of their peers who drink (Hansen, 1992, 1993, 1994). Scientific evaluations of these programs have produced mixed results with generally modest effects that are short-lived unless accompanied by ongoing booster sessions. Some programs include both individual-level education and family- or community-level interventions. Evaluations suggest that even these comprehensive programs may not be sufficient to delay the initiation of drinking, or to sustain a small reduction in drinking beyond the operation of the program.

Public service announcements (PSAs) are messages prepared by nongovernmental organizations, health agencies, and media organizations that deal with responsible drinking, the hazards of drinking-driving, and related topics. Despite their good intentions, PSAs are an ineffective antidote to the high-quality pro-drinking messages that appear much more frequently as paid advertisements in the mass media (see Ludwig, 1994; Murray et al., 1996).

Counter-advertising involves disseminating information about a product, its effects, and the industry that promotes it, in order to decrease its appeal and use. Tactics include health-warning labels on product packaging, such as those that explain that alcohol may cause birth defects when consumed during pregnancy. Although a significant proportion of the population reports seeing these warning labels, research indicates that exposure produces no change in drinking behavior per se (Grube & Nygaard, 2001; Agostinali & Grube, 2002).

In sum, the impact of education and persuasion programs tends to be small at best. When positive effects are found, they do not persist.

6.7. Treatment and Early Intervention Services

In addition to its value in the reduction of human suffering, treatment can be considered a form of prevention. Treatment for alcohol problems typically involves a set of services, ranging from diagnostic assessment to therapeutic interventions and continuing care. Researchers have identified more than 40 therapeutic approaches, called treatment modalities, which have been evaluated by means of randomized clinical trials (Miller et al., 1995). These modalities are delivered in a variety of settings, including freestanding residential facilities, psychiatric and general hospital settings, outpatient programs, and primary health care.

There is no consistent evidence that intensive in-patient treatment provides more benefit than less intensive outpatient treatment, although residential treatment may be indicated for patients who: 1) are highly resistant to treatment; 2) have few financial resources; 3) come from environments that are not conducive to recovery; and 4) have more serious, coexisting medical or psychiatric conditions (Finney et al., 1996). Regarding specific treatment modalities, the weight of evidence suggests that behavioral treatments are likely to be more effective than insight-oriented therapies (Miller & Hester, 1986). Recent research also indicates that Twelve Step Facilitation, which is based on the principles of Alcoholics Anonymous, is as effective as more theory-based therapies (Babor & Del Boca, 2002; Ouimette et al., 1999). In general, when patients enter treatment, exposure to any treatment is associated with significant reductions in alcohol use and related problems, regardless of the type of intervention used.

Interest on the part of the pharmaceutical industry in medications to treat alcohol dependence has increased in the past decade, and several compounds are now available in the US and Europe. In the 1990s, naltrexone, an opioid antagonist, became available for medical management of alcohol dependence, following positive studies showing incremental benefits of psychotherapy combined with this medication (O'Malley et al., 1992). Acamprosate (calcium acetylhomotaurinate), an amino acid derivative, has also shown positive effects in the prevention of relapse. It is now in widespread clinical use in Europe (Kranzler & Van Kirk, 2001).

Although mutual help societies composed of recovering alcoholics are not considered to be formal treatment, they are often used as inexpensive substitutes, alternatives, and adjuncts to treatment (McCrady & Miller, 1993). Mutual help groups based on the Twelve Steps of AA have proliferated throughout the world (Mäkelä, 1993). Research suggests that AA itself can have an incremental effect when combined with formal treatment, and that AA attendance alone may be better than no intervention at all (McCrady & Miller, 1993; Babor & Del Boca, 2002; Ouimette et al., 1999; Walsh et al., 1991).

In contrast to treatment provided in specialized settings, brief interventions consist of one to three sessions of counseling or advice delivered in general medical settings. The cumulative evidence of randomized controlled trials (conducted in a variety of settings) indicates that clinically significant changes in drinking behavior and related problems can follow from brief interventions with non-alcoholic heavy drinkers (Bien et al., 1993; Kahan et al., 1995; Wilk et al., 1997).

Although treatment and early intervention can be considered an effective means of secondary prevention, specialized services (other than mutual help organizations) tend to be expensive and may not be affordable in developing countries unless they are integrated with the system of primary care.

7. THE INTERNATIONAL CONTEXT OF ALCOHOL POLICY

In a world of increasing trade globalization, national and local alcohol policies, predicated on the extraordinary nature of alcohol, have increasingly come under pressure at the international level. The last 50 years have seen a convergence in alcohol policies in Europe. There have also been converging trends with regard to taxing alcoholic beverages, although excise duties are still clearly lowest in wine-producing countries, and highest among the Nordic countries, Ireland, and the United Kingdom. In North America there has been a gradual decline in alcohol control in most jurisdictions in recent decades, with more dramatic changes such as privatization of alcohol retail sales. Alcohol taxes have not been raised to match inflation. In contrast, there have been extensive education and law enforcement efforts to control drinking-driving.

Similar developments have taken place in other parts of the world. For instance, the collapse of the communist system in the former Soviet Union and Eastern Europe has meant that alcohol control, especially the control of alcohol availability, has lost much of its effect in these countries. On the other hand, in the 1990s, under the impetus of the European Alcohol Action Plan, many Eastern European countries adopted national alcohol programs or participated in projects aimed at strengthening local alcohol control (Gual & Colom, 2001).

In many developed countries, general alcohol policies affecting the whole population and oriented to the collective good have been weakened or dismantled, often under pressure from the 'structural adjustment' programs of international development agencies. Policies remaining from the past have been gradually eroded (e.g., privatization of monopolies, erosion of taxes by inflation, extension of closing hours). At the same time, however, popular concern about alcohol-related problems has risen, although it has only fitfully found political expression. In many countries there has been an increase in educational programs, despite research on their lack of effect, along with some interventions to curtail drinking-driving.

One factor behind the weakening of national and local alcohol policies has been the impact of international trade agreements and common markets. To the extent that alcohol is considered to be an ordinary commodity, these agreements and treaties often become severe obstacles for conducting purposeful and efficient alcohol control policies.

8. THE POLICY ARENA

Who makes alcohol policy? The answer differs among countries and between different levels of government within countries. Within each jurisdiction of the policy arena, there is an interplay of different interest groups.

A national level legislative and regulatory framework is essential to the promotion of effective measures to curtail alcohol-related problems. Federal and national laws often establish the legislative framework pertaining to alcohol. In many nations there is a vacuum in advocacy for the public interest, leaving members of non-governmental organizations as the most likely candidates to represent the public (Craplet, 1997). These have occasionally involved interest groups representing victims of alcohol-related harm, such as Mothers Against Drunk Driving (DeJong & Russell, 1995). More recently, alcohol issues have increasingly become the concern of health professionals.

The mass media can have a significant influence on the policy debate at the national and local levels, given their dominant role in contemporary culture (Milio, 1988). Media coverage influences whether policymakers perceive a problem and how salient that problem is. This is an 'agenda-setting' function (Erbring et al., 1980).

Groups involved in for-profit production and sales are often key players in policy debates. Supported by free market values and concepts, the alcoholic beverage industry has become increasingly involved in the policy arena in order to protect its commercial interests. In some countries, the industry is the dominant nongovernmental presence at the policymaking table. Although the alcoholic beverage industry is not monolithic in terms of its motives, power, or operations, its commercial interests often come into conflict with public health measures.

An appreciation of the various players in the alcohol policy arena can heighten our understanding of the following fundamental conclusion: alcohol policy is often the product of competing interests, values, and ideologies. The process of alcohol policy creation needs to be better understood, more transparent, and more responsive to the needs of the citizens who are the end consumers of emerging policies.

9. ALCOHOL POLICIES: A CONSUMER'S GUIDE

The difference between good and bad alcohol policy is not an abstraction, but very often a matter of life and death. Research has the capacity to indicate which strategies are likely to succeed in their public health intentions, and which are likely to be less effective or even useless, diversionary, and a waste of resources. Building on previous work in this area, Babor et al. (2003) rated 32 policy options in *Alcohol: No Ordinary Commodity* according to four major criteria: 1) evidence of effectiveness; 2) strength of research support; 3) extent of testing across diverse countries and cultures; and 4) relative cost in terms of time, resources, and money.

In general, effectiveness is strong for the regulation of physical availability and the use of alcohol taxes. Given the broad reach of these strategies, and the relatively low expense of implementing them, the expected impact of these measures on public health is relatively high. Most drinking-driving countermeasures received high ratings on effectiveness as well. Not only is there good research support for these programs, but they also seem to be applicable in most countries and are relatively inexpensive to implement and sustain.

In contrast, the expected impact is low for school-based education and for public service messages about drinking. Although the reach of educational programs is thought to be excellent (because of the availability of captive audiences in schools), the population impact of these programs is poor. Similarly, while feasibility is good, cost-effectiveness and cost-benefit are poor.

Treatment and early intervention strategies have, at best, medium effectiveness. At the population level, their impact is limited, since specialized treatment for alcohol problems can only benefit the relatively small fraction of the population who come to treatment. While treatment provision is an obligation of a humane society, its effect on the actual drinking problem rates of the population at large is necessarily limited.

Strategies directed at altering the drinking context are primarily applicable to on-premise drinking in bars and restaurants, which somewhat limits their public health significance. In most developed countries, only a minority of drinking is done on-premise, although frequently this drinking is trouble-prone. One recurring theme in this literature is the importance of enforcement.

The following 10 policy options stand out as 'best practices': minimum legal purchase age, government monopoly of retail sales, restrictions on hours or days of sale, outlet density restrictions, alcohol taxes, sobriety check points, lowered BAC limits, administrative license suspension, graduated licensing for novice drivers, and brief interventions for hazardous drinkers.

Alcohol policies can be effective at both the community level and the national level. Within each of these levels, policies can be targeted at the general population, at high-risk drinkers, and at people already experiencing alcohol-related problems. Alcohol policies rarely operate independently or in isolation from other measures. Complementary system strategies that seek to restructure the total drinking environment are more likely to be effective than single strategies. Full-spectrum interventions are needed to achieve the greatest population impact.

In sum, opportunities for evidence-based alcohol policies that better serve the public good are more available than ever before. But the policies to address alcohol-related problems are too seldom informed by science, and there are still too many instances of policy vacuums filled by unevaluated or ineffective strategies and interventions. Because alcohol is no ordinary commodity, the public has a right to expect a more enlightened approach to alcohol policy.

10. AFFILIATIONS

Thomas F. Babor, Ph.D., MPH is Professor and Chairman of the Department of Community Medicine and Health Care at the University of Connecticut School of Medicine, Farmington, CT, USA

11. NOTES

[1] The Alcohol and Public Policy Group consists of Thomas Babor, Raul Caetano, Sally Casswell, Griffith Edwards, Norman Giesbrecht, Kathryn Graham, Joel Grube, Paul Gruenewald, Linda Hill, Harold Holder, Ross Homel, Esa Österberg, Jürgen Rehm, Robin Room, and Ingeborg Rossow.

The writing of this book was sponsored in part by the World Health Organization (WHO Regional Office for Europe and Geneva Headquarters) and the Society for the Study of Addiction. The findings and conclusions represent the consensus views of its 15 authors, none of whom received either direct or indirect support for their participation from any of the sponsoring organizations or any other organization that might represent a conflict of interest. This article, with minor changes, includes substantial portions of a paper originally printed in Addiction (The Alcohol and Public Policy Group, *Alcohol: No Ordinary Commodity. A Summary of the Book,* October, 2003). It is reprinted here with permission from Blackwell Publishing.

12. REFERENCES

Agostinelli, G., & Grube, J. (2002). Alcohol counter-advertising and the media: A review of recent research. *Alcohol Research and Health, 26,* 15-21.

Babor, T. F., & Del Boca, F. K. (Eds.) (2002). *Treatment Matching in Alcoholism.* Cambridge, UK: Cambridge University Press.

Babor, T. F., Caetano, R., Casswell, S., Edwards, G., Giesbrecht, N., Graham, K., Grube, J., Gruenewald, P., Hill, L., Holder, H., Homel, R., Österberg, E., Rehm, J., Room, R., & Rossow, I. (2003). *Alcohol: No Ordinary Commodity - Research and public policy.* Oxford and London: Oxford University Press.

Baggott, R. (1989). Regulatory reform in Britain: The changing face of self-regulation. *Public Administration, 67,* 435-454.

Begg, D. J., Alsop, J., & Langley, J. D. (2000). The impact of graduated driver licensing restrictions on young driver crashes in New Zealand. In *Proceedings of the 15th International Conference on Alcohol, Drugs and Traffic Safety.* Stockholm, Sweden: International Council on Alcohol, Drugs and Traffic Safety (ICADTS).

Bien, T. H., Miller, W. R., & Tonigan, S. (1993). Brief intervention for alcohol problems: A review. *Addiction, 88,* 315-336.

Botvin, G. J., Baker, E., Dusenbury, L., Botvin, E. M., & Diaz, T. (1995). Long-term follow-up results of a randomized drug abuse prevention trial in a white middle-class population. *Journal of the American Medical Association, 273,* 1106-1112.

Bruun K., Edwards G., Lumio M., Mäkelä K., Pan, L., Popham R.E., Room R., Schmidt W., Skog O.-J., Sulkunen P., Österberg E. (1975) *Alcohol Control Policies in Public Health Perspective.* Helsinki: The Finnish Foundation for Alcohol Studies.

Campbell, A. J. (1999). Self-regulation and the media. *Federal Communications Law Journal, 51,* 711-746.

Carvolth, R. (1995). The Contribution of Risk Assessment to Harm Reduction through the Queensland Safety Action Approach. Proceedings of the 'Window of Opportunity Congress', Brisbane, Australia.

Cook, P. J. (1981). The effect of liquor taxes on drinking, cirrhosis and auto fatalities. In M. Moore, & D. Gerstein (Eds.), *Alcohol and Public Policy: Beyond the Shadow of Prohibition* (pp. 255-285). Washington, DC: National Academy of Sciences.

Dawson, D. A. (1998). Beyond black, white and Hispanic: Race, ethnic origin and drinking patterns in the United States. *Journal of Substance Abuse, 10,* 321-339.

Dawson, D. A. (2000). Drinking patterns among individuals with and without DSM-IV alcohol use disorders. *Journal of Studies on Alcohol, 61,* 111-120.

DeJong, W., & Russell, A. (1995). MADD's position on alcohol advertising: a response to Marshall and Oleson. *Journal of Public Health Policy, 16,* 231-238.

Demers, A. (1997). When at risk? Drinking contexts and heavy drinking in the Montreal adult population. Contemporary Drug Problems 24, 449-471.

Edwards, G., Anderson, P., Babor, T.F., Casswell, S., Ferrence, R., Geisbrecht, N., Godfrey, C., Holder, H., Lemmens, P., Makela, K., Midanik, L., Norstrom, T., Osterberg, E., Romelsjo, A., Room, R., Simpura, J., Skog., O. Alcohol and the Public Good. Oxford University Press, 1994.

Erbring, L., Goldenberg, E., & Miller, A. (1980). Front page news and real world cues: a new look at agenda setting by the media. *American Journal of Political Science, 24,* 16-49.

Ezzati, M., Lopez, A. D., Rodgers, A., Vander Hoorn, S., Murray, C. J. L., & the Comparative Risk Assessment Collaborating Group (2002). Selected major risk factors and global and regional burden of disease. *Lancet, 360,* 1347-1360.

Finney, J. W., Hahn, A. C., & Moos, R. H. (1996). The effectiveness of inpatient and outpatient treatment for alcohol abuse: The need to focus on mediators and moderators of setting effects. *Addiction, 91,* 1773-1796.

Grube, J. W., & Nygaard, P. (2001). Adolescent drinking and alcohol policy. *Contemporary Drug Problems, 28,* 87-131.

Greenfield, T. K., & Rogers, J. D. (1999). Who drinks most of the alcohol in the US? The policy implications. Journal of Studies on Alcohol 60, 78-89.

Gual, A., & Colom, J. (1997). Why has alcohol consumption declined in countries of southern Europe? *Addiction, 92* (Suppl. 1), 21-31S.

Gual, A., & Colom, J. (2001). From Paris to Stockholm: where does the European Alcohol Action Plan lead to? *Addiction, 96,* 1093-1096.

Hansen, D. J. (1992). School-based substance abuse prevention: A review of the state of the art in curriculum, 1980-1990. *Health Education Research, 7,* 403-430.

Hansen, D. J. (1993). School-based alcohol prevention programmes. *Alcohol Health & Research World, 17,* 54-61.

Hansen, D. J. (1994). Prevention of alcohol use and abuse. *Preventive Medicine, 23,* 683-687.

Hauritz, M., Homel, R., Townsley, M., Burrows, T., & McIllwain, G. (Eds.) (1998a). *An Evaluation of the Local Government Safety Action Projects in Cairns, Townsville and Mackay: A Report to the Queensland Department of Health, the Queensland Police Service and the Criminology Research Council.* Australia: Griffith University, Centre for Crime Policy and Public Safety; School of Justice Administration.

Hauritz, M., Homel, R., McIlwain, G., Burrows, T., & Townsley, M. (1998b). Reducing violence in licensed venues through community safety action projects: The Queensland experience. *Contemporary Drug Problems, 25,* 511-551.

Henstridge, J., Homel, R., & Mackay, P. (1997). *The Long-Term Effects of Random Breath Testing in Four Australian States: A Time Series Analysis.* Canberra, Australia: Federal Office of Road Safety.

Hibell, B., Andersson, B., Bjarnason, T., Kokkevi, A., Morgan, M., & Narusk, A. (1997). *The 1995 European School Survey Project on Alcohol and Other Drugs (ESPAD Report: Alcohol and Other Drug Use among Students in 26 Countries.* Stockholm: Swedish Council for Information on Alcohol and Other Drugs (CAN).

Hibell, B., Andersson, B., Ahlström, S., Balakireva, O., Bjarnason, T., Kokkevi, A., & Morgan, M. (2000). *The 1999 ESPAD Report: Alcohol and Other Drug Use among Students in 30 European Countries.* Stockholm: Swedish Council for Information on Alcohol and Other Drugs (CAN).

Holder H.D. and Edwards G. (eds.) (1995) *Alcohol and Public Policy: Evidence and Issues.* Oxford University Press.

Homel, R. (1981). Penalties and the drink-driver: A study of one thousand offenders. *Australian and New Zealand Journal of Criminology, 14,* 225-241.

Homel, R., Tomsen, S., & Thommeny, J. (1992). Public drinking and violence: Not just an alcohol problem. *Journal of Drug Issues, 22,* 679-697.

Howard-Pitney, B., Johnson, M.D., Altman, D.G., Hopkins, R., & Hammond, N. (1991). Responsible alcohol service: A study of server, manager, and environmental impact. *American Journal of Public Health, 81,* 197-199.

Kahan, M., Wilson, L., & Becker, L. (1995). Effectiveness of physician-based interventions with problem drinkers: A review. *Canadian Medical Association Journal, 152,* 851-859.

Kranzler, H.R., & Van Kirk, J. (2001). Naltrexone and acamprosate in the treatment of alcoholism: A meta-analysis. *Alcoholism: Clinical and Experimental Research, 25,* 1335-1341.

Lang, E., Stockwell, T., Rydon, P., & Beel, A. (1998). Can training bar staff in responsible serving practices reduce alcohol-related harm? *Drug and Alcohol Review, 17,* 39-50.

Lemmens, P. H. (1991). Measurement and distribution of alcohol consumption (dissertation). Maastricht: University of Limburg.

Levine, H. G. (1985). The birth of American alcohol control: prohibition, the power elite, and the problem of lawlessness. *Contemporary Drug Problems, 12,* 63-115.

Ludwig, M. J. (1994). Mass media and health education: a critical analysis and reception study of a selected anti-drug campaign. *Dissertation Abstracts, International, 55,* 1479A.

Mäkelä, K. (1993). International comparisons of Alcoholics Anonymous. *Alcohol Health & Research World, 17,* 228-234.

Mäkelä, P., Fonager, K., Hibell, B., Nordlund, S., Sabroe, S., & Simpura, J. (1999). *Drinking habits in the Nordic countries.* SIFA Rapport 2/99. Oslo: National Institute for Alcohol and Drug Research.

Mayhew, D. R. (2000). Effectiveness of graduated driver licensing. In T. Kursius, W. Bullock, N. Edwards, J. Holt, M. King, T. Lake, K. Redford, M. Sheehan, & R. Tay (Eds.), *Proceedings of Conference: Road Safety - Research, Policing and Education, November 26-28, 2000* (pp. 5-10). Brisbane, Queensland, Australia.

McCrady, B. S., & Miller, W. R. (Eds.) (1993). *Research on Alcoholics Anonymous: Opportunities and Alternatives*, pp. 41-78. New Brunswick, NJ: Rutgers Center of Alcohol Studies.

McKnight, A. J., & Voas, R. B. (2001). Prevention of alcohol-related road crashes. In Heather N., Peters T.J., & Stockwell T. (Eds.), *International Handbook of Alcohol Dependence and Problems*, pp. 741-770. Chichester, UK: John Wiley and Sons.

Milio, N. (1988). Making healthy public policy; developing the science by learning the art: an ecological framework for policy studies. *Health Promotion, 2,* 263-274.

Miller ,W. R., & Hester, R. (1986). Inpatient alcoholism treatment. Who benefits? *American Psychologist, 41,* 794-805.

Miller, W. R., Brown, J. M., Simpson, T. L., Handmaker, N. S., Bien, T. H., Luckie, L. F., Montgomery, H. A., Hester, R. K., & Tonigan, J. S. (1995). What works? A methodological analysis of the alcohol treatment outcome literature. In R. K. Hester, & W. R. Miller (Eds.), *Handbook of Alcoholism Treatment Approaches: Effective Alternatives*, 2nd edn. (pp. 12-44). Boston, MA: Allyn and Bacon.

Mohan, D., & Sharma, H. K. (1995). India. In D. W. Heath (Ed.) *International Handbook of Alcohol and Culture* (pp. 128-141). Westport, CT: Greenwood Press.

Moskowitz, J. M. (1989). Primary prevention of alcohol problems: A critical review of the research literature. *Journal of Studies on Alcohol, 50,* 54–88.

Murray, C. J. L., & Lopez, A. (1996). Quantifying the burden of disease and injury attributable to ten major risk factors. In C. J. L. Murray, & A. Lopez (Eds.), *The Global Burden of Disease: A Comprehensive Assessment of Mortality and Disability from Diseases, Injuries and Risk Factors in 1990 and Projected to 2020* (pp. 295-324). Boston: Harvard School of Public Health on behalf of the World Health Organization and the World Bank.

Murray, J. P., Jr., Stam, A., & Lastovicka, J. L. (1996). Paid- versus donated-media strategies for public service announcement campaigns. *Public Opinion Quarterly, 60,* 1-29.

O'Malley, S. S., Jaffe, A. J., Chang, G., Schottenfeld, R. S., Meyer, R. E., & Rounsaville, B. (1992). Naltrexone and coping skills therapy for alcohol dependence: A controlled study. *Archives of General Psychiatry, 49,* 894-898.

Ouimette, P. C., Finney, J. W., Gima, K., & Moos, R. H. (1999). A comparative evaluation of substance abuse treatment: examining mechanisms underlying patient-treatment matching hypotheses for 12-step and cognitive-behavioral treatments for substance abuse. *Alcoholism: Clinical and Experimental Research, 23,* 545-551.

Putnam, S. L., Rockett, I. R. H., & Campbell, M. K. (1993). Methodological issues in community-based alcohol-related injury prevention projects: Attribution of program effects. In T.K. Greenfield, & R.

Zimmerman (Eds.), *Experiences with Community Action Projects: New Research in the Prevention of Alcohol and other Drug Problems* (pp. 31-39). Rockville, MD: Center for Substance Abuse Prevention.

Rehm, J. (2000). Alcohol consumption and mortality. What do we know and where should we go? *Addiction, 95,* 989-995.

Rehm, J., & Sempos, C. T. (1995a). Alcohol Consumption and mortality - questions about causality, confounding and methodology. *Addiction, 90,* 493-498.

Rehm, J., & Sempos, C. T. (1995b). Alcohol consumption and all-cause mortality. *Addiction, 90,* 471-480.

Rehm, J., Greenfield, T. K., & Rogers, J. D. (2001a). Average volume of alcohol consumption, patterns of drinking and all-cause mortality. Results from the US National Alcohol Survey. *American Journal of Epidemiology, 153,* 64-71.

Rehm, J., Gutjahr, E., & Gmel, G. (2001b). Alcohol and all-cause mortality: a pooled analysis. *Contemporary Drug Problems, 28,* 337-361.

Room, R., Jernigan, J., Carlini Marlatt, B., Gureje, O., Mäkelä, K., Marshall, M., Medina Mora, M. E., Monteiro, M., Parry, C., Partanen, J., Riley, L, & Saxena, S. (2002). *Alcohol in Developing Societies: A Public Health Approach.* Helsinki: Finnish Foundation for Alcohol Studies.

Rossow, I. (2000). The validity of political arguments in the Norwegian alcohol policy debate: associations between availability of liquor and consumption of illegal spirits. *Contemporary Drug Problems, 27,* 253-269.

Saffer, H. (1991). Alcohol advertising bans and alcohol abuse: An international perspective. *Journal of Health Economics, 10,* 65-79.

Shults, R. A., Elder, R. W., Sleet, D. A., Nichols, J. L., Alao, M. O., Garande-Kulis, V. G., Zaza, S., Sosin, D. M., Thompson, R .S., & the Task Force on Community Preventive Services (2001). Reviews of evidence regarding interventions to reduce alcohol-impaired driving. *American Journal of Preventive Medicine, 21* (Suppl. 1), 66-88.

Skog, O.-J. (1985). The collectivity of drinking cultures. A theory of the distribution of alcohol consumption. *British Journal of Addiction, 80,* 83-99.

Skog, O.-J. (1988). Effect of introducing a new light beer in Norway: substitution or addition? *British Journal of Addiction, 83,* 665-668.

Skog, O.-J. (2001). Commentary on Gmel and Rehm's interpretation of the theory of collectivity in drinking culture. *Drug and Alcohol Review, 20,* 325-331.

Stewart, L., & Conway, K. (1999). Community Action to reduce rural drink driving crashes: encouraging sustainable efforts in changing environments. In S. Casswell, H. Holder, M. Holmila, S. Larsson, R. Midford, H. M. Barnes, P. Nygaard, & L. Stewart (Eds.), *Fourth Symposium on Community Action Research and the Prevention of Alcohol and Other Drug Problems: Based upon Kettil Bruun Society Thematic Meeting* (pp. 233-246). Auckland, NZ: Alcohol and Public Health Research Unit, University Of Auckland.

Tobler, N. S. (1992). Prevention programs can work: Research findings. *Journal of Addictive Diseases, 11,* 1-28.

Toomey, T. L., Kilian, G. R., Gehan, J. P., Perry, C. L., Jones-Webb, R., & Wagenaar, A. C. (1998). Qualitative assessment of training programs for alcohol servers and establishment managers. *Public Health Reports, 113,* 162-169.

Ulmer R. G., Preusser D. F., Williams A. F., Ferguson S. A., & Farmer C. M. (2000). Effects of Florida's graduated licensing program on the crash rate of teenage drivers. *Accident Analysis and Prevention, 32,* 527-532.

Wagenaar A. C., & Holder H. D. (1995). Changes in alcohol consumption resulting from the elimination of retail wine monopolies: Results from five US states. *Journal of Studies on Alcohol, 56,* 566-572.

Wagenaar A. C., Gehan J. P., Jones-Webb R., Wolfson M., Toomey T. L., Forster J. L., & Murray D. M. (1998). *Communities Mobilizing for Change on Alcohol: Experiences and Outcomes from a Randomized Community Trial.* Minneapolis, MN: University of Minnesota.

Walsh D. C., Hingson R. W., Merrigan D. M., Levenson S. M., Cupples L. A., Heeren T., Coffman G. A., Becker C. A., Barker T. A., Hamilton S. K., McGuire T. G., & Kelly C. A. (1991). A Randomized Trial of Treatment Options for Alcohol-Abusing Workers. *The New England Journal of Medicine, 325,* 775-781.

Wells-Parker E. (2000). Assessment and screening of impaired driving offenders: An analysis of underlying hypotheses as a guide for development of validation strategies. In *Proceedings of the 15th International Conference on Alcohol, Drugs and Traffic Safety.* Stockholm, Sweden: International Council on Alcohol, Drugs and Traffic Safety (ICADTS).

Wilk A. I., Jensen N. M., & Havighurst T. C. (1997). Meta-analysis of randomized control trials addressing brief interventions in heavy alcohol drinkers. *Journal of General Internal Medicine, 12,* 274-283.

World Health Organization (1999). *Global Status Report on Alcohol. WHO/HSC/SAB/99.11.* Geneva: WHO Substance Abuse Department.

World Health Organization (2000). *International Guide for Monitoring Alcohol Consumption and Related Harm.* Geneva, Switzerland: WHO Department of Mental Health and Substance Dependence, Noncommunicable Diseases and Mental Health Cluster.

T. STOCKWELL

HARM REDUCTION: THE DRUGIFICATION OF ALCOHOL POLICES AND THE ALCOHOLISATION OF DRUG POLICIES

Key words: harm reduction, supply reduction, drinking patterns, prevention

ABSTRACT

The concept of Harm Reduction emerged from the drug field in the 1980s in the context of reducing the risk of the spread of blood-borne viruses without necessarily reducing drug use. The concept has since become increasingly influential in the alcohol and even tobacco fields. In Australia, for example, most state liquor acts now identify Harm Reduction (or Harm Minimisation) as a principal objective. The concept of Harm Reduction has been highly controversial and there have been many attempts to redefine it towards politically acceptable positions.

In the alcohol field the concept has sometimes been proposed as an alternative to the view that the prevention of alcohol related harm can only be achieved through a reduction of the total population consumption of alcohol. This paper will present evidence to suggest that most effective interventions to reduce alcohol-related harm require reductions in the quantity of alcohol consumed per occasion. Furthermore, it is highly unlikely in most modern drinking societies that significant reductions in alcohol-related harm can occur without also a significant drop in total population consumption. Nonetheless, Harm Reduction is an important and influential principle in alcohol policy that can be incorporated alongside controls on the physical and economic availability of alcohol.

It is recommended that the term Risk Reduction be applied to the many strategies that fall between Harm Reduction and abstinence-based approaches that require a reduction in amount of alcohol consumed. Finally, emerging evidence regarding common risk and protection factors for adolescent substance use as well as other mental health and behavioural problems is briefly discussed. It is recommended that the concept of Risk here is broadened to include a wide range of social and economic factors which, when addressed, can have multiple benefits in relation to the reduction of both substance use other adolescent problems.

R. Müller and H. Klingemann (eds.),
From Science to Action? 100 Years Later - Alcohol Policies Revisited, 49–58.

INTRODUCTION

In this chapter the expression provided by the book's editor of 'drugification of alcohol policies' is used as code for the emergence of the concept of Harm Reduction as a significant perspective in alcohol policy (e.g. Plant, Single & Stockwell, 1997). Discussion of a broad Risk and Harm Reduction perspective will form the main agenda of this paper. The symmetrical concept of the 'alcoholisation of drug policies' will be interpreted as code for moving towards a regulated legal market for drugs that are currently illegal in most countries. Rather than venturing far into this last difficult last area some observations regarding commonalities in alcohol and other drug policy will be provided with particular reference to risk and protection factors among young people.

The concept of Harm Reduction emerged from the illicit drug field in the 1980s in the context of reducing the risk of the spread of blood-borne viruses without necessarily reducing drug use. Primary examples include the provision of clean needles for injecting drug users, the use of opiate antagonists to treat heroin overdose (Lenton & Hargreaves, 2001) and oral methadone as an alternative to injecting (Wodak & Moore, 2002). The advent of HIV/AIDS demanded that the policy response sought ways of reducing risk to the wider community by encouraging the many people who continued to use drugs to do so more safely. A sea-change in treatment priorities occurred so that, for example, methadone was no longer used merely as a means of assisting withdrawal from heroin but also as a much safer long-term substitute (Ward, Mattick & Hall, 1992). Harm Reduction is often controversial. Some countries such as the USA and Sweden have national policies that are explicitly opposed to the principles of Harm Reduction (Wodak & Moore, 2002). Even today, the provision of clean needles is discouraged in many US cities and the use of methadone is controversial (Wodak & Moore, 2002). Even in countries like Australia with an explicit acceptance of 'harm minimisation' in its national policy statements (Commonwealth Department of Health and Aged Care, 1999), there have been major political controversies surrounding a proposed trial of heroin prescription following the leadership of Swiss policy (Wodak & Moore, 2002) and the recent introduction of a safe-injecting facility in Sydney, New South Wales (Van Beek & Gilmore, 2000). In the public discourse around these issues, a central concern among opponents such as Prime Minister Howard has been the fear that such programs will "send the wrong message to young people" regarding the acceptability of using illegal drugs.

These debates are not unique to the currently illegal drugs but have echoes in relation to both tobacco and alcohol also. Despite the overwhelming consensus that any level of smoking is potentially damaging to health and that "Quit' is the main message for health campaigns, there have been efforts in Australia to develop a Harm Reduction approach to smoking (Borland & Scollo, 1999). These efforts include wanting to recognise reduced smoking as a worthwhile (if second best) treatment outcome and also considering the marketing of alternative nicotine delivery systems that do not require the inhalation of smoke. Such views are usually fiercely opposed by mainstream anti-tobacco protagonists as, again, 'delivering the wrong message'.

In relation to alcohol policy, the application of the Harm Reduction paradigm has also had its share of controversy. A specific example was the opposition from Australian nutrition experts to the proposal of adding thiamine to beer in the late 1980s for fear that it would encourage beer drinkers to consume more if it was viewed as a kind of 'health product'. In more general terms, Harm Reduction has sometimes been viewed as a challenge to the more orthodox public health view that alcohol-related harm can only be lowered by a reduction in the total population consumption of alcohol (Bruun *et al.*, 1975; Edwards *et al.*, 1994). The suggestion that there can be benefits that do not depend upon a reduction of all alcohol consumption is seen by some as sending the wrong message – this time to the policy makers.

Despite the fears and controversies, there are signs that the concept of Harm Reduction has come to have a significant place in discourse about alcohol policy. In Australia, these signs include a) the inclusion of an explicit harm minimisation objective in most state liquor laws following a national review of such legislation (Stockwell, 1995) b) mention in the recent National Alcohol Action plan of examining safer alcohol containers and glassware to prevent glass-related injuries from violent incidents (Commonwealth Department of Health and Aged Care, 2001) and the recommendation of breath-ignition interlocks for recidivist drink-drivers (see Voas, Blackman, Tippetts & Marques, 2002).

WHAT IS ALCOHOL HARM REDUCTION?

There have been many learned discussions regarding what the term Harm Reduction really means. For example, it has been argued that the term should be restricted to strategies that have been demonstrated to reduce drug-related harm (e.g. Lenton & Midford, 1996). While an evidence base is an important consideration for any strategy, one problem here is that it allows the inclusion of abstinence approaches which also will inevitably reduce harm. As such the term is emptied of any distinctive meaning. Another difficulty with an empirical definition is that the evidence base usually lags behind innovations in practice and it is still necessary to discuss the intent of strategies as well as to (later) determine their actual effectiveness. In this paper, the proviso of 'without necessarily reducing use' will be retained as the distinctive feature of Harm Reduction as an overall approach.

Taking this strict definition of Harm Reduction, it is clear that many applications of the term to the field of alcohol policy might better be described as Risk Reduction since rather than seeking to "make the world safer for drunks" they require the reduction of alcohol intake to less risky levels. By way of illustration, most of the examples of Alcohol Harm Reduction provided by Plant *et al.* (1997) in their book on this topic require a reduction in alcohol intake for their effect. For example, controlled drinking for people with drinking problems relies almost exclusively on teaching people to drink less per drinking occasion (Cameron, 1997). Nearly all drink-driving enforcement programs require people to drink less alcohol or not at all when they are driving – though admittedly some will find alternative forms of transport and maybe drink even more (Stewart & Sweedler, 1997; Loxley, Saunders, Blaze-Temple & Binns, 1990). Labelling alcohol containers with their content in terms of standard drinks is designed to assist drinkers wishing to drink within low risk drinking guidelines (Stockwell & Single, 1997). Responsible alcohol service training as traditionally described aims almost single-mindedly to cut-off service to drinkers before they become intoxicated and to completely deny service to underage drinkers (Saltz, 1997). Perhaps the only legitimate example of true Harm Reduction provided in that book relates to the range of emerging strategies around making licensed premises less violent by such means as training security staff to calm rather than aggravate potential trouble, limiting crowding and providing plastic or shatter-proof glassware – none of these require any reduction in alcohol intake for their effectiveness (Graham & Homel, 1997).

Another false application of the principle of Harm Reduction to alcohol policy is in relation to the idea that a focus on high risk drinking patterns is more appropriate than a focus on total population consumption. This is a false application not because the idea has no theoretical merit (Stockwell Single Hawks & Rehm, 1997) but because this strategy still requires a reduction in alcohol consumption for effectiveness and hence does not constitute Harm Reduction. It is also false if it is taken to mean that the evidence for a link between per capita alcohol consumption and levels of alcohol-related harm is equivocal. If anything, the evidence has mounted that there are mostly very strong relationships between population rates of serious alcohol-related harm and per capita consumption (see Norstrom & Skog, 2001; Gruenewald & Treno, 2000). The idea that a focus on 'drinking patterns' (Stockwell, 2001) somehow frees up alcohol policy from the need to measure and control per capita alcohol consumption is unfounded, however convenient such a view might be for commercial alcohol producers (Grant & Litvak, 1998). There is anyway solid evidence of a positive relationship between changes in level of per capita consumption in a given population and changes in the number of high risk drinkers (Edwards *et al.*, 1994). Furthermore, a recent analysis of Australian drinking patterns suggests that at least 67% of all alcohol consumed that was reported drunk in a 1998 national alcohol consumption survey (with only 46.5% coverage of actual per capita consumption) was by people exceeding the current national drinking guidelines. For persons aged 18 to 29 years of age this proportion was 90% (Stockwell, Dietze, Chikritzhs, Catalano & Heale, 2002). In short, it is difficult to imagine circumstances under which levels of risky drinking could change without per capita consumption also being similarly affected. A drinking patterns perspective if applied accurately to high risk drinking patterns is clearly in direct conflict to the interests of alcohol producers since so great a proportion of their products are consumed in high risk ways.

A further area of an apparent application of a harm reduction approach to alcohol-related problems in Australia has been in relation to school-based alcohol education. A well-controlled study of a program known as the School Health Alcohol and Harm

Reduction Project or 'SHAHRP' demonstrated significant reductions in both drinking behaviour and reports of incidents of alcohol-related harm e.g. hangovers, injuries, embarrassing incidents (McBride, Midford, Farringdon & Phillips, 2000). It is true that the program involved learning to avoid problems such as getting into a car with a drunk driver but a significant component of the program was focused on training children to count standard drinks, monitor their drinking and to not get intoxicated. The measured reductions were of for risk behaviours and harms and both were likely to be related to reported reductions in alcohol use, especially risky alcohol use. SHAHRP really looks more like Risk Reduction than Harm Reduction – or at least a strong cocktail of the two.

So what then is left in this small corner of alcohol policy that can be genuinely designated as Harm Reduction in the pure sense of the term? Is the influence of Harm Reduction on alcohol policy more apparent than real? Thiamine fortification of flour, regular beer and bulk wine (Drew & Truswell, 1998)) late night public transport schemes for patrons of licensed premises, using plastic or shatter-proof glassware in potentially violent venues, limiting crowding and training security staff to defuse arguments (Graham & Homel, 1997) all do meet the criterion of not requiring some reduction in alcohol consumption for their effectiveness. There is one other genuine Harm Reduction initiative that borrows substantially from the illicit drugs area: training of young people to care for friends who have lost consciousness (e.g. Youth Research Centre, 1995). In Australia, around 100 people are recorded as dying each year (many of them young) from some form of alcoholic 'overdose' ie poisoning or choking on vomit while unconscious (Chikritzhs *et al.*, 2000). A Western Australian study of the drinking behaviour of university students found that among a significant group that had reported participating in drinking games, 89% had witnessed a drinking companion lose consciousness and that in two-thirds of cases they had left them to sleep off the effects (Polizotto *et al.*, in press). As is the case with heroin overdose such instances create an increased risk of a fatality and steps should be taken to keep the individual awake and, if necessary, call for medical assistance (e.g. Darke, Ross & Hall, 1996). The principle of looking after friends is attractive to young people and can be extended to looking out for a whole range of other risks associated with intoxication such as getting behind the wheel of a car, unprotected sex, suicide attempts and violent disputes. It might be that a preoccupation with reducing alcohol use sometimes gets in the way of ensuring that attention is given to the possibility of 'making the world safer for drunks'.

In summary, it has been argued that despite the increased adoption of Harm Reduction in name in relation to alcohol policy and prevention, in practice there has been only limited application of the true principle of not requiring reduction in use for effectiveness. There has been a tendency over the last decade to bracket any approaches that are alternatives to abstinence (e.g. controlled drinking) or to a public health focus on reducing per capita alcohol consumption as being in someway Harm Reduction. It is argued here that there is in reality a substantial gulf between abstinence approaches and Harm Reduction - and that this gulf is occupied by an enormous variety of strategies that in some way depend on reduced alcohol consumption. The term Risk Reduction is recommended as a descriptor for these other strategies (Stockwel, Single, Hawks and Rehm, 1997)). The final section of this paper contains a brief discussion and illustration of a broader concept of Risk and the allied concept of Protection in relation to predictors of adolescent drug use and risky drug use.

CONVERGENCE OF ALCOHOL AND OTHER DRUG POLICIES

While we are very used to a dichotomy of legal versus illegal drugs, there is of course some significant middle ground. Some use and sale of 'legal drugs' such as alcohol and tobacco is illegal and may even involve criminal sanctions e.g. sales of alcohol to minors and to the intoxicated, drinking to excess before driving. In an increasing number of jurisdictions in Europe and Australia, the use of cannabis in small quantities for personal use has been decriminalised (Lenton *et al.*, 2000).

Another important middle ground for alcohol, tobacco and other drug policies is in relation to what have come to be known as the social determinants of drug use and related harm as well as a constellation of common risk and protection factors for adolescent problem behaviours (e.g. conduct disorders, unprotected sex, depression, binge drinking and illicit drug use). Bond, Thomas, Toumbourou, Patton and Catalano, (2000) applied a scale developed by Hawkins, Catalano and Miller, (1992) to a sample of over 9,000 Victorian school children which had been designed to measure adolescent risk and protection factors variously including: poverty, family dysfunction, school failure, peer influences, parental drug use and drug availability. They found strong relationships between the risk/protection scale scores and the probability of adolescents also reporting drinking 5 or more drinks on an occasion, smoking cigarettes, smoking cannabis, using other illicit drugs, depression and trouble with the police. Findings such as these have been influential in encouraging the view that effective prevention policies need to address underlying social problems (unemployment, poor housing, community functioning) and address risk factors in the lives of young people that are common across a range of mental health, crime and substance use issues (e.g. Spooner, Hall & Lynskey, 2001).

More careful analysis and comparison of such issues across the legal and illegal drugs reveals an important disparity, however. Smoking tobacco and heavy sessional use of alcohol are more mainstream activities being found mostly among adolescents with low and/or middle-range scores on the Bond *et al.* (2000) Risk and Protection Scale. Re-analysis of the Victorian adolescent data set revealed that the Prevention Paradox held in relation to tobacco and 'binge' drinking but did not do so for smoking cannabis and, in particular, for the use of other illicit drugs (Loxley *et al.*, in press). While high risk adolescents were more likely to smoke and drink excessively, by age 16 years the greatest number engaging in these behaviours on a weekly basis were low and medium risk individuals. In relation to cannabis, there was an increasing trend with age for those smoking weekly to be low or medium risk but the majority were still classified as high risk. In later teenage years and in early adulthood it is likely, at least in Australia, that regular cannabis smoking would be most prevalent in 'mainstream' rather than high risk populations.

A further line of evidence from longitudinal studies of adolescent drug use suggests mutual benefits from targeting the use of legal drugs in prevention programs. A systematic review of such studies by Toumbourou and colleagues (see Loxley *et al.*, in Press) found strong evidence for early smoking and alcohol use predicting a range of later problems in early adulthood such as alcohol dependence, illicit drug use and mental health problems. These relationships were evident even when adjustments were made for a wide range of potentially confounding social, demographic and behavioural variables.

The above pattern of results, suggests two important conclusions for shared future directions in alcohol and other drug policies: (i) a major focus on universal, whole of population interventions targeting the use of legal drugs by people of all ages and (ii) targeted interventions on high risk families and young people to reduce later adolescent use of illegal drugs. Both of these directions should yield reciprocal benefits in terms of reducing rates of risky use and harm of both legal and illegal drugs. These arguments and their implications have been developed in far greater detail elsewhere (Loxley *et al.*, in press). Clearly, the concept of Risk Reduction should be expanded beyond a concern with amounts consumed and levels of intoxication.

CONCLUSIONS

The theme of mutual influences between alcohol policy on the one hand and illicit drug policy on the other has been briefly explored with particular reference to the related concepts of Harm and Risk Reduction. While the term Harm Reduction has emerged from the illicit drugs field in the past twenty years and is frequently applied to alcohol policy, in most instances the yardstick of *not necessarily requiring reduced alcohol use* does not usually apply but there are still some potentially important examples of Harm Reduction to be recommended in modern alcohol policy. In most instances, there has been little progress with their implementation. It has been argued that the concept of Harm Reduction does not in isolation offer an alternative conceptual basis though it does have a small place alongside universal or whole of population approaches to reducing risk and harm. Rather than just considering whether the alcohol and illicit drugs fields have had reciprocal influences on each other it has been suggested that there are significant developments in relation to understanding common risk and protection factors for both these problem areas as well as others from the fields of mental health and crime prevention.

REFERENCES

Bond, L., Thomas, L., Toumbourou, J. Patton.G.C. & Catalano, R. (2000) Improving the lives of Young Victorians in Our Community: A survey of risk and protective factors. Centre for Adolescent Health Report prepared for Community Care Division, Department of Human Services.

Borland, R. & Scollo, M. (1999) Opportunities for harm minimization in tobacco control. *Drug and Alcohol Review,* 18, 345-353.

Bruun K. , Edwards G., Lumio M., Makela K., Pan L., Popham R.E., Room R., Schmidt W., Skog O-J., Sulkunen P. & Osterberg E. (1975) *Alcohol control policies in public health perspective, vol. 25.* Finnish Foundation for Alcohol Studies.

Cameron, D. (1997) Harm minimisation in clinical practice. In M. Plant, E. Single, & T. Stockwell. (Eds.), *Alcohol: Minimising the Harm.* (pp. 233-247). London: Free Assoc. Books Ltd.

Chikritzhs, T., Jonas, H., Heale, P., Stockwell, T., Dietze, P., Hanlin, K. & Webb, M. (2000) *Alcohol-caused deaths and hospitalisations in Australia, 1990-1997.* National Alcohol Indicators Technical Report No. 1. National Drug Research Institute, Curtin University of Technology, Perth, Western Australia.

Commonwealth Department of Health and Aged Care (1999) *National Drug Strategic Framework 1998-99 to 2002-03: Building partnerships.* Canberra: Commonwealth of Australia.

Commonwealth Department of Health and Aged Care (2001) *National Alcohol Action Plan.* Canberra: National Drug Strategy Framework.

Darke, S., Ross, J. & Hall, W. (1996) Overdose among heroin users in Sydney, Australia. I. Prevalence and correlates of non-fatal overdose. *Addiction*, 91(3), 413-417.

Drew, L.R. & Truswell, A.S. (1998) Wernick's encephalophathy and thiamine fortification of food: time for a new direction? *Medical Journal of Australia,* 168(11), 534-535.

Edwards, G.A.P., Babor, T.F., Casswell, S., Ferrence, R., Giesbrecht, N., Godfrey, C., Holder, H.D., Lemmens, P., Mäkelä, K., Midanik, L.T., Norström, T., Österberg, E., Romelsjö, A., Room, R., Simpura, J. & Skög, O.-J. (1994) *Alcohol Policy and the Public Good.* New York: Oxford University Press.

Graham, K. & Homel, R. (1997) Creating safer bars. In E. Single, & T. Stockwell. (Eds.), *Alcohol: Minimising the Harm. What Works?* (pp. 171-192) New York: Free Association Books Ltd.

Grant, M. & Litvak, J. (1998) (Eds.) Introduction: Beyond per capita consumption, In M. Grant. & J. Litvak. *Drinking patterns and their consequences.* Washington DC: Taylor & Francis.

Gruenewald, P. & Treno. A. (2000) Local and global alcohol supply: economic and geographic models of community systems. *Addiction*, 95(S4), S537-S549.

Hawkins, J.D., Catalano, R.F. & Miller, J.Y. (1992) Risk and protective factors for alcohol and other drug problems in adolescence and early adulthood: Implications for substance abuse prevention. *Psychological Bulletin,* 112, 64-105.

Lenton, S. & Hargreaves, K. (2001) *The naloxone feasibility study: a study in to the provision of naloxone hydrochlride, for peer administration, as an aid in the prevention of fatal heroin-overdose. Technical report.* Perth, Western Australia: National Drug Research Institute, Curtin University of Technology.

Lenton, S. & Midford, R. (1996) Clarifying 'harm reduction'? *Drug and Alcohol Review*, 15(4), 411-414.

Lenton, S., Heale, P., Erickson, P., Single, E., Lang, E. & Hawks, D.V. (2000) *The regulation of cannabis possession, use and supply: a discussion document prepared for the Drugs and Crime Prevention Committee of The Parliament of Victoria. Monograph No. 3.* Perth, Western Australia: National Drug Research Institute, Curtin University of Techonology.

Loxley, W., Saunders, B., Blaze-Temple, D. & Binns, C.W. (1990) Drinking and driving in Western Australia: Perceptions of practices, priorities and preventives. *Australian Journal of Social Issues*, 25(2), 120-136.

Loxley, W., Toumbourou, J., Stockwell, T., Haines, B., Scott, K., Godfrey, C., Waters, E. & Patton, G. (In Press) *The prevention of substance use, risk and harm in Australia: A review of the evidence. A report prepared for the Commonwealth Department of Health and Ageing.* National Drug Research Institute and the Centre for Adolescent Health.

McBride, N., Midford, R., Farringdon, F. & Phillips, M. (2000) Early results from a school alcohol harm minimization study: the school health and alcohol harm reduction project. *Addiction,* 95(7), 1021-1042.

Norström, T. & Skög, O.-J. (2001) Alcohol and mortality: Methodological and analytical issues in aggregate analyses. *Addiction,* 96(S1), S5-S17.

Plant, M., Single, E. & Stockwell, T. (1997) *(Eds.) Alcohol: Minimising the Harm.* London: Free Assoc. Books Ltd.

Pollizotto, M., Saw, M., Tjhung, I., Chua, E. H., Straton, J. & Stockwell, T. (In press) Fluid skills: the role of drinking games in the alcohol consumption patterns of Western Australian youth. *Contemporary Drug Problems.*

Saltz, R.F. (1997) Prevention where alcohol is sold and consumed: server intervention and responsible beverage service. In M. Plant, E. Single. & T. Stockwell. (Eds.), *Alcohol: Minimising the Harm. What Works?* (pp. 72-84). New York: Free Association Books Ltd.

Spooner, C., Hall, W., Lynskey, M. (2001) *Structural Determinants of Youth Drug Use.* Woden, ACT: Australian National Council on Drugs.

Stewart, K. & Sweedler, B.M. (1997) Driving under the influence of alcohol. In M. Plant, E. Single, & T. Stockwell. (Eds.), *Alcohol: Minimising the Harm.* (pp. 10-25) London: Free Assoc. Books Ltd.

Stockwell, T. (1995) Alcohol, violence and licensed premises: the nature of the relationship. In T. Stockwell. (Ed.), *Alcohol misuse and violence report 5: An examination of the appropriateness and efficacy of liquor licensing laws across Australia.* (pp. 105-118), Canberra: Australian Government Publishing Service.

Stockwell, T. (2001) Overview of Section IV: Drinking patterns and types of alcohol problem. In N. Heather, T. Peters, & T. Stockwell. (Eds.), *International Handbook of Alcohol Dependence and Problems.* (pp. 376-378), West Sussex, UK: John Wiley & Sons Ltd.

Stockwell, T. & Single, E. (1997) Standard unit labelling of alcohol containers. In M. Plant, E. Single, & T. Stockwell. (Eds.), *Alcohol. Minimising the Harm. What Works?* (pp. 85-104), London: Free Association Press.

Stockwell, T., Dietze, P., Chikritzhs, T., Catalano, P. & Heale, P. (2002) How much alcohol is drunk in Australia in excess of the new Australian alcohol guidelines? Letter to the Editor. *Medical Journal of Australia,* 176(2), 91-92.

Stockwell, T., Single, E., Hawks, D. & Rehm, J. (1997) Sharpening the focus of alcohol policy from aggregate consumption to harm and risk reduction. *Addiction Research,* 5(1), 1-9.

Van Beek, I. & Gilmore, S (2000) Preferences to have used a medically supervised injecting centre among injecting drug users in Kings Cross, Sydney. *Australian and News Zealand Journal of Public Health*, 24(5), 540-542.

Voas, R.B., Blackman, K.O., Tippetts, A.S. & Marques, P.R. (2002) Evaluation of a program to motivate impaired driving offenders to install ignition interlocks. *Accident, Analysis and Prevention*, 34, 449-455.

Ward, J., Mattick, R. & Hall, W. (1992) *Key issues in Methadone maintenance treatment.* Sydney: National Drug and Alcohol Research Centre.

Wodak, A. & Moore, T. (2002) Modernising Australia's Drug Policy. Sydney: University of New South Wales Press Ltd.

Youth Research Centre. (1995) *Rethinking Drinking,* Parkerville: University of Melbourne.

Professor Tim Stockwell
Director
National Drug Research Institute
GPO Box U1987
Perth, 6845
Western Australia

IRMGARD EISENBACH-STANGL

FROM TEMPERENCE MOVEMENTS TO STATE ACTION: AN HISTORICAL VIEW OF THE ALCOHOL QUESTION IN INDUSTRIALISED COUNTRIES

Key words: alcohol, temperance movements, alcohol policy in industrialised countries

It was only in industrialised countries that social mass movements developed pointing to problems related to the consumption of psychoactive substances and demanding self reform and social reform. The temperance and abstainer movements aiming at the reduction and eradication of alcohol consumption are the most prominent examples and the United States are the part of the industrialised world were the most powerful anti-alcohol organisations were established in the course of the 19th century. The national states more or less hesitantly took over the request of the movements and transformed them according to their own interests and their own structure and societal position. Three stages are discussed: the alcohol policy of the total nation-state predominating before WWII, the alcohol related measures of the national welfare state developing after WWII and the state reactions to alcohol and other drug related problems at present, at the time of "globalisation", when the nation state is loosing power.

1. INTRODUCTION

A symposium on alcohol policies will not astonish too many citizens living in industrialised countries today. That drinking is linked to a variety of problematic consequences, which need to be addressed by appropriate state measures, is taken to be self-evident in this part of the world. Yet, such was not always the case. 100 years ago, when the Swiss Institute for the Prevention of Alcoholism and Other Drug-Related Problems was being founded, the public responsibility for dealing with alcohol-related problems had just been established. And it still was rather novel about 30 years later, as illustrated by the considerations presented below. They are taken from the novel "Matto regiert" ("Matto rules"), by the Swiss author Friedrich Glauser, published in 1936. "Matto regiert" deals with murder in a mental asylum inhabited by the ghost of Matto, who rules the world and is able to bring about war whenever he wishes. The vice director of the asylum, Dr. Laduner, a psychiatrist trained in psychoanalysis by August Aichhorn in Vienna, frames the alcohol question in one of his talks to the police detective Studer investigating the murder:

> "In the asylum we have three cases of chronic alcoholism. One of the cases, a man, now forty years old, lost his job because of inebriety. He has given seven children to the world, all of them alive, the state has to maintain his wife and children and has to pay

R. Müller and H. Klingemann (eds.),
From Science to Action? 100 Years Later - Alcohol Policies Revisited, 59–69.

> for the man here. The second case: a handy-man, with the familiar wage of eighty Rappen an hour, who married because he too wanted something of what we call life today, that is a place to call home and a woman who belonged to him. Eighty Rappen an hour doesn't get you far. The man was orderly, at first; his wife as well. Three children. He didn't have enough. The man went boozing, the wife went laundering. Two more children. Snaps is the cheapest. Bätziwasser is twenty Rappen a glass. Could he be expected to drink Waadtländer, for five Franks a bottle? Not really, could he? The man had a home. The burden became too heavy, he wanted to forget.....Is it possible to force men to always face their misery? I don't know. The gentlemen of the welfare office are convinced, they have their wages......I don't want to go too far.....But Bätziwasser isn't healthy, can lead to a splendid alcohol delirium, and that's just what happened. The result? The man is here, his wife is supported by a small benefit from the municipality, the children live on the breadline..... And the third case is even sadder.....Let's pass it over, it would only repeat the first two. In short, in the third case five children. The municipality and the state care for them. Work it out, Studer: seven children in the first case plus five in the second and five in the third. That makes seventeen children, and also six adults, who also have to be cared for..." (1989; 100-101).

The most interesting part of the extract above with regard to the topic of this paper relates to the duty of the state to care for the alcoholic as well as for his wife and children. The state is considered to be responsible for the fate of its citizens even if they have been behaving in an irresponsible way, such as drinking too much. However, the extract also illustrates that the societal responsibilities were perceived as a burden and that the attribution of responsibilities to the individual on the one hand and to the state on the other were not easily separated. To put it another way: in the 1930s in Switzerland it was still not entirely self evident for the state to take responsibility for drunkards and their families. This leads us to the first phenomenon mentioned in the title: to the modern temperance movement in industrialised countries that emerged at the turn of the eighteenth century and lost its influence, at the latest, after World War II, i.e. 150 years later.

2. THE TEMPERANCE MOVEMENT

The modern temperance movement in industrialised countries is to be understood, among other things, as a movement establishing the general public awareness of and responsibilities for alcohol-related issues. We know that the temperance movement was supported by different interest groups, and also taken up by old status groups and other modern social movements, which always understood how to hijack the alcohol question in order to further their own interests. In some countries, the old aristocracy tried to retain their economic privileges and their social status by accusing the rising classes of irresponsible drinking (Gusfield, 1963; Eisenbach-Stangl, 1993). In other countries, the bourgeois classes presented their way of life as a model to the workers. The Swiss historian Jakob Tanner talks about the propaganda for such "new, genuine bourgeois concepts of order as cleanliness, hygiene, rational lifestyles, frugality and time discipline", used to enforce moral standards centred around factory work (Tanner, 1986).

Just as the bourgeois classes used temperance to make workers more disciplined, and thus more profitable, women used sobriety in attempts to make their husbands more disciplined and profitable (Levine, 1980; Appelt, 1991). Some of them later joined the women's rights and suffrage movement and tried to gain political power for themselves. Others extended the fight against alcohol to the bars and to everything that kept their husbands out of the home and spending money outside the home. This, at least, is the well described case of the United States; yet, women became active against alcohol in other countries, too (e.g. Anderson 1992).

Temperance was linked to emancipation not only in the case of women; the abolition and workers movements also often overlapped with it. The socialist movement ultimately discovered temperance as a step on the way to a better society – a more egalitarian consumer society, as Sulkunen (1997) puts it. And those who opposed the socialist movement explained social problems not in terms of societal structures but from the perspective of biological heritage – that is mainly the soiling of the race – and began to appreciate sobriety as a means to improve the quality of the physical equipment of their race and thus its position in the fight of the fittest.

Many social movements devoting themselves to sobriety tried to contribute to the building of the nation (Levine, 1980; Sulkunen, 1997, 2002). Thus, the fight against alcohol was also linked to xenophobia – the downside of nationalism. Minorities and immigrants were accused of drinking in an uncivilized way and were suspected of inducing – to their advantage – the natives to drink excessively (Gusfield, 1963; Eisenbach-Stangl, 1993). And in many counties – especially in mainly Protestant lands – temperance became a concern of the church and of religious movements aiming to improve both the sinful citizen and society as a whole (Gusfield, 1963; Fahrenkrug, 1984; Olson, 1986; Eriksson, 1990).

Temperance concerns were therefore combined with all major modern social movements and their ideologies, concerning class, gender, nationality, ethnicity and religion, and also with the social interests and conflicts they expressed. In the special case of the United States, all major interests and conflicts were articulated within the temperance movement itself, which thus became the most powerful social movement of modern times. Yet, regardless of whether temperance was thought to be the main cure of social problems, or merely a means among others in the pursuit of societal and personal happiness, the movements concerned with temperance increasingly demanded the state to intervene according to their proposals. And they were successful. The Swiss temperance movement, for instance, formulated a petition to the federal government in 1882, which was answered in 1885: a partial monopoly on spirits was established and the so-called 'Alkoholzehntel' introduced, with the effect that 10 percent of alcohol-related tax revenue had to be spent on prevention (Tanner, 1986). The Austrian temperance movement later took up the Swiss demands, but was only able to elicit appropriate alcohol-related state action during the first decades of the twentieth century (Eisenbach-Stangl, 1991).

It was, of course, nothing new for the state to intervene in 'intoxication issues'. For instance, the import of tobacco and coffee had been prohibited or strongly restricted in many countries in earlier centuries. In the seventeenth century, King James I of England raised the duties on tobacco by 4000% – with the effect that smuggling spread rapidly (Austin, 1981). Although state intervention during the seventeenth century was a 'top down' phenomenon, so to speak, in the nineteenth century it took the opposite direction, i.e. 'bottom up'. Social movements demanded that the state respond. The state, however, was quite often not so eager to oblige, even though intervention could serve its own interests, as historical lessons taught: for instance, King James very quickly replaced the high duties on tobacco by a profitable monopoly. Today we know that state intervention in the field of intoxicants did serve more than fiscal interests, that it also promoted centralisation, strengthened bureaucratic power and provided the state with opportunities to develop control measures for intervening in the everyday life of its citizens.

Yet, it was not only the direction of the societal action that had changed, but also its principal agent: the character of the state at the end of the nineteenth century was fundamentally different from that of earlier centuries, its power no longer curtailed by the church. Instead of being doubted in the name of God, the state itself had become the focus of beliefs. The ideologies developing at the end of the nineteenth century increasingly assumed a religious character, and amidst the so-called 'political religions' the state became the principal source of hope. The respective transformations taking place at both an ideological and a practical level were favoured by the shortcomings of the liberal state in solving the acute economic crisis and the increasing societal conflicts expressed by the social movements (Hautmann & Kropf, 1974; Ley 1999). The changed character of the societal power structure intervening with regard to alcohol-related issues informed the character of the actions taken, and deserves closer examination.

3. THE TOTAL NATION-STATE AND TOTAL STATE RESPONSES TO 'INTOXICATION ISSUES'

The nineteenth century witnessed the creation of the nation-state. Those living within the borders of a state were conceived to be of one nation. Language, history and the arts, among other things, were used to present and confirm the common roots, the unity and the singularity of a nation. The notions of the 'fatherland' and 'motherland' were born. The historian Schulze (1994) demonstrates that it needed an enemy to create a nation-state, that the perfect stimulus was a threat from the outside – from another state. In other words, the stuff that nations were made of contained xenophobia, and this had impact on the state – the worldly organ of the nation's power.

During the last decades of the nineteenth century, the nation-state changed from being an essentially democratic organ of power into an 'imperial' one. Patriotism developed, and democratic values and structures became gradually dissolved. During this period, the nation became absolute, nationalistic, totalitarian: "Du bist nichts. Dein Volk ist alles", "La France d'abord", "Right or wrong, my country" was the order, legitimising physical violence against enemies, non-believers and strangers both outside and, increasingly, also within the borders. "The often irrational feelings of threat and inferiority in the societal sphere, which shaped not only the public atmosphere but increasingly also governmental actions, were counterbalanced by feelings of superiority and of a mission, occasionally leading to missionary activities" (Schulze, 1994, p. 269). During the period of the two world wars, the imperial nation-state was finally transformed into the total nation-state, whose prevailing characteristics became the following: official totalitarian ideologies, centralised mass movements serving as uniform political parties, the total control of all means of compulsion and communication, the bureaucratic control of the economy by *dirigisme*, and its transformation into societal or state property.

The state thus became active in respect to alcoholism when its societal and political position became central, when it became at first imperial and later totalitarian towards both the exterior and also the interior. Through the formulation and enforcement of alcohol-related controls, the state intervened in the economy *and* in the private lives of its citizens – in their pleasures, their desires and their sufferings – and expanded its responsibilities in the realms of social order to individual discipline, health, wealth and happiness, as were thought to be threatened by drinking. The demands of the temperance movement, as well as the alcohol-related measures actually taken, mirror the development towards the imperial and total position adopted by the state. Production, distribution and consumption were increasingly submitted to state controls, though the divergence between the alcohol-related control policies of different industrialised countries remained enormous.

The most extreme, and therefore the most interesting, examples of alcohol-related control policies are prohibition, the Bratt System in Sweden, and the policies of the Third Reich, which have never been ascribed a special name. In the case of prohibition, the policies were aimed at reversing the attitudes towards intoxicants that for millennia had been deeply embedded in the social structure, the culture and the main religion of industrialised societies, and eradicating their use (Levine, 1986; Hauge, 2000). The social and religious cult of inebriety was to be transformed into a social and religious cult of sobriety, of the total renouncement of a pleasurable habit on the part of all citizens for the sake of the nation and of new immanent and material values.

In the case of the Bratt System, the state action was total in another way: on the surface it aimed at the complete control of individual drinking, and more profoundly focussed on moral education. Those behaving orderly and in accordance with the requested norms received the alcohol ration which had been especially designated for them in advance; those who did not, lost it, and were compelled to undergo intensified education. Through the Bratt System, and thus through alcohol-related controls, the country as a whole seems to have been partially transformed into a 'total institution', as Goffman (1961) defined it: "Their encompassing or total character is symbolized by the barrier to social intercourse with the outside and to departure that is often built right into the physical plant ....". Moreover, all the types of total institutions mentioned by Goffman (1961 p. 16) seem to have been realised at a single stroke: institutions established to care for persons felt to be incapable of looking after themselves and/or to be a threat to the community; institutions to protect the community against what are felt to be intentional dangers to it, institutions purportedly established the better to pursue some work like task and establishments designed as retreats from the world even while often serving also as training stations for the religious.

As regards the Third Reich, it might be better to talk about a race-state instead of a nation-state: the sacred entity was the Aryan race, and the value of individuals was judged accordingly – their drinking being no exception. Those whose alcohol consumption appeared to be disquieting but whose biological heritage was thought to be worthy were considered to be curable and were submitted to treatment. Excessive drinkers who were diagnosed as ethnically inferior were considered to be incurable and were excluded: in practice, they were sterilised and sent to labour camps. Since the Aryan race was thought to have been soiled for centuries, and accordingly judgements based on pure racial characteristics impossible, the diagnosis or selection was based on the capacities and readiness of the individuals to conform and to achieve. The alcohol policy of the Third Reich was thus total in its exclusion of deviant individuals, and rejected supply restrictions, although supply restrictions were introduced in the war – although not for the army (Hamann, 1996; Hauschildt, 1997).

Switzerland during this period proved to be a moderate country with regard to totalitarian policies, including alcohol controls. There was an element of prohibition, an element of education and one of exclusion, but all elements were modest. Prohibition only concerned absinth – the 'fée verte' of the French-speaking population. Fahrenkrug (1993, 1995) studied the process of stigmatisation of this beverage, which was forbidden in Switzerland by democratic vote in 1908 – years before France. In 1938, a penal law was enforced which allowed for the sending of 'Gewohnheitstrinker' (habitual drinkers) to alcohol asylums, in cases where they had committed a crime connected to their drinking habits. Imprisonment could be suspended in favour of compulsory treatment and remitted if the offender was cured. As Klingemann (1986) put it: the hidden aim of the law was to control those inclined towards an 'immoral life' – a 'liederliche Lebenswandel' as it was the termed in German – and to improve them by compulsory treatment for alcoholism. Incidentally, treatment at this time was already professionalized: a modern treatment system had been built up from the middle of the nineteenth century, including residential and out-patient care and patient clubs, based on professional methods and serving as a model for German-speaking countries at least (Klingemann, 1992).

4. THE WELFARE STATE AND ITS DOUBLE FACE

After 1945, alcohol policies are known to have changed direction, and now concentrated on deviant individuals. As many studies illustrate, the treatment of those perceived to be problem-drinkers increased in all industrialised countries (e.g. Mäkelä *et al.*, 1981). In some countries treatment was mainly compulsory, in others mainly voluntary; in some it was mostly organised in the private sector, in others it was mostly public; in some countries – as in the United States – it was based on self-help models, whilst in others – as in European countries – it was based on professional concepts. At first sight, the state seems to have been purified and reformed: from a total nation-state, a sacred entity of far greater importance than its individual citizens, to a welfare state working as a provider of manifold services. However, as usual, appearances are misleading.

The temperance movements had been successful in establishing public awareness and responsibilities for alcohol-related issues. The state had taken over, and the temperance movements – having lost their attraction and their social weight during the period of the two world wars – after 1945 accordingly expired. Yet, the state had not only taken over alcohol issues, it also took over the social conflicts to which the alcohol issue was linked. The total nation-state had suppressed the major social conflicts in the name of a superior entity; the welfare state compensated, neutralised and de-differentiated these conflicts (Eisenbach-Stangl, 1999). Treatment proved to be a good means in this process: it allowed the respective problems to be ascribed to vulnerable individuals and scientific theories to be developed explaining their vulnerability in terms of social, psychical and biological causes. The alcohol question had first been successfully delegated by the temperance movements to the state, and now it was being delegated by the state to the experts.

The majority of citizens seem to have appreciated this political solution: otherwise it would not have worked. The new perception of alcohol-related issues and the morals linked to it had been taken over by the individual citizens. As a result, the system of treatment continuously expanded, and became increasingly diversified. At least on the surface, alcoholism had become an illness related to individual problems and stimulating those suffering to look for an appropriate cure. The solution was to be approached from the perspective of the consumer, as Sulkunen (2002, p. 81) expressed it: "Responsibility should be placed on the individual, and the state's role is to wake the consumer's own interest in protecting their health".

The welfare state was less permissive behind the scenes. Parallel to the expansion of the treatment system for alcoholics, an increasing number of regulations, decrees and laws were enforced which restricted or even prohibited alcohol consumption in connection with specific activities or on specific occasions. The most prominent regulations concern drinking and driving, others concern the workplace, and all of them are continuously tightened up and diversified. Those who violate them are often indirectly forced into treatment. Seen from another perspective, an increasing number of the patients of the treatment system do not come forward voluntarily, though they are not treated 'compulsorily', in the usual sense of the term. The state behind the scenes and with its caring face for consumers thus remained involved in the expansion and enforcement of individual discipline in the interests of the economy, the state itself and society as a whole.

The alcohol-related controls of the welfare state impinged on the private, individual sphere – possibly even more so than previous measures, since consumption was not directly restricted. Therefore, one should assume that they settled alongside consumer desires and colonized the 'Lebenswelt'. Alcohol consumption consequently served to fulfil a personal wish to drink, but also led to anxieties over self-reliance and health; it responded to social pressures to drink, but also to those to refrain from drinking in order to avoid problems. In other words, drinking increasingly became shaped by contradictions.

One good example to illustrate these contradictions and their inherent confusions is the attitudes of Austrians towards the BAC level of 0.08 percent introduced in 1960 for "drinking when driving". A survey carried out 20 years later examined respondents' knowledge of this level. Two thirds of those questioned knew the BAC level, and less than one quarter knew the 'permitted' number of drinks. More than 30 years later, in 1993, acceptance was quite high and knowledge about the level had improved substantially (98% were informed), although consumption itself was still guided by different principles: almost one quarter admitted having violated the regulations at least once in their life and 6% during the previous 3 months (Uhl & Springer, 1993). Five years later, the BAC level was reduced to 0.05 percent.

The example given above also addresses the reasons for the crisis in the welfare state: in taking over most social conflicts and problems, it had to deal with their enforcement and therefore with their internalisation by the individual citizens. Moreover, the welfare state even became active with regard to the definition of the problem, as Barbara Lucas (2001) puts it, and the solutions offered consisted mainly of bureaucratic and professional means that were far removed from everyday life. For this reason, the welfare state consequently became vulnerable itself.

5. THE END OF DELEGATION? TOWARDS RISK MANAGEMENT

If the conflicts and problems are taken over by the state, then the state itself becomes vulnerable to reproach. In the field of addiction, the policies relating to illegal drugs are the most prominent example of such a process. Yet, further examples can be found in respect to alcoholism, often concerning treatment – the most prominent branch of alcohol control policies after World War II. Treatment is expensive and uneven; it comes late and is ineffective; it deals only with illness, not with health; it applies to only a tiny part of all alcohol-related problems. State intervention in industrialised countries has consequently changed over the last two decades, and the new type of controls taking shape on the horizon can cautiously be termed 'risk management'. At the same time, the social conflicts and problems linked to alcohol have become less neutralised and more articulated.

The philosopher Heintel (1998) comments positively on the changes in state intervention. He states that the delegation of conflicts to the state was superior to their private resolution, as it meant subsumption to general rules, and thus abstraction. (One also could talk about the superiority of universalism over particularism.) However, the delegation to the state also brought high costs: individuals were expropriated of their conflicts, and became detached from their emotions linked to these conflicts. Individuals consequently became handicapped, if not even incapable of dealing with their emotions and of solving their problems in a socially competent way. The withdrawal of the delegation to the state therefore contributes to the empowerment of the citizens. If Heintel's considerations are transferred to the alcohol issue, it becomes apparent that in the period of the total state, as well as that of the welfare state, citizens were submitted to powerful organisations which, besides controlling and supporting them, also disempowered them. They first became moulded elements of larger units, and later turned into patients and ignorant violators of common rules. Under these premises, self-control and self-change – on an individual as well as an organisational and regional level – had to remain utopian concepts.

Nevertheless, self-control and self-change become important concepts within a society and a state interested in risk management. Risk management also relies on individual empowerment, including the right to decide how to manage through to the right not to manage or to take the risk. Yet, as Heintel (1998) pointed out, in order for the shift of responsibilities from the state to the citizen to function it has to take place voluntarily. What one can actually observe is mostly the opposite: there are shifts taking place only on the surface. Alcohol prevention, for instance, is still determined by the state, although it increasingly appears in a new, individual guise. In the case of other shifts, the citizens have not been asked in advance and presumably do not agree. The privatisation of treatment is an appropriate example. The political discussion concerning those areas in which a shift would be favourable and those in which state intervention should be retained or even extended is generally lacking. Instead, those in favour of state intervention stand up against those in favour of raising responsibilities on less aggregate levels. And the growing tensions are accompanied by increasing social conflicts and by a reawakening of social movements dealing with alcohol issues. Are we simply regressing to the situation before Matto?

We cannot go back; we have changed over the last 100 years. Besides state controls, self controls with regard to drinking have evolved. We are no longer able to drink as the Greeks did at their Symposia or as those living in the North American colonies described by Levine (1986). Even the southern European "wine eaters" are going to die out. This is one argument in favour of shifting selected responsibilities to smaller entities than the national state. Another argument of equal weight concerns the development of supranational structures with even greater powers, known as 'globalisation': countries with soft alcohol controls now have to deal with countries with tight controls or even with prohibition, i.e. total controls. Within the same process, alcohol control policies are confronted with drug control policies still in a totalitarian state or in the state of Planwirtschaft, as Scheerer (2001) expressed it. In this conflict-prone development, humble solutions – and that includes solutions for smaller entities – become increasingly necessary. Switzerland may serve as an example in this respect, too. The political autonomy of the cantons has enabled the establishment of a range of control systems for legal and illegal drugs, and the development of surprising and innovative experiments.

Glauser and his heroes Matto and Doctor Laduner also provide us with a motto for humble change. On the last pages, Laduner again talks to the policeman Studer:

> " 'Where does Matto's empire end?' asked the doctor softly. 'At the palisades of the asylum Randlingen? You once spoke about the spider being on the watch in the middle of her net...The threads reach further. They reach over the whole world. ... Matto throws his balls and paper garlands..... You might consider me to be a poetical psychiatrist.....That would not be bad..... We do not want much....To bring a small piece of reason into the world.... Not the reason of the time of the French Enlightenment, but another kind of reason – that of our time... The reason that like a lantern would be able to light the obscure interior and to elucidate a little... To scare away the lie a little..... To push aside the big words: duty, truth, honesty... To make us more modest.....' " (1989;191)

BIBLIOGRAPHY

Anderson, H. (1992). *Utopian Feminism, Women's Movements in fin-de-siecle Vienna*. Yale University Press.

Appelt, Ch. (1991) *Frauen, Alkohol, Gesellschaft. Zur Relevanz und Aktualität der amerikanischen Temperenzbewegung*. Freiburg im Breisgau: Lambertus.

Austin, G. (1981) Die Revolution im europäischen Drogengebrauch des 16. Jahrhunderts (Tee, Kaffee, Tabak) im Vergleich zur heutigen Situation. In G. Völger (Ed.) *Rausch und Realität. Drogen im Kulturvergleich* (pp. 64-72). Cologne: Rautenstrauch-Joest-Museum für Völkerkunde.

Eisenbach-Stangl, I. (1991) *Eine Gesellschaftsgeschichte des Alkohols. Produktion, Konsum und soziale Kontrolle alkoholischer Rausch- und Genußmittel in Österreich 1918 – 1984*. Frankfurt am Main: Campus.

Eisenbach-Stangl, I. (1993) The beginnings of Galician and Austrian Alcohol Policy: A common discourse on Dependence, *Contemporary Drug Problems*, 20, 705-718

Eisenbach-Stangl I. (1999) Community action in "Red Vienna" 1918-1934 – lessons to be learned from history. In S. Larsson & B. S. Hanson (Eds.) *Community Based Alcohol Prevention in Europe – Methods and Strategies* (pp. 110-126). Lund: Lunds Universitet.

Erikson, S. (1990) Drunken Danes and Sober Swedes? Religious Revivalism and the Temperance Movements as Keys to Danish and Swedish Folk Cultures. In B. Strath (Ed.) *Language and the Construction of Class Identities. The Struggle for Discursive Power in Social Organisation: Scandinavia and Germany after 1800*. University of Gothenburg, Department of History.

Fahrenkrug, H. (1984) *Alkohol, Individuum und Gesellschaft. Zur Sozialgeschichte des Alkoholproblems in den USA*. Frankfurt am Main: Campus

Fahrenkrug; H. (1993) Das wundersame Ende der "grünen Fee". Überlegungen zu einer gelungenen Drogenprohibition in der Schweiz, *travers*, 0, 39-48

Fahrenkrug, H. (1995) What happened to the "Fée verte". Notes on the lost drinking of Absinthe in Switzerland, *Addiction Research*, 3, 271-277

Glauser, F. (1936/ 1989) *Matto regiert*. Zürich: Arche Verlag AG

Goffmann, E. (1961) *Asylums. Essays on the Social Situation of Mental Patients and Other Inmates* (German translation 1972. Frankfurt am Main: Suhrkamp).

Gusfield, J. R. (1963) *Symbolic Crusade. Status politics and the American Temperance Movement* (fourth printing 1976). Urbana, Chicago, London: University of Illinois Press.

Hamann; B. (1996) *Hitlers Wien. Lehrjahre eines Diktators*. Munich: Piper.

Hauge, R. (2000) *One Thousand Years of Alcohol Policy in Norway*, paper presented at the 26th Annual Alcohol Epidemiology Symposium of the Kettil-Bruun-Society in Oslo, June 2000

Hauschildt, E. (1997) Zusammenschlüsse: Von der Reichshauptstelle gegen den Alkoholismus bis zur Reichsstelle gegen die Alkohol- und Tabakgefahren - 1921 bis 1944. In Deutsche Hauptstelle gegen die Suchtgefahren (Ed.) *Suchtkrankenhilfe in Deutschland, Geschichte, Strukturen, Perspektiven* (pp. 30-41). Freiburg im Breisgau: Lambertus.

Hautmann, H. & Kropf, R. (1974) *Die österreichische Arbeiterbewegung vom Vormärz bis 1945. Sozialökonomische Ursprünge ihrer Ideologie und Politik*. Vienna: Europaverlag.

Heintel, P. (1998) Mediation. Veränderung in der Konfliktkultur. In G. Falk, P. Heintel & Ch. Pelikan (Eds.) *Die Welt der Mediation* (pp.17-58). Klagenfurt: Alekto Verlag.

Klingemann, H. (1986) Von der Kontrolle liederlichen Lebenswandels zur kontrollierten therapeutischen Maßnahme ? Veränderte schweizerische Rechtsnormen zur Zwangsunterbringung, *Kriminologisches Journal*, 3, 182 - 201

Klingemann, H. (1992) The Role of Alcohol Treatment in a Consensus Democracy: The Case of the Swiss Confederation. In H. Klingemann, J. P. Takala & G. Hunt (Eds.) *Cure, Care and Control. Alcoholism Treatment in Sixteen Countries*. (pp. 151-172). State University of New York Press.

Levine, H. (1978) The Discovery of Addiction. Changing Conceptions of Habitual Drunkenness in America, *Journal of Studies on Alcohol*, 39, 143-174

Levine, H. (1980) Temperance and Women in 19th-Century United States. In O. J. Kalant (Ed.) *Alcohol and Drug Problems in Women* (pp. 25-67). New York: Plenum Press.

Levine, H. (1986) Das "gute Geschöpf Gottes" und der "Dämon Rum". Vorstellungen über Alkohol, Verbrechen und Unfälle in Amerika während der Kolonialzeit und im 19. Jahrhundert. In I.

Eisenbach-Stangl (Ed.) *Teufel Alkohol, Kriminalsoziologische Bibliografie 50 – 51* (pp. 3-38). Vienna: Institut für Rechts- und Kriminalsoziologie.

Ley, M. (1999) Politische Religionen in der Moderne. In Universität Wien, Institut für Politikwissenschaft (ed.) *Polis und Psyche*. University of Vienna, Institute of Political Sciences.

Lucas, B. (2002) *Reducing Complexity: Discourse Formulation and State-Society Relationships. The case of Alcohol policies in Europe (1850 - 2000),* paper presented at the 28th Annual Alcohol Epidemiology Symposium of the Kettil-Bruun-Society in Paris, June 2002

Mäkelä, K, Room, R., Single, E., Sulkunen, P. & Walsh, B. (1981) *Alcohol, Society and the State. A comparative study of alcohol control.* Toronto: Addiction Research Foundation.

Olson, G. W. (1986) Anglikanische Mässigkeits- und Enthaltsamkeitsvereine, 1835 - 1914: Ein Überblick, *Drogalkohol*, 3, 228-236.

Scheerer, S. (2001) Planwirtschaft und neue Perspektiven in der Drogenpolitik. In Verein für Bewährungshilfe und Soziale Arbeit (Ed.) *6. Christian Broda Vorlesung 2001*. Vienna: Association for Parole and Social Work.

Schulze, H. (1994) *Staat und Nation in der europäischen Geschichte.* Munich: C.H. Beck.

Sulkunen, P. (1997) From pastoral welfare state to consumers emancipation. The case of Nordic alcohol control. In S. Henderson & S. Petersen (Eds.) *Consuming health - the commodification of health care* (pp. 66-87). London: Routledge.

Sulkunen, P. (2002) Ethics of alcohol policy in a saturated society, *Addiction*, 92 (9), 1117-1122.

Tanner, J. (1986) Die "Alkoholfrage" in der Schweiz im 19. und 20. Jahrhundert, *Drogalkohol*, 3, 147-168.

Uhl, A. & Springer, A. (1993) *Studie über den Konsum von Alkohol und psychoaktiven Stoffen in Österreich unter Berücksichtigung problematischer Gebrauchsmuster.* Vienna: Federal Ministry for Health and Consumer Protection.

AFFILIATION

Ludwig Boltzmann-Institut für Suchtforschung, Wien (LBISucht)
Mackgasse 7 – 11
A- 1237 Vienna, Austria
Phone: +43 1 880 10/ 113; Fax: +43 1 880 10/ 77;
c-mail: irmgard.eisenbach-stangl@api.or.at

B. LUCAS

REDUCING DISCURSIVE COMPLEXITY: THE CASE OF ALCOHOL POLICIES IN EUROPE (1850 – 2000)

Key words: alcohol policy, discourse analysis, welfare state, comparative history, European countries

Abstract: Since the end of 19th century, alcohol policies have passed through three main phases: in all the western European countries, the interpretation shifted from moral redemption and public order to medical concern and, more recently, risk prevention. This evolution of alcohol discourse can be understood as a process of reduction of discursive complexity, i.e. articulation of some elements and exclusion of others. This process can be related to the changing place and role of the state in the welfare system: keeping social order in a minimal intervention logic, then providing reparation of damages in a centralised and planned way, and finally, promoting public health through the creation and co-ordination of policies networks. In order to illustrate that point, the first part of the paper describes the diffusion of *temperance discourse* at the turn of the century and the elaboration of the first political frame (1830-1930). In the second part, we discuss the way the *disease model* became hegemonic and resisted to challenging interpretations (1930-1975). In the third part, we observe the coming out of the *public health model* and the opening of a new discursive conflict (1975-1990); more recently (from the 1990s), we may see a redefinition of discourses and coalitions around the new concept of *harm reduction*. From the liberal state of the 19th century to the contemporary "network society", still one question remains: does the policy making institutions and the democratic claims really support a more opened discursive space?

1. INTRODUCTION

Why all this noise about wine and strong drink? The year is 1772, and the remark comes from Benjamin Rush, one of the founders of American psychiatry. (Rush, 1772: 22)[1]. Rush's remark anticipates future criticisms, revealing the consensus prevailing at the time. For until the late 18th century, alcohol was seen in positive terms: as a valuable medicinal product, an important element in social rituals, a nutritious substance, a "good creature of God". Neither the steady increase in the amount of alcohol consumed, nor the frequent incidence of public intoxication, appeared to give rise to any concern in American or European society (Levine, 1978). Symbolically, Rush's observation thus launched the debate on alcohol policy, both in the United States and in Western Europe.

When we look at how this debate unfolded, it is immediately apparent that, throughout Europe, there were striking similarities in the way the central issue was transformed over time. Initially, the focus of concern was the excessive drinker, *the drunkard*. Then, in the second half of the 19th century, the drink out-shadowed the drinker: all Europe was now concerned about the *alcohol question*. After the Second World War, however, alcohol vanished as a theme in itself, to be replaced by *the alcoholic* – a person suffering from a now defined illness. Later on, in the 1970s, a rival campaign was launched, based on the general concept of public health.

R. Müller and H. Klingemann (eds.),
From Science to Action? 100 Years Later - Alcohol Policies Revisited, 71–100.

Whereas at the beginning, the focus was on *total consumption*, alcohol policy throughout Europe has tended more recently to look at the issue in terms of *alcohol related problems* or *risks.*

In order to demonstrate the importance of this interpretative processes in the transformation of alcohol policies in Europe, I propose to link public policy analysis with discourse theory. Maarten Hajer (1997, 2003) and Carole Lee Bacci (1999) are among the few theorists on the contemporary scene who have attempted to do this. For the most part, research in the two fields has run in parallel. On the one hand, public policy researchers have been increasingly concerned, since the 1980s, by the role of ideas in the policy-making process (Busch&Braun, 1999). The so called "cognitive approaches" (Muller&Surel, 1998) stress the importance in public policy of "paradigms" (Hall, 1993), "belief systems ", (Sabatier&Jenkin-Smith, 1993 ; Sabatier, 1998) or "référentiel" (Jobert&Muller, 1987; Faure and al. 1995). These new approaches to public policy underline that what is at issue is not only a matter of *problem solving*, but also, and perhaps more significantly, a matter of *constructing meanings.* However, there is no reference in this literature to discourse theory, nor is any use made of discourse analysis.

On the other hand, discourse theorists have increasingly been addressing themselves to social and political issues. As Nancy Fraser (1997: 154-155) explains, in the structuralist model (put forward, among others, by Lacan) language was studied as a symbolic system or code – abstracted, that is, from practice and context. In the current, more "pragmatic" model, language is considered at the level of discourse, as a historically specific social practice. Fraser (1997: 152) argues that, by investigating discourse in these terms, we can address four general political issues: the way social identities are fashioned and altered; how, under conditions of inequality, social groups are formed and dissolved; how the cultural hegemony of the dominant group is secured and contested; and, finally, what prospects there are for emancipatory social change and practice. This model is apparent in the work of Michel Foucault and Pierre Bourdieu, and more recently in Laclau and Mouffe's *New Theory of Discourse* (Howarth, 2000). However, these works focus principally on general political and sociological issues, and do not address the specific field of public policy.

By drawing on both public policy research and discourse analysis, I will seek to show how a field of public policy, such as that relating to alcohol, can be framed as a *conversation.* As Jane Jenson (1989: 238) puts it:

> The terrain on which actors struggle for representation is *the universe of political discourse*, a space in which socially constructed identities emerge in discursive struggle (...) At issue are conflicts over the representation and reproduction of power relations based on difference.

Focussing on the similarities between countries, my intention here is to give an account of the way in which alcohol policy discourses developed and were transformed over time in Europe. In order to understand this common shift, I propose to explore two hypotheses. First, I suggest that the dynamic in the European discourse on alcohol *has to do with the evolution of the welfare state.* I argue that there is coincidence, in terms of discursive structure, between the development of alcohol policy and the changing forms of welfare in Western Europe, as far as *relations between state and society* are concerned. In brief, we can observe a shift from subsidiarity to planning, and thence to networking in public policy (Butschi&Cattacin, 1994; Cattacin&Lucas, 1999; Willke, 1991, 1992; Freiburghaus, 1991; Morand, 2000). Inspired by system theory, the authors cited here are mainly concerned with the issue of *managing societal complexity* (Papadopoulos, 1995). Following Willke (1991), we may say that this complexity is ignored by the "subsidiarity state", drastically reduced by the "interventionist state", and recognised and organised by the "reflexive state". This historical perspective is based on a functional interpretation of change: as society grows in complexity (Luhmann, 1982), so the welfare state has to change, as each successive model of state intervention is confronted with its limits.

My suggestion is that we should understand this process of policy making in terms of discourse: as a political *debate* that aims to deal with *discursive* complexity. And this leads to my second hypothesis: as far as the structure of its discourse is concerned, the development of alcohol policy has been characterised by a permanent process of *reducing complexity*. Thus what we need to understand more precisely, when considering the evolution of the Welfare state, is the way in a which a given discourse becomes *hegemonic* in a particular historical context: the way in which it contributes to fixing power relationships at a discursive level, and thus to maintaining the social order.

This occurs first through the *articulation* of alternative discourses or elements of discourses. Articulation has been described by Laclau&Mouffe (1985: 105) as "any practice establishing a relation among elements such that their identity is modified as a result of the articulatory practice." It occurs also thought the *exclusion of alternative discourses*. In the process, the three faces of power are revealed (see Lukes, 1973). For exclusion can be the result of an open conflict that ends up with a winner and a loser, but "power may be, and often is, exercised by confining the scope of decision making to relatively safe issues" (Lukes 1973: 18). And finally, "the crucial point [is] that the most effective and insidious use of power is to prevent such conflict from arising in the first place" (*op cit.*: 23).

I argue that the way in which the frame of reference for alcohol policies in western Europe are formulated can be explained as a result of certain shared practices of articulation and exclusion. If the construction of a hegemony is threatened by discursive contest, new strategies will be deployed in the field of discourse in order to preserve the existing power relationships. The common recourse to this kind of discursive strategy in Europe may help to explain the relative consistency of alcohol policies. Their different timing and content will depend on the relative success of these strategies.

My approach to social policy could be qualified as relational (Donati, 1991), in the sense that the object of research is not defined *a priori*. "The field of alcohol is identified by the limits of its effects or, in other words, by the network of relations that it produces", Bütschi&Cattacin (1994: 42, my translation). In relation to a given social policy field, this implies a shift in focus from the *welfare state* to the *welfare society* or (according to Evers, 1990) the *welfare mix*. This perspective allows us to characterise the relations between actors of different types (public or private) and to consider the emerging effects of the relationship itself. Just as it is possible to identify a political field, so, I believe, it is possible to identify a *discursive field*, which reveals a particular distribution both of discourses and of power relations (see Bourdieu, 2000). From a relational perspective, a given discourse is definable only to the extent that it is part of an environment in which it can be identified in *relation* to the number of past, present or even future discourses. Following Hajer, I understand discourse as:

> a specific ensemble of ideas, concepts and categorisations that are produced, reproduced and transformed in a particular set of practices and through which meaning is given to physical and social realities" (Hajer, 1997: 44).

We can study the way in which discursive hegemony has been constructed, and challenged, in the field of alcohol policy in Europe by considering two dimensions that in each country concerned link the characteristics of the welfare state to those of the alcohol policy debate: (1) The *discourse formulation process*: who are the actors that formulate discourses about alcohol and, more specifically, who are the actors that formulate the political frame of reference? To what extent is this an open process? What are the rules of discourse formulation, and what do they tell us about the relationship between State and society? (2) The *discursive context*: what is the structure of the discursive field of alcohol policy? what is the global frame of reference, in term of social policy the so called "référentiel global" (Jobert&Muller, 1987)? Is the discourse "institutionalised", i.e. translated into rules and practices (Hajer, 1997)?

Methodologically, the analysis is based on a comparison of thirteen European countries (Austria, Denmark, Finland, France, Germany, Great Britain, Italy, the Netherlands, Norway, Spain, Sweden, Switzerland and Portugal), in which I look, on the one hand, at similarities in the structuring of the discourse in each case, and, on the other, at policy design and policy network. I should emphasis that in this chapter I present only the preliminary results of an ongoing research, with a view to supporting a theoretical exploration which I assume may be of interest to anyone concerned with alcohol research, public policy or discourse analysis[2]. I have aimed to reconstruct at a meso-level the common discursive field among these countries, on the basis both of secondary literature and some significant sources. For this purpose, I have taken into account published speeches and writings, but also material relating to the concrete practice of actors (such as information about a type of treatment). I have considered both types of sources from the point of view of discourse, aiming to infer from them a global framework for interpretation. From this perspective, discourse must be understood as an "ideal typical" construction. My account of the organisational characteristics of alcohol policy is based on information about policy networks and institutions in the alcohol field in each particular country, and focuses especially on the relationship between state and society (see also Cattacin&Lucas, 1999).

I organise my argument following three main historical phases. For each, I start considering social policy as a whole and then the specific alcohol question. I first argue that the diffusion and transformation of the *temperance discourse* fits the model of subsidiarity (I). In the second part (II), I argue that the hegemonic construction of the *Disease Model* fits the institutional setting of the interventionist welfare state. Finally (III), I argue that the recent focus on "alcohol problems" - as part of a more general discourse on public health - fits the new tendency towards networking (III). I suggest that after the *total consumption model* which came out in the 1970s, the notion of *harm reduction* may soon become the focus of a new hegemonic discourse on alcohol policy. In the conclusion (IV), I summarise the main historical developments, and question an assumption often made in the literature about new forms of governance: do the new policy network designs and the role of the state in providing information and inciting change really lead to a more open discursive space?

2. CONSTRUCTING HEGEMONY IN THE CONTEXT OF SUBSIDIARITY: THE TEMPERANCE DISCOURSE (1830-1930)

If one were allowed only one criterion to mark the birth of a distinct era in the 19th century in Europe, it might be, as Polanyi (1983) has argued, the advent of liberalism, as manifested in the differentiation between the political and the economic systems, and the idea of self-regulation. The term self-regulation refers to the regulation of the economy by the market, i.e. by the price mechanism. Moreover, the operation of a free market economy entails a "market society": one in which there are markets not just for goods, but also for land, labour and capital. The relations between the political system and the economic system are based on the principle of *non-intervention* and *the guarantee of self-regulation*. Nothing should disturb the workings of the market, and, in particular, there should be no state interference in the mechanisms of price, supply and demand. "Only policies and measures which contribute to assuring the self-regulation of the market in creating conditions which make the market the only organisational power in economic matters are suitable" (Polanyi, 1983: 104, my translation).

Following the logic of economic policy, this liberal vision presupposes that society, too, be self-regulating. But some persistent enigma, an anomaly, would reveal soon the specificity of the social. In practice, this anomaly took the form of *pauperism* (Castel, 1995). The negative effects of industrialisation - the disorganisation of a traditional way of life, brought about by the liberalisation of work and fluctuations in trade - were *not* compensated for by the advantages of a market free from restrictions. To the consternation of 19th century society, it appeared that pauperism was undeniably associated with abundance.

In the light of the "social question" to which it gave rise, state intervention in society took on a new meaning: the liberal principle of self-regulation was now reinforced by the principle of *subsidiarity*, enshrined at the beginning of the 20th century in Christian social doctrine. According to this principle, the state or higher authorities should concern themselves only with those tasks that cannot be accomplished by inferior units. In other words, it circumscribed the central authorities' sphere of competence. The well-being of the individual was the criterion by which every state action should be measured. State intervention was thus legitimised by the *incapacity of inferior social units to resolve social problems* (Kissling-Naëf&Cattacin, 1997).

The first protective social measures taken in Europe were indeed carried out independently of the state. 19th century liberals devised a number of strategies (like charity, creation of mutual-help associations, patronage) meant for the working class, which soon became the main object of concern. But although it was recognised as a social problem, pauperism in the first instance was addressed in exclusively moral terms - see Castel (1995), and Ashford (1986), Rosanvallon (1989), Ewald (1996). Initially at least, the social contract proposed by liberal thinkers eliminated the need for a more global consideration of the way in which labour was organised. It was only with the establishment of the labour movement that the model of social protection, offered by a moralistic bourgeoisie that had an interest in securing social harmony without state intervention, was contested. The failure of this strategy of "assimilation", which presupposed that the dominated classes would adhere to dominant norms, transformed the perception of the deviant: no longer repentant, he had become the enemy (Gusfield, 1967). Here, then, state intervention was legitimised by the requirement of *social order*.

The state intervened in two ways to protect order in society. First, it employed the traditional threat - or practice - of *violence* (Freiburghaus, 1991). The principal role of the state was to guarantee public order through the use of a traditional police force. Measures of coercion or punishment were used against individuals whose behaviour was judged deviant. Generally speaking, the state responded to social problems by employing a strategy of exclusion, i.e. by recourse to mental asylums and prisons. As Castel argues, the establishment of liberal society coincides with the reactivation of total institutions: poorhouses, prisons, insane asylums or, in the case of England, workhouses.

> The use of these modern versions of internment, which were justified by the ideologies of reparation or recovery, was their solution" for the most resistant and desocialised groups. (Castel, 1995: 383, my translation).

Legal measures represented the second means by which the state intervened to protect the social order (Freiburghaus, 1991; Morand, 2000). Here, the liberal state appears as the guarantor of certain liberties. The limitation of working hours, the establishment of a legal minimum age for working, or the setting of minimal hygiene standards in the late 19th century were the first signs that a notion of social citizenship was beginning to be practised (Cattacin&Lucas, 1999). Thus positive law, designed to establish a framework for economic activity, can be seen as the liberal state's first instrument of systematic intervention in the social field. Generally speaking, however, the use of the law was for a long time identified with restraint or punishment (Morand, 2000). Following Willke (1991), we can say that the principles of both self-regulation and subsidiarity allowed the state to contain complexity in the economic and social systems and, in this way, limit public involvement in societal regulation once "social problems" where first identified.

How, meanwhile, did the discourse on alcohol policy evolve? The first construction of the alcohol problem, like for other social issues, occured at the "organisational level" of the civil society (Cattacin, 1996), through an important dialogue involving some churches, temperance movements, philanthropic associations, labour organisations, medical community, newspapers, but also industrial and commercial interests. In Germany, a bibliography is published in 1904, listing the woks related to the moral, medical, scientific and social dimensions of alcohol and alcoholism and it contained no less than 504 pages! (Bynum, 1984). This dialogue, in which the state's role was extremely confined, gave rise to the first temperance discourse, which soon became *hegemonic.* But in order to keep its hegemonic position, the temperance discourse had to transform itself and build a new discursive alliance with the state: in its second incarnation (as the second temperance discourse) it called for public intervention, following the principle of subsidiarity. Inspired by temperance movements, the first policy designs also reflected the liberal model, with the state, in the name of public order, expanding its capacity for prohibition and repression. Let us look at these three points in more detail.

During the 18th century, alcohol consumption was first interpreted as a problem through a moral discourse formulated by the Church, which stigmatised the "sin of drunkenness" or the "vice of drunkenness" and was mainly concerned with the redemption of drunkards. State intervention, meanwhile, was largely confined to the punishment of individuals (or tax raising). Alcohol abuse was not yet interpreted as a specific form of deviance, and drunkards were included in the general category of "poor", "mentally ill" or "delinquent" individuals (Levine, 1978, Cattacin&Lucas, 1999). The first temperance discourse went a step further, shifting the burden of responsibility from the will of the subject to the product, alcohol, itself, which was understood to generate compulsive behaviour. As a discourse which called for the regulation of the amount of alcohol consumption, temperance grew out of a combination of scientific (medical) and religious arguments.

Actually, the growing discursive complexity of the 19th century was reduced by this very ambivalent and undifferentiated discourse, which could articulate a multiplicity of interests in an expanding discursive coalition. As Roberts (1985) puts it, temperance occupied such a prominent place on the social and political agenda of the 19th century precisely because it appealed to a great many people for a great many different reasons. At the same time, the first temperance discourse excluded the idea of state intervention - an option that still lacked legitimacy and therefore had no place in the argument, and ignored any alternative interpretation: as alcohol abuse was framed as a cause to social problems, and as social problems were framed as an addition of individual failures, it was difficult to argue that social inequalities or economical order where responsible for alcohol abuse.

Let us consider first the *articulation process* that leads the first temperance discourse to extend the coalition around it, and then turn to the exclusionary process. The temperance discourse first relied on two concepts: *addiction* and *abstinence* (Levine, 1984). The articulation of those concepts allowed for the construction of a discursive hegemony that would help to preserve the social order in a changing society. The notion of addiction illustrates well the importance accorded to loss of control and to the annihilation of willpower. The counterweight to addiction, willpower, remained a key value in the discourse of religious people and manifested itself in the practice of abstinence or sobriety. It was the discursive cohabitation of these two traditions that characterised the emergence of the temperance discourse: "The temperance press has always regarded drunkenness as a sin and a disease. A sin first, then a disease." (National Temperance Society 1873, quoted by Levine, 1978: 157). Besides appealing to doctors and churchmen, this concept also attracted aspiring entrepreneurs who were looking for ways to win success in an increasing competitive society. The first temperance discourse thus provided a means for the elite of the 19th century to assert their social legitimacy.

Significantly, this first discursive coalition - initiated by a bourgeoisie that was concerned with its own self control - was able further to expand as a result of a second and decisive discursive articulation, in which the temperance discourse was linked to a more global frame of reference - the so-called "social question". Alcohol, already recognised as the cause of individual dependence, was now identified as the cause of *all the social problems* confronting European societies. During this period, a causal link between "alcohol" and "pauperism" was established in various countries, like in the USA (Levine, 1984), Switzerland (Bütschi&Cattacin, 1994), Sweden (Rosenqvist&Takala, 1985), Germany (Spode, 1997), France (Mitchell, 1987), Italy (Cottino, 1985) and Great Britain (Berridge, 1993). Henceforward the temperance discourse would address itself to the *working classes*, who now became the main focus of attention. From the early 20th century onwards, the notorious "alcohol question" in Europe was made synonymous with the problem of the consumption of alcohol by the lower classes (Roberts, 1984).

What is very striking at this point is the undecidability or ambiguity of the first temperance discourse. What was its "real" meaning? Depending on the context and one's perspective, it can be interpreted as a mechanism of social control or as a force for emancipation. This discursive ambiguity accounts for the two different readings of temperance history in the literature - one sympathetic, the other more critical (Robert, 1984). For example, we will see that the fear of degeneration that haunted the bourgeoisie was one motivating factor in prompting people to join the temperance movement; conversely, aspiration towards higher things and belief in human perfectibility inspired many among the working classes to rally to the same discourse. Thus a discourse that was generated by an elite in search initially of legitimisation, and subsequently of social control, would eventually be appropriated by the working class itself!

For the Left was obviously confronted with a dilemma: on the one hand, it was bound to defend a programme based on the need for structural changes in the battle against pauperism. On the other, it agreed with the factual premise of the middle class temperance discourse - that there was an alcohol-related problem among the lower classes. In view of their concern about the problem, left-wing leaders were under pressure to come up with a solution to it. They fell back on the attitude that alcoholism was an individual moral failing, later on tempering this view with demands for regulation. This position, defined as "abstinent socialism", came to dominate the European left (Roberts, 1985).

Let us now turn to the way in which this first temperance discourse *excluded* alternative interpretations. What was true for the problem of pauperism was also true for alcohol-related problems: the solutions formulated at the beginning of the 19th century adhered to the principle of societal self-regulation and individual rehabilitation. In the first place, it was mainly through the organisation of civil society that the temperance discourse spread. Temperance associations multiplied, first in Great Britain and the USA, and subsequently throughout the rest of Europe, particularly Protestant Europe (Mäkelä and al, 1996). Second, it is clear that the discourses of the temperance movements were underpinned by a desire for social rehabilitation. Their principle of action was based on self-help: they advocated moral persuasion and the temperance pledge (Roberts, 1984). This motivation can also be seen in the practices of the first specialised care institutions, which were most often created by "temperance doctors" or those working in mental asylums where "moral treatment" was applied (Baumohol&Room, 1987). Thus, the solutions were prescribed exclusively at the level at which the problems were immediately manifest, namely at the level of the individual. On the whole, the discourses were addressed *to* the drinkers, in the form of a "social programme" for "moral achievement" (Room, 1998).

The notion of state intervention had no legitimacy within this discursive context; nor did it figure in any significant way in the debate on the alcohol question -at least before the middle of 19$^{th.}$ Moreover, this first temperance discourse make it difficult to link alcohol consumption and social organisation. Thenceforth, one of the only remaining discourses to offer any opposition to this prevailing view will be that of socialism, as formulated, notably, by Kautsky, but only at the end of the century. Still at that time, the socialists were alone in posing the question: *why do people drink?* and in attempting to link the phenomenon with the question of living and working conditions. Their discourse inverted the causal relationship, finding the cause of alcohol abuse in the bad social conditions of the working class. In the view of socialists such as Kautsky, whose interpretation was based on an extrapolation from Germany's structural conditions, the road to a solution lay through class struggle. But this view proved influential only among the Left in Germany (Roberts, 1985) and Italy (Cottino&Morgan, 1987).

As far as the debate on alcohol was concerned, the first temperance discourse succeeded in closing the gate (for a while) to the political conflict, social antagonism and power relationships that characterised societal development at that time, while nevertheless offering, behind the apparent neutrality of its moral (and sometimes scientific) premises, a strong *political* interpretation. In an increasingly complex context, however, this hegemonic position would come up against new challenges. The failure to achieve complete discursive hegemony on solving the problem of alcohol through societal self-regulation led the social actors involved to ask for and legitimise *public intervention*, calling for the adoption of *restrictive legislation*. In all Europe, we can observe from the mid-19th century onwards a general *shift* in the temperance discourse from a moral to a coercive view of the problem. How can we explain the content of this second temperance discourse?

At the level of the "lived world" (Habermas, 1981), i.e. of everyday practice, the moral argument – even the argument that the leftist elite had espoused – had come up against an opposing view of life, a form of resistance, that legitimised or at least tolerated drinking. People continued to drink, and it was not until the turn of the century that we can observe any change in drinking habits (Edwards & al., 1995: 33-

34). In some cases – for example among the Catholic minority in the U.S. (Gusfield, 1963) - this resistance was explicitly formulated in a political discourse that used alcohol consumption as a cultural symbol. Moreover, discussion of the social question did not disappear along with the first Temperance discourse – the concept of alcohol as an explanation of social problems could not achieve to reduce the debate about social question. With the spread of universal suffrage and, more specifically, after the revolutions of 1848 and 1871, other points of view were brought to bear on the issue of pauperism: mainly as part of the new question of social *rights* (such as the right to work).

This generated the fear (or hope) of political subversion: the law had lost its consensual face (Donzelot 1984). In this context, a shift took place in the temperance discourse: the alcohol question was no longer seen as a social problem that had to be solved by social means, but as a political problem that required state intervention. As far as argumentation was concerned, putting the alcohol question on the political agenda, in the specific context of subsidiarity, meant, on the one hand, discursively identifying a societal *failure* (which would legitimise state intervention) and, on the other, finding an appropriate frame of reference in which to articulate the need for intervention and the form it should take.

Society's failure to stem the alcohol problem was identified in terms of *social degeneration*. At the political level, this discourse expressed the fear of a level of social degeneration that could lead to a nation's defeat in rivalry or war with other nations. The French, for example, feared that France would become depopulated compared to imperial Germany (Mitchells, 1987). In Great Britain, the medical profession and the temperance movement were jointly concerned about the impact of degeneration on national efficiency, notably in the context of the Boer War and, later on, the First World War (Weir, 1984); while in Germany degeneration was going to be seen as a racial problem (Giles, 1995). In each case, the discourse of degeneration aroused public fears and hence legitimated state intervention for the sake of *public order*.

In articulating the need for intervention and the form it should take, the second temperance discourse made a radical call for the state's traditional forces – the police and the law - to be activated. The production, distribution and consumption of alcohol should be regulated, and drunkards punished. There was thus, in my view, no real paradox (*pace* Sulkunen&Warpenius, 2000), in the fact that the second temperance discourse at one and the same time appealed for individual self control *and* called for legal regulation. Given the context of subsidiarity, this was a logical evolution of the argument, as a discursive way to expand its coalition and preserve its hegemony.

Concretely, however, this discursive move led to a "dislocation" of temperance (Laclau&Mouffe 1985). The addiction concept loose its importance, and the second temperance discourse relied on a new articulation, between "abstinence" or "temperance" and "public order". This open the possibility for two discourses to distinguish: the medical one (alcoholism as a disease) and the liberal one (let us consume!). Moreover, the shift towards state intervention and the demand for restrictive measures had created a new opportunity for both conflict and competition between discourses.

The possibility for conflict is obvious. The demand that the consumption, sale and production of alcohol be regulated was directly contested by a liberal discourse that championed the liberty of producers, consumers and traders to act as they wished. Thus in Germany, for example, the powerful brewing industry engaged in a real war of ideas against the temperance movements, issuing a series of tracts and pamphlets in which they argued that alcohol did harm only to those who were already sick or degenerate (Giles, 1995). This conflict reached its height in the 1920s due to the reference of American' prohibition.

But the second temperance discourse called not only for state intervention but for financial support for its activities. This gave rise to a new concurrence between organisations. In particular, the medical strand within the temperance movement appealed for financial support to set up systematic treatment for alcoholics. Those who supported this idea aimed to establish a specialised niche within the structure of the medical profession, seeking to define alcoholism as an illness. The paradigm of degeneration would also be used in this new scientific context. It helped in establishing alcoholism as a specific object of study that appeared to lend itself well to research and seemed to offer good therapeutic prospects (Bynum, 1984). This shift towards a *specific* medical discourse would mark, in some cases, the end of the old discursive alliance with the temperance movement.

As we now today, the disease model will "hegemonize" the alcohol field after the second world war. For the time being, however, this new medical interpretation of alcoholism as a specific disease remained relatively insignificant, both within the discursive field as a whole and within the specific discourse of the medical profession. Generally speaking, alcoholism continued to be treated as a form of mental illness, and the specific nature of the problem had yet to be recognised. Moreover, the medical discourse could not find any allies among state authorities (Baumohol&Room, 1987), because it did not fit easily with the public order frame of reference. Except in the Nordic countries (Rosenqvist&Takala, 1985) and Austria (Eisenbach-Strangl, 1992), in which there was already a strong tradition of state intervention and in which it was possible to envisage implementing a system of coercive care. In these countries, the discursive coalition between doctors and temperance movement could be saved once doctors started to play an important role in the promotion of a restrictive system for the regulation of alcohol -defending even the approach according to which alcoholism *was not* a sickness and developing a system of care based on enforced treatment, as in Sweden (Sutton, 1998) and in Finland (Bruun, 1971).

By contrast, in Great Britain, the medical profession did not see it as part of their role to help enforce restrictions, and they opposed, for example, the move to close pubs on Sundays (Berridge, 1993), an issue which opened a marked rift between the temperance movement and the medical profession. In this instance, a system of control was introduced in the early 20th century that restricted the times at which alcohol could be sold – a system that was legitimised by reference to public order, but no move was made to authorise forced treatment for alcoholism, and any doctors who undertook to treat alcoholics did so outside the auspices of the state. (Berridge, 1992, Baumohol&Room, 1987).

Thus, throughout Europe, during the period that ended definitely with the Second World War, the need for public order dominated discussion and was seen as the prime justification for state intervention, in regards to societal failure. Within this context, the second temperance discourse can be seen partially to have succeeded in its aims: after the First World War, almost all European countries legislated on alcohol regulation (Cattacin&Lucas, 1999). But the state invested only marginally in the areas of care or prevention, which for the most part were left to civil society organisations or private clinics.

Actually, the new policy designs on alcohol were manifested in two kinds of measures. The first were addressed to deviant behaviour and took the form of sending alcoholics to mental asylums or prisons. The majority of European countries also criminalised drunkenness (Cattacin&Lucas, 1999). Finland offers a prime example of this kind of coercive approach. Right up until 1950, alcohol-related problems in Finland were dealt with by police intervention, prisons and enforced care (Mäkela and al. 1981: 41).

The second type of measure involved implementing a legal framework to limit access to alcohol. In Europe, the Nordic countries again took the lead here, with Sweden, Norway and Finland all establishing a state monopoly on the production and sale of alcohol. But this state instruments had nothing to do which the present reference to public health. As Sutton (1998:42) recall us, "the state retail monopoly for alcohol (…) was initially established as a means of controlling purchases by individual." Similarly, the regulations imposed on taverns in Italy, for example, were clearly motivated more by concerns about public order and political control (taverns were perceived as hotbeds of revolution) than about individual or public health (Cottino, 1985).

3. STATE CONTROL OF DISCOURSE (1930 – 1975): FROM HEGEMONY TO THE CRISIS OF LEGITIMISATION

After the 1920s, the relation between state and society was called into question[3]. In fact, neither the private actor nor the *Etat de droit* were in a position to respond to the growing demands for the resolution of social problems – demands expressed through trade unions and, more generally, through the extension of the means for democratic participation. In this regard, the crisis of 1929 represented a crucial event that allowed the welfare state to gain legitimacy. But the development of a more visible and active state was also stimulated by the radicalisation of social confrontation (which required the state to intervene as a conciliator), two World Wars (which gave rise to modern bureaucracy and large scale social programmes) and technological innovations (which enlarge the scope for systematic intervention in social problems) (Cattacin, 1996).

Between the 1950s and the 1970s, some version of the welfare state model was developed in all the West European countries. The traditional political frame of reference, which was based, as we have seen, on the notion of public order, was thus modified, or rather *completed*, by the elaboration of the first state policies on social and health issues. The repressive approach and the use of legal regulation still played a conspicuous role. However, "reparation" policies, designed directly to address the effects of social problems, were juxtaposed – although not integrated – with these more traditional forms of intervention. The aim was to compensate for the negative effects of industrial growth by a corresponding increase in public expenditure. The principle of social risk insurance spread (Ewald, 1986) and the response to social problems was increasingly medicalised (Gehradt, 1991). Psychosocial intervention, which was now increasingly professionalised, highlighted moreover the need for specialised institutions that would enlarge the role of medicine in treating social problems.

The state began to intervene more and more directly. It developed existing public institutions, created new ones and (by means of large subsidies) assimilated those private organisations whose aims and functions accorded with the its own standards, while marginalising others. From then on, the solution to social problems was elaborated and implemented mainly by the state, using as its instrument large-scale planning, such as the planning of hospitals during the 1960s, which was based on the expertise of social and health professionals.

This shift in state-society relations was also visible in the discursive field. In this model, civil society was now relegated to the status of audience, while the debate itself was conducted within the state by political parties and, at the level of programme elaboration, by scientists and experts. As Claus Offe argues:

> The implicit sociological premise underlying the constitutional accords of the liberal Welfare State, was that the models of private life - the family, work and consumption - would absorb the energy and aspirations of the majority of people and that participation in public life and in conflicts concerning them had as a result only a marginal importance in the life of the vast majority of citizens. This constitutional definition of the activities respectively of capital and labour, of the state and civil society, correlated with the centrality accorded to the values of growth, prosperity and the redistribution of resources. (Offe, 1997: 101, my translation)

In this way, the role of defining the problems to be addressed was now transferred to the sphere of state control. The political parties acquired a monopoly over public debate and conflict, at the cost of a significant reduction in the diversity of the problems formulated (Willke, 1991). On the other hand, the fact that the state had now taken responsibility for social questions guaranteed, in principle, that the response to social problems would be universal and that services would be developed in each case for the entire country. The result was a de-politicisation of social stakes and a de-differentiation of problems and solutions.

Let us look now at how this evolution was reflected in the structuring of discourses on alcohol. What is striking here is the relative *absence*, during this period, of social debate on this question throughout Western Europe – the apparent confidence that, in some way, the "alcohol question" had been resolved. In every European country the drink question vanished from the social and political agenda. In 1931, for example, the Royal Commission on Licensing concluded that the problem of alcohol in Great Britain was no longer a gigantic evil" (Weir, 1984: 93). This optimistic perspective appeared to correspond to the fall in consumption, particularly of spirits, recorded in Europe between the turn of the century and the Second World War (Edwards et al., 1995).

However, my hypothesis is that the reinterpretation of the alcohol question that took place between the 1930s and 1970s was once again part of a more general reframing process that was linked to the relations between state and society. After the re-opining of conflict and competition that started with the second temperance discourse, we notice now a new process in which discursive complexity is radically reduced. The alcohol issue would again be radically simplified, with the *disease model* taking over almost entirely. The new liberal discourse on alcohol contributed to the dominance of this model. "Alcoholism" was now seen as an illness in itself; "addiction" was rediscovered and the ordinary consumption of alcohol was left to "normal consumers". I will first look briefly at the historical process that led to the dominance of this model, and then illustrate some of the ways that it functioned to exclude other discourses.

The disease model spread to Europe from the USA after the Second World War. Many authors have discussed this model, but Robin Room's account (1983: 54) reveals its main arguments:

> 1.There is a new scientific approach to alcohol issues which replaces the old moralistic approach.
> 2.This approach involves the recognition that there is a well-defined singular entity called "alcoholism" which some people have and others don't.
> 3.Those who have "alcoholism" will always be different in their drinking from the "normal" drinker and therefore should never drink again.
> 4.The entity should be thought of as a disease in itself (and not, for instance, as just a symptom of another underlying disease) which the alcoholic suffers from involuntary.
> 5. It is therefore both rational and humane to help and treat alcoholics as sick, rather than as immoral or criminal.
> 6. Providing treatment for alcoholism is the most urgent priority for and most adequate method of handling society's "alcohol-related problems."

The discursive field was virtually monopolised at that time by three discourses, each of them being *articulated* by this same model. First, there was the work of the Yale Research Centre for Alcohol Studies, which was circulated by *The Quarterly Journal of Studies on Alcohol*, founded in 1940. The slogan "Alcoholism is a disease" was introduced in this context for the explicit purpose of "de-moralising" the political debate on alcohol consumption (Conrad&Schneider, 1980). Second, Alcoholics Anonymous, founded in 1935, grew rapidly in the United States and subsequently in Europe (Mäkelä et al., 1996). Their discourse was also based on the concept of alcoholism as an illness and on the view that total abstinence was essential to recover. Finally, in a seminal article on the subject, the researcher E. M. Jellinek identified and described the various phases of alcoholism (Jellinek 1952), making the illness more easily identifiable. Symbolically, this new definition of the problem was sanctioned by the World Health Organisation's adoption of the disease model in 1951.

The impressive success of the disease model, in terms of its diffusion and acceptance, can be related to the evolution of the welfare state. The fall in alcohol consumption that was recorded between the two World Wars proved not to be lasting. From the 1950' onwards, two parallel trends can be observed throughout Western Europe: a renewed rise in per capita production and consumption of alcohol, sometimes to the level reached in the 19th century (Edwards et al, 1995) and a concomitant rise in most alcohol-related health problems (Mäkelä, 1987). But, now, there was no more concern about the direct causal relationship between these trends. The state stood in the middle, and drew a new and more indirect relationship between economical or technological progress and the development of a health system. The disease model had made alcoholism an identifiable illness that affected an identifiable population, for whom it was possible to identify an effective treatment, one that was based on expert advice and which the state could implement through developing an appropriate health policy and financing it in the context of the new Keynesian compromise. The problem was thus redefined according to the logic of technocratic management that characterised the welfare state – redefined, in other words, in terms of its *solution*.

The disease model was to prove extraordinarily resilient and resistant to challenge. It effectively *excluded* any opposing discourse, systematically rejecting the old temperance discourse and everything associated with it. Indeed, with the repeal of American prohibition in 1933, the disease model was established precisely in terms of its *opposition* to the model on which prohibition was based. Alcohol as a product of consumption was no longer to blame, and nor was the consumer. The disease model built its hegemony on the rejection of the temperance discourse. This mechanism of rejection influenced the scientific field as much as the political debate. Thus, throughout the period in which the disease model prevailed in the alcohol policy network (i.e. until the mid 1970s), the critical discourses that emanated from the scientific community came under heated political attack (Room, 1999). For example, the "total consumption" approach advocated in the 1950s by Ledermann was not taken seriously because of its political implication: to design a policy aiming a reducing the global consumption instead of focussing on some sick persons (Berridge, 1996).

The unusual willingness of scientists to break with the past helps also to explain what has been called an "eclipse of knowledge" in the scientific field (Katcher, 1992): the tendency among the medical profession to dismiss knowledge accumulated since the beginning of the century. Suddenly, the importance of most alcohol-related health problems - for example, cirrhosis of the liver and cancer of the oesophagus - was minimised, precisely because they had been the focus of the now-discarded temperance discourse[4]. Moreover, since alcohol was seen as an individual, as opposed to a social problem, the spotlight was once again turned on the old concept of addiction, which in turn limited the exploration of the causal link between alcohol and a whole series of social or medical problems.

Another kind of eclipse also occurred at this time. In the disease model, only a small percentage of the population was constructed as a problem. The majority - the social drinkers - were now excluded from scientific and hence political concern. In a way, the medical-administrative community succeeded in sharing the discursive field –as a market– with the alcohol industry: with the former addressing the problematic drinkers, the latter focusing on the social drinkers.

Every attempt to question this dominant interpretation in the name of prevention or general public health was equated with a return to the temperance discourse and as such discredited. This phenomenon can be seen in relation to methods of state regulation, which were now dismissed *a priori* as mechanisms of social control. Repressive or regulatory measures did not disappear completely during this period, but their status was much reduced. Public drunkenness, for example, was decriminalised, and in terms of public order drinking was now deemed a criminal offence only in relation to driving (Cattacin&Lucas, 1999). Alcohol was seen in socio-economic terms as a product that was subject to regulation like any other foodstuff. Under pressure from industrial lobbies, and with the enlargement of the European Community, there was a general reduction in taxation on alcohol, and the development of tourism, the growth of supermarkets, and the increased number of points of sale led to a liberalisation in the system of licence-granting.

The state played an active part in the production of discourses on alcohol. In collaboration with medical experts, it was now responsible for defining the problem of alcoholism and determining how it should be resolved[15]. The use of "half knowledge" (Marin, 1981) made it possible to establish a homogeneous framework for shaping and implementing policy. The wholesale rejection of the old temperance discourse meant that it gradually lost its legitimacy among civil society organisations and within the medical profession, which, on the contrary, sought to distance itself from this previous model by referring to the discourse of scientific and administrative experts. In order to survive, in other words, organisations aligned themselves with the officially-sanctioned discourse (Butschi&Cattacin, 1994). Private organisations that had played a key role in the temperance movements (including those in Nordic countries) either professionalised, went into decline, or disappeared completely.

Moreover, the implementation of "reparation" policies contributed to the hegemony of the new discourse in the field and ensured that individuals with a "problem" were reoriented towards the health system. This institutionalisation of the new discourse (Hajer, 1997) also explains its resistance to change. Fully-developed health systems now integrated the question of alcohol treatment within their individually-oriented approach. From the 1950s onwards, the majority of countries offered state support to cover the costs of treating recognised "alcoholics". The medical field established a new, specialised field of "alcohology". The model was perfectly adapted to the insurance and reparation policies of the post-war period.

It was only when the place and role of the state in the production of welfare began to be questioned, as a result of the crisis of the welfare state in the mid-1970s, that the disease model encountered a serious challenge. The re-evaluation of the state's role could be observed in the new discourses on alcohol. The new debate, which essentially mobilised the scientific community, followed the contested diffusion of neo-liberal ideology in Europe (Jobert, 1994). After a period of relative consensus, the global frame of reference for the formulation of social policy appeared to be divided, and this would provide a window of opportunity (Kingdom, 1984) for the *public health model* to emerge and challenge the hegemony of the medical model in the field of alcohol.

4. NETWORKING: FROM A DISCURSIVE CONFLICT TO AN OVERLAPPING CONSENSUS (1975 – 2000)?

The crisis that the European welfare states underwent in the late twentieth century has been interpreted differently: as a crisis of finances (O'Connors, 1973), governability (Crozier and al., 1975), bureaucratic management (Nozick, 1974), modern forms of domination (Ewald 1986) and solidarity (Rosanvallon, 1981), or as a crisis in the welfare state project itself (Habermas, 1985). Comparative neo-institutionalist studies conducted in the early 1990s, however, have also emphasised the resilience of the welfare states (Pierson, 1994; Esping-Anderson, 1996). From this perspective, the various reforms in social policy have been no more than adjustments to the basic model.

If we look at social policy during the late twentieth century, however, it seems undeniable that a transformation has taken place in the role of the state, its relationship to society and its methods of intervention. Kenis & Schneider (1991) have identified the main aspects of this evolution in policy-making: the growing importance of the organisation of civil society; the blurring of boundaries between public and private; the transformation of state instruments: see for example the new concepts of the "animator state" (Donzelot, 1994); the "reflexive state" (Willke, 1992); the "propulsive State" (Morand, 1991); the "incitor State" (Bütschi&Cattacin, 1993); the loss of state centrality and the pluricentralisation of political and social processes; the fragmentation of the state; the growing internationalism and interdependence of national stakes; and the increasing recourse to information – notably scientific expertise – as a political instrument. The coincidence of growing societal complexity and the internal complexity of state components likewise constitutes the principal problem confronting the current welfare state (Willke, 1992).

The new relational nature of current policy-making may be seen in the growing role played by political networks and by communication. This *networks* are characteristically informal, decentralised and horizontal. According to Volker Schneider:

> In the context of policy making, this means that a policy emerges not from a centrally concerted or programmed action but from the autonomous interaction of a plurality of interdependent organisations or individuals. (Schneider, 1992: 110).

Moreover, *information and communication* are now used as an important public policy instrument. Notable phenomena in this context are the promotion of public debate through the state's organisation of discussion *forum* and dissemination of knowledge, but also the active participation of private organisations in designing and implementing social programmes. The state no longer has exclusive responsibility for producing well-being in society, but is one player among a whole network of others. Similarly, it has lost its monopoly over legitimate discourses on the nature of well-being and how to achieve it.

From this perspective, the increased role played in recent years by civil society may imply —but not necessarily —a renewal of liberal-style self-regulation. I may also point to a deficit in the legitimacy and efficiency of the welfare state, such that the process of defining and resolving social problems has been transferred to what Beck (1992) refers to as the level of sub-politics. What is new in this form of self-regulation is that the state, principally in its administration, seeks to retain an *active role* in social politics. In order to do this, it relies on the resources available (mainly in the realm of information and communication) to intervene in society. The ability of the state administration to command these resources is thus a necessary condition for this new form of regulation. The result sought here is a higher degree of social acceptance of state intervention.

As far as the elaboration of current political discourses is concerned, this new context helps to account for what Fischer and Forester (1995) have called "the argumentative turn in policy and planning", i.e. the growing importance of the discursive dimension in policy making. At the same time, there is a tendency within the framework of these new relations between the state and society to develop new discourses through "overlapping consensus" (Rawls, 1993). This tends to guarantee the identification of actors of the public policy and of the targets groups with the programs that are promoted. This urge towards consensus is also the Achilles heel of such societies, however, in so far as it blocks action when positions are irreconcilable. Nevertheless, the advantages of this type of regulation are that it allows the groups directly concerned, in partnership with established organisations, to take charge of solving their own problems, and in doing so resolves the issue of legitimisation both in relation to the partisan political arena, and in relation to the groups within the population to whom the programmes in question are addressed (Cattacin&Lucas, 1999).

Hence, during the 1970s and '80s health policies in Europe gradually shifted away from a medical and curative approach towards a more preventive perspective. There were social, scientific and financial reasons for this: citizens themselves demanded more psycho-social and preventive measures; the research community provided arguments for a more information-based health system, and politicians and policy-makers were looking for a strategy that would reduce the costs of the health care system. In this new context, the dominant biomedical conception of social ills was called into question, opening a fresh debate about the need for a new paradigm (Engel, 1977). Whereas public order, and later on individual health, were once at the centre of the discourse, it was now in the name of the *New public health* that the state seeks to legitimise its intervention in the social field (for a discussion of this concept, see Peterson&Lupton, 1996). Prevention in this context represented a significant alternative to the medicalisation of individuals, to the uniform system of treatment, and, finally to the costly expansion of the care sector (hospitals and so on.).

How, meanwhile, did the discourse on alcohol evolve over the same period? Generally speaking, the alcohol issue since 1975 has been actually included within the paradigm of *public health.* In summary, this discourse organises prevention around three elements: the host, the environment and the agent (Holder, 1994). In re-interpreting the alcohol question, three conceptual shifts have occurred (Mosher&Jernigan, 1989). First, attention is no longer centred exclusively on the minority of alcoholics, but on the entire population. This new approach is based on the results of epidemiological research concerning the implications of global consumption for public order, health and security. This statistical data suggest that although the majority of the population is not alcohol-dependent, their consumption at an aggregate level can be linked to the national level of alcohol-related social and medical problems. Thus, the "old" idea, developed in the 1950' by Ledermann, gets a late recognition in the context of this new paradigm.

Second, fresh consideration has been given to the impact of alcohol consumption on health. As we saw earlier, this field of research was neglected during the period when the disease model, which focused on individual dependence, dominated the discourse on alcohol. The integration of the alcohol question within the paradigm of public health has allowed a resumption of research into problems such as cirrhosis of the liver, or the long-term results of consumption, such as cancer. From this perspective, the consumption of alcohol is constructed as a problem of health risk factor.

Finally, the recasting of the alcohol question in terms of public health has resulted, politically, in preventive health campaigns aimed at reducing consumption among the entire population, i.e. in the adoption of a *population-based model* or *total consumption model:* the scientific argument, based on the epidemiological studies, has first been used to legitimise measures taken to control access to alcohol or increase taxes on it. But more recently, we can observe a new tendency toward the adoption of *harm reduction* arguments.

If we consider now the dynamic of the discourse on alcohol since it has been included within the paradigm of public health around 1975, we can discern two stages. First, we have noted the re-opening of a *conflict* over the interpretation of the alcohol issue and, later, the elaboration of a new kind of *consensus.* Let's begin with the construction of a new antagonism during the first period. This debate first took place within the international epistemic community (Haas 1992). This reflects the growing influence on alcohol policies of inter- or super-national dynamics, which have taken the debate onto an international level. It was thus at this level that two political dynamics came first into direct opposition.

On the one side, the integration of European countries in the "super-national State" – the European Union - had the effect of promoting the discourse generated by the alcohol industry, in which alcohol was presented as a product of commonplace consumption. Indeed, this economic logic forced the Nordic countries to relax their interventionist methods (Holder, et al., 1998) and to reconsider their political frame of reference (Sulkunen et al., 2000). On the other side, the public health model was supported by the World Health Organisation (WHO), which since 1992 had developed a plan of action for Europe that was directly inspired by the public health discourse (the European Alcohol Action Plan, WHO, 1993). One of the objectives of this plan was to reduce global alcohol consumption. It should be clear by now that this new discursive dynamic was initiated in a context in which the resilient disease model and, more generally, the biomedical paradigm still prevailed and determined concrete national policies. "The biomedical paradigm is a powerful idea that continues to contribute significantly to health-policy making, as does the associated continued emphasis on individual treatment provided by individual doctors" (Lewis, 1999).

The hegemony and institutionalisation of the disease model, which was supported by liberal discourse and tacitly accepted by public opinion, meant that the new, public-health-oriented discourse on alcohol was obliged to take up an offensive position *against* this dominant interpretation, a position exemplified in an emblematic publication known as *The Purple Book* (Bruun, 1975). The new approach argued not so much against the notion of alcoholism as an illness, but more significantly against the implications of this concept in political terms, that is, against the way in which it excluded the majority of the population from legitimate concern. This was a pathbreaking contribution: since 1975, a growing body of literature came to support the scientific argument in favour of control measures (Giesbrecht, 1995): thus, for example, Edwards et al, in their book *Alcohol Policy and the Public Good* (1995) took up the argument first broached in 1975 by Kettil Bruun, presenting the results of new research and seeking, in the name of scientific objectivity, to legitimise a restrictive policy. But the more important point may be this one: in seeking to construct "social drinkers" as a problem, the population-based model encroached on a terrain that until then was part of the taken for granted sphere of consumption.

The liberal discourse on the free market and the right to free consumption was directly threatened, in period of "welfare state crisis". Given this favourable discursive context, the industry started to play an open part in the conflict from the 1980s —apart from traditional lobbying activities. The debate took the form of a confrontation between the supporters of an active state intervention in public health and the supporters of the free market. Ranged against one another were, on the one hand, arguments in defence of the welfare state and against the assaults of the liberalised economy and, on the other, anti-temperance and anti-coercion arguments that clearly represented the interests of the alcohol industry.

Once again, the "alcohol question" has been *articulated* with a more general frame of reference concerning welfare –in that case, with two of them. The creation of such an antagonism between the public health advocates and the alcohol industry' agents can also be understood looking at their respective discursive *positioning*. In terms of the way in which its arguments were structured and successfully diffused and imposed, the new public-health, population-based model followed a similar trajectory to that of the alcoholism movement that had prevailed some forty years previously. Like its predecessor, it drew an opposition between the objectivity of modern science and the falsity of old-fashioned interpretations. This view was neatly captured in what has been considered the first manifesto of the disease model:

> The chief obstacle to the progress in the scientific solution of problem lies in the existence of a prevailing body of public opinion which is apathetic to this approach. (Anderson 1942, quoted by Room, 1983: 48).

Now, we can find similar arguments in recent references to the role of alcohol in public health:

> By the end of this book the reader will have been acquainted with what is *objectively* known about which measures (...). This exposition will also have served a purpose if in passing it corrects misapprehensions which in the past have too often coloured policy thinking on alcohol" (Edwards and al. 1994: 2).

This argumentative line tends to construct an *normative* distinction between what is called scientific and what is not. And as a matter of fact, the alcohol industry started with an offensive strategy, trying to contest directly the epistemic community on it's own legitimacy terrain —that is: following scientific arguments to promote public health ! To do this, it financed scientific projects or scientific foundations, like the Foundation for Alcohol Research (SAR) in Netherland, or the Alcohol Education and Research Council in United-Kingdom (see Lemmens, 1997) and, as we will see later, even got involved in prevention. Just as the disease model imposed itself against the temperance discourse, so the population-based model presented itself in strong opposition to the discourse of its new enemy, the alcohol industry: their arguments were presented as the "ideological" side as opposed to scientific objectivity.

New alliances between alcohol industries where created, having the same strategy in mind. In 1989, for example, the Portman Group was founded, involving the most important drinks distributors in the United Kingdom, officially with the aim of "promoting a reasonable usage of alcoholic beverages, to reduce damages caused by alcohol and to develop a better awareness of alcohol abuse" (Communication, 1995). This discursive strategy allowed the industry to position itself on an equal footing with advocates of public health, and thus directly to combat their arguments. Thus the Portman Group in this case sought to discredit the book *Alcohol Policy and the Public Good* and to contest directly the WHO plan of action, which they criticised especially for not concentrating on the abusers of alcohol. Another influential international group in recent years has been the Amsterdam Group, founded in 1990. In 1993 it published a report entitled *Les Boissons Alcoolisées et la Société Européenne (Alcoholic Drinks and European Society)* (Amsterdam Group 1993), which was characterised as a "demolition of objectives and methods of the WHO plan of action" by the Eurocare Association in 1995[6]. In joining the discursive war, the association Eurocare produced its own report, significantly entitled: *Counterbalancing the Drink Industry.*

This battle also issued in several articles, particularly in the British press. In United-Kingdom, one of every four or five alcohol research project is linked to the industry (Lemmens, 1997). It is the publicity over some incident concerning the anonymous reviews in 1994 which contributed to the process of demonising all discourses produced with the support of alcohol interests, and casted doubt on the credibility of scientific research financed by the alcohol industry (Lemmens, 1997). Thus, by the mid-1990s, the discursive field was neatly polarised into two opposing sides, so that any discourse that did not exactly reproduce the arguments put forward by one side was immediately accused of playing the "enemy" game of the other.

> Alcohol producers are engaged in a campaign to capture the heart and mind of alcohol research and public health people, as part of a major effort to win the *war of ideas* that shapes alcohol policy at national and international level" (Editorial, *Addiction* 2000 (95) 2: 179).

This dualism had the effect of *excluding alternative discourses* from the discursive field – such as the new harm reduction model which started to diffuse from the1990s in the illegal drug epistemic community.

Since the mid-1990s, there appears however to have been a greater willingness to move beyond this polarisation of the field into "good" and "bad". I will argue here that the outline of this new consensus can also be linked to transformations in the nature of state regulation, in particular to the growing tendency towards networking and to the influence of the new instruments used by the state in influencing actors of the field and public opinion and/or behaviour: namely information and persuasion. An evolution towards the constitution of a new discourse in the alcohol field, the *harm reduction model,* is now apparent. This has been made possible by the forging of new discursive alliances.

The harm reduction movement in relation to alcohol refers to a political answer originally developed in the illegal drugs field. As a discourse, it relies on three interdependent concepts (Cattacin and al., 1994): the concept of *harm reduction* or *harm minimisation* (to reduce the risks related to a context of consumption); the concept of *low threshold* (to guarantee that everybody can have an easy access to the services or treatment); the concept of *normalisation* (to accept the reality of the alcohol or drug problem and treat the dependant persons as normal citizens). As far as public policy is concerned, a model of harm reduction can be characterised with reference to the experience gained in German and Dutch cities:

> This model is based on a hierarchy of aims which favours the reduction of risks at each stage of the drug addiction process and in each domain of activity. Faced with the complexity of the problem, this model tries to favour and guarantee prevention and is seen to stimulate a large diversity of proposed solutions for drug addicts, as well as implicated actors, both public and private. Because of this, particular attention is attached to the co-ordination of networks. The appropriateness of this model in its environment is guaranteed by a continuous process of experimentation/adaptation." (Cattacin et al., 1994: 215, my translation).

Today, several factors suggest that the discourse on harm reduction, though it as yet plays only a minor role in the field of alcohol, may gradually gain significance. First, there has begun to be some scientific discussion of the premises on which the population-based model is implicitly based. There has been a renewed interest in "drinking patterns" as an alternative way of conceiving alcohol problems (Heath, 2002). As far as epidemiological research is concerned, some researchers have suggested "desegregate" the different categories of consumption in order both to respect social plurality and to focus more specifically on particular categories (Stockwell et al., 1997). This discourse has been presented as a contribution to the scientific debate, but its implications, and perhaps its justification, are political (see Rehm et al., 1996). In terms of the way in which it has emerged, the discourse of the harm reduction model is not dissimilar to that of the population-based model. Once again, as we have seen before, it is the political context that has opened the way for a greater differentiation in policy design and implementation within a complex society, and thus offered an opportunity for a new scientific trend to emerge.

Second, a number of controversial initiatives -as far as the prevention field is concerned- have been undertaken in order to forge a common discourse. This "desire" for reconciliation inspired the National College of Industrial Relations and the International Centre for Alcohol Policies, founded in 1995, to convene three meetings of experts (Dublin 1997, Geneva 2000, Dublin 2002), for the sole purpose of developing collaboration between the industry and the public health community. The priority was, officially, to find a "common language" (ICAP, 1999). The discursive result of this exercise has been formulated in a series of common principles of co-operation between the alcohol industry, governments, scientific researchers and public health services (The Dublin Principles, 1997). Thus this discourse has been drafted according to the principle of overlapping consensus.

Naturally enough, however, not all those who have been active in the field of prevention or treatment have been convinced of the desirability of overcoming, by this method, the discursive divide between the public health discourse and that of the industry. The research community is also split over the appropriateness of conducting research financed by the alcohol industry, and in its attitude towards the industry in general. Some argue in favour of maintaining an independent position, free from vested commercial interests, in order to keep their credibility *vis à vis* the public. This new divisions within the epistemic community may contribute to breaking up the old discursive coalition around the public health approach to alcohol, based on the global reduction of consumption through restrictive measures.

As far as the alcohol industry is concerned, the same shift in strategy – from dualism to a willingness to forge a minimal consensus - can be observed. Initially, its discursive strategy was clearly based on its opposition to the discourse of the population-based model. For example, the industry responded to public health warnings about the dangers of alcohol by financing and circulating research demonstrating, on the contrary, the beneficial effects of moderate consumption. In addition, it countered directly arguments in favour of reducing the global level of consumption by arguing that the focus should be exclusively on chronic alcoholics. This strategy of counter-argument continues to this day, but it is complemented now by a more indirect attempt to *reframe* the alcohol debate —and research— around more consensual issues (like pregnant women, young people, drinking and driving).

Third, even if this new harm-reduction discourse is being formed within the framework of a supposedly scientific debate (see, for example, the report in France on the evaluation of the Evin Law, published by Entreprise et Prévention, 1993), and even if it is politically legitimated by a declared wish to forge consensus between public health workers and the industry means, I think it emerges as a more pragmatically result of new form of policy making. For the common tendency of European countries now is to integrate the alcohol question within the more global concept of prevention of illness (in relation to legal *and* illegal drugs), and to develop programmes of health promotion in an integrative way that takes into account the interests of all sectors. We have seen over the last few years the participation of a wider range of social actors, from both the *profit* and *non-profit-making* sectors, in developing and implementing alcohol-related policies. In this new context we have seen that the state acts as a mediator, seeking to reconcile different arguments. In the administering of policy, there has been also a tendency to greater co-ordination between departments (Cattacin&Lucas 1999). From this perspective, the discourse on harm reduction has allowed a new punctual coalitions to form between certain members of the research community, the industry, supporters of public health and the politicians and administrators concerned.

This strategy is motivated by the need to overcome both the tendency towards paralysis or blocked action in a highly complex society, and the financial limitations of public intervention. Indeed, I would suggest here that the harm reduction discourse has emerged as the result of this new form of governance, shifting the debate from ideological considerations to *concrete negotiations* around specific problems (for example: how do we all — public, for profit, non profit organisations —guaranty the security of the young people during a concrete public manifestation?). In the context of a welfare state that has greater recourse to private organisations and discursive strategies, we have noticed that policy emerges not from a centrally concerted or programmed action, but from the interaction of a plurality of interdependent organisations. As far as alcohol is concerned, the development of the harm reduction model has resulted from concrete cases of policy-making, involving the co-operation and direct participation of the industry in prevention projects. Once a minimum consensus is attained, the industry can become involved in developing programmes on a pragmatic basis according to the harm reduction principle[7]. Of course, in doing so, "the industry seeks to promote [its] long-term commercial interest" (Rae, 1993), seeing its participation in prevention as a way both of reinforcing its credibility and of promoting an approach to the problem that is favourable to its interests.

The fundamental criticism that has been made of this growing tendency towards integration and overlapping consensus is that it completely excludes the political (Mouffe, 1996). In other words, it excludes from the discursive field the essential conflict between the interests of health and those of commerce, perhaps removing that conflict to the level of personal ethics. Furthermore, it is clear that the participation of industry in *forum* organised by the state or non-profit organisations contributes to the legitimisation of its discourse - including, by extension, its promotional discourse. Lastly, networking is not going to provide democracy and efficiency as if by magic. Likewise, in this new context, the state must be strong, but not in the traditional sense of centralised and interventionist authority. It must be strong enough to guaranty the democratic participation of all actors concerned, the production and diffusion of minority discourses and the condition of a real *debate*. But it must also use its legitimacy to talk for the "general interest" and its capacity to diffuse information and co-ordinate meetings and discussion in order to maintain its *leadership* in the "organisation of the self organisation" of a complex society. A weak state, in term of information, communication resources and networking capacity may be reduced merely to supporting the strongest discourse — that is, today, the one promoted by the industry.

5. CONCLUSION

In this paper, I have tried to link an analysis of discourse and an analysis of public policy, in order to explain historical shifts in alcohol policy that have occurred throughout Europe. This constructivist perspective tends to underline the influence of the interpretative process in the evolution of alcohol policy. I have tried to suggest that the evolution of the alcohol discourse has to do with the construction of a discursive hegemony, understood as a process of reducing discursive complexity in the context of specific relations between state and society in the production of welfare.

I have argued that alcohol policies up until the Second World War followed the logic of subsidiarity. First, the discursive field was structured according to the relationships between the principal social groups. In this context, the temperance discourse functioned as a discursive alliance that guaranteed the dominance of the bourgeoisie, in the name of moral defence. Significantly, the only real alternative interpretation, the socialist discourse, was excluded from the process of defining the alcohol problem. Second, the argumentation gradually changed because of its failure to solve the "alcohol question" at a discursive level i.e. to achieve its hegemonic project. The second temperance discourse called for state involvement, justifying state intervention on the basis of its own logic, i.e. as a means of maintaining public order. In doing so, it excluded the medical interpretation of alcoholism (which nevertheless continued at this stage as an autonomous discourse). As a result, the first public frame of reference for alcohol policies in Europe adhered to the principle of the liberal state, which was required only to guarantee public order and hence to focus on only one dimension -the legal dimension- of the problem.

During the period of the welfare state, the formulation of the discourse was monopolised by the state and by experts. The discursive field now appeared homogeneous: the liberal discourse addressed "social drinkers", while the disease model addressed "alcoholics". This sharing of the public space created a consensual framework that was very difficult to contest. Moreover, the institutionalisation of the dominant discourse reinforced its hegemony and its ability to resist change. Hence, the principle dynamic of change came not from the discourse itself but from a crisis of legitimacy within the welfare state, which in this case was the actor principally responsible for defining and resolving the problem. It was only this that afforded a new opportunity for discursive transformation.

The crisis in the legitimacy of the welfare state opened a discursive window for the public health model. The initial debate, although conducted in the name of science, took place at an ideological level and brought two main poles of opinion into opposition: public health promotion vs. neo-liberalism. More recently, in the new context of network policy-making, the discursive field has been generated by a variety of actors in the public policy network (scientists, politicians, policy-makers and those involved in care and prevention) and has been elaborated at a more pragmatic level. This plurality has affected the scientific field as well, which exhibits multiple different trends and is concerned with an object of recognised complexity. In this context, the discursive coalitions that were originally built around two antagonistic sides seem to start being reorganised around a new, more consensual discourse focusing on harm reduction.

But the integration of organised civil society in policy-making and the new role played by negotiation, which is used to a much greater extent than in previous periods, does not automatically guarantee the democratisation and openness of the discursive field: integration within the existing networks is very selective, the discourse remains the product of an elite, and the consensual dynamic that has developed around the concept of harm reduction tends to exclude conflict *a priori* rather than recognising or resolving it. In so far as a neo-liberal discourse constitutes the global frame of reference for policy making, the arguments promoted by the industry *in the name* of science or public health may exert quite a strong appeal. Finally, the position of the state in the welfare mix is not necessarily strong enough in each country for it to act as a real manager of societal complexity and to promote the realisation of an innovative discursive procedure through networking. In this sense, the apparent organisational opening could well represent a new form of discursive closure.

6. AFFILIATION

Department of Political Science
University of Geneva, Switzerland
Barbara.Lucas@politic.unige.ch
and
IEPI, University of Lausanne, Switzerland

7. NOTES

1I would like to thank Sandro Cattacin, who initiated the project and provided important theoretical input. Similar description of welfare state' evolution, can also be find in Cattacin&Lucas 1999. I also thank the Kettil Bruun Society for its support, and all its members for our fascinating discussions about alcohol question. Last, but not least, thank you to Hanspeter Kriesi, Léa Sgier, Pekka Sulkunen, Robin Room, Geoffrey Hunt, Louise Nadeau, and to the participants of the Workshop "Policy, Discourse, and Institutional Reform" of the European Consortium for Political Research (ECPR) Joint Sessions, 2001, for their constructive comments on some earlier or partial version of the paper.
1 This research is carried out for my PhD. in Political Science, Department of Political Science, University of Geneva, under the direction of Hanspeter Kriesi. Parts of the project have recieved financial support from the Swiss Foundation for Alcohol Research and the Swiss National Foundation for Research.
1 The short account of welfare development that follows is also formulated in Cattacin&Lucas 1999.
1 At the same time, the dominant medical paradigm changed. It was now inspired by a microbiological approach to illness. In contrast to the degenerationist paradigm, this new view led to difficulties in interpreting alcohol-related problems.
1 To cite a few examples in France, the High Committee for the Study of and Information on Alcoholism was created in 1954. In Sweden, two governmental Commissions carried out research which was published and had a considerable political impact (Armyr, 1982). In Switzerland the Federal Commission against Alcoholism was created during this period, for the specific purpose of remedying the one-sided approach of the Federal Authority of Alcohol, which was above all a management unit.
1 This association brings together active private European organisations in the domain of the prevention of drug and alcoholism.
1 This has been the case for example in the Netherlands, in Denmark or even in France. In the Netherlands, the organisation STIVA, which brings together Dutch alcohol producers, contributed to both the definition and the implementation of preventative schemes regarding drink-driving. On the other hand, owing to lack of agreement, prevention policies aimed at reducing consumption had been drawn up without the participation of the industry.

8. REFERENCES

Armyr, G., Elmer A. & U. Herz (1982). Alcohol in the world of the 80 s. Habits, attitudes, preventive policies and voluntary efforts. Stockholm: Solber Förlags AB.

Ashford, Douglas E. (1986). The Emergence of the Welfare States. Oxford: New-York, Basil Blackwell.

Baumohl, J. & R. Room (1987). "Inebriety, Doctors and the State: Alcoholism Treatment Institutions before 1940", in Marc Galanter (ed.), Recent Developments in Alcoholism. Vol. 5, New-York: Plenum, 135-174.

Beck, Ulrich (1994). Risk Society. London, Thousand Oaks, New Delhi: Sage Publication.

Berridge, Virginia (1996). "Research and Policy: What Determines the Relationship?", Policy Studies, 17 (1), 23-34.

Berridge, Virginia (1993). "The nature of the target disorder: an historical perspective", in G. Edwards and al. Drugs, Alcohol and Tobacco: Making the Science and Policy Connections. Oxford: Oxford University Press, 179-186.

Berridge, Virginia (1992). "Alcool et drogue en Grande Bretagne: histoire et politique", in Alain Ehrenberg (ed). Drogues, politique et société. Paris: Descartes.

Bourdieu, Pierre (2000). Propos sur le champs politique. Paris: Presses Universitaires de Lyon.

Bruun, Kettil et al. (1975). Alcohol Control Policies in Public Health Perspective. FORSA, Fondation finlandaise pour l'étude de l'alcoolisme, Vol. 25.

Bruun, Kettil (1971). "Finland: the non medical approach", in L. G. Kiloh and D.S Bell (eds). 29th International Congress on Alcoholism and Drug Dependance, Sydney, Australia, February 1970. Australisa, Butterwoths, 545-559.

Busch, Andreas & Dietmar Braun (1999). "Why ideas matter: A theorical starting point", in Braun, D. & Busch A. (eds). Public Policy and Political Ideas. Cheltenham: Edward Elgar, 1-7.

Bütschi, Danielle et Sandro Cattacin (1994). Le modèle suisse du bien-être. Coopération conflictuelle entre Etat et société. Le cas de l'alcoolisme et du vih/sida. Lausanne: Réalités sociales.

Bynum, W. F. (1984) "Alcoholisme and degeneration", in 19th Century European Medicine and Psychiatry, British Journal of Addiction, 79, 59-70.

Castel, Robert (1995). Les métamorphoses de la question sociale. Paris: Folio, Essais.

Cattacin Sandro et Barbara Lucas (1999) "Autorégulation, intervention étatique, mise en réseau: les transformations de l'Etat social en Europe", Revue Française de Science Politique, 49 (3), 379-398.

Cattacin, Sandro (1996). "Organiser les solidarités", in Marc-Henry Soulet (éd.). Crise et recomposition des solidarités. Fribourg: Presses Universitaires, 147-171.

Cattacin, Sandro, Barbara Lucas & Sandra Vetter (1996). Modèles de politique en matière de drogue. Paris: l'Harmattan.

Communica (1995). Publication trimestrielle de la Régie Fédérale des Alcool, Berne, 2 .

Conrad, Peter & Joseph Schneider (1980). Deviance and Medicalization. From Badness to Sickness. St Louis: the CV Mosby Company

Cottino, Amadeo (1985) "Science and class structure: notes on the formation of the alcohol question in Italy (1860-1920)", Contempory Crises, 9, 45-53.

Cottino A., Morgan P. (1987). "Italie", in Marcus GRANT (sous la dir. de). La lutte contre l'alcoolisme. OMS, Publications régionales, Série européenne 18, 89-97

Crozier, Michel, S. Huntington & J. Watanuki (1975). The Crisis of Democracies, Report on the Governability of Democracies. New York: University Press.

Donati, Pierpaolo (1991). Teoria relazionale delle società. [Relational Theory of Society]. Milano, Angeli.

Donzelot, Jacques (1994). L'Etat animateur. Paris, Esprit.

Edwards, Griffith & al. (1995). Alcohol Policy and the Public Good. Oxford/New York: Oxford University Press.

Eisenbach-Strangl, Ingmar (1992). "Treatment-Seeking and Treatment Reluctant Alcoolics: A Two – Class Treatment System iun Austria", in H. Klingemann et al. (eds). Cure, care or control. Alcoholism treatment in sixteen countrie. State University of New York Press, 173-189.

Engel, Georges (1977). "The need for a new medical model: a challenge for biomedine", Science, 196, 129-136.

Entreprise et Prévention (1993) La loi Evin. Premier bilan. Entreprise et prévention, Paris.

Esping-Andersen, Gösta (1996). Welfare Sates in Transition. National Adaptation in Global Economies. London: Sage.

Eurocare (1995). Contrebalancing the drink industry. Cambrideshire
Evers, Adalbert (1990). "Shifts in the Welfare Mix - Introducing a New Approach for the Study of transformations in Welfare and Social Policy", in: Adalbert Evers et Helmut Wintersberger (éd.), Shifts in the Welfare Mix. Frankfurt am Main/Boulder, Colorado: Campus/Westview, 7-29.
Ewald, François (1996). Histoire de l'Etat Providence. Paris: Grasset, Poche Essais.
Ewald, François (1986). L'Etat-providence. Paris: Grasset.
Fauré, Alain, Pollet Gilles & Philippe WARIN (1995). La construction du sens dans les politiques publiques. Débats autour de la notion de référentiel. [The construction of meaning in public policy: Debates about the concept of referentiel]. Paris, L'Harmattan, Logiques Politiques.
Fischer, Frank et John Forester (eds.) (1993). The Argumentative Turn in Policy Analysis and Planning. London: Duke University Press.
Fraser, Nancy (1997). Justice Interruptus. Critical Reflexion on the Postsocialist Condition. New-York and London: Routledge.
Freiburghaus, Dieter (1991). "Le développement des moyens d'action étatiques", in Charles-Albert Morand, L'Etat propulsif, Paris: Publisud, 49-64.
Gerhardt, Ute (1991). Gesellschaft und Gesundheit, Begründung der Medizinsociologie. Francfort: Suhrkamp
Giesbrecht, N., Greenfield, Thomas K. & Ann Kaskutas (1995). "Assessing and interpreting emerging development in alcohol policy in Canada and the United States: suggestions for future research", paper presented at the 21th Annual Alcohol Epidemiology Symposium, Porto.
Giles G. J. (1995). "Are Alcoholic beverages the cause of alcoholism? Degeneracy and the paradigm of the Alcoholic in Germany, 1990-1945", paper presented at the 21th Annual Alcohol Epidemiology Symposium, Porto.
Groupe d'Amsterdam (1993). Les boissons alcoolisée et la société européenne.
Gusfield, Joseph R. (1996). Contested meanings. The construction of Alcohol Problems. Madison: The University of Winsconsin Press.
Gusfield, Joseph R. (1967). "Moral passage: The symbolic process in public designations of deviance", Social Problems, 15, 175-183.
Gusfield, Joseph R. (1963). Symbolic crusade: Statuts politics and the American temperance movement. Urbana, University of Illinois Press.
Hass, Peter (1992). "Introduction:epistemic communities and international policy coodination", International Organization, 46 (1), 1-35.
Habermas, Jürgen (1985). "Die Krise des Wohlfahrtsstaates und die Erschöpfung utopischer Energien", in Jürgen HABERMAS. Die Neue Unübersichtlichkeit. Frankfurt M: Suhrkamp, 141-163.
Habermas, Jürgen (1981). Théorie de l'agir communicationnel. Paris, Fayard.
Hajer Maarten A. (2003). "A Frame in the Field. Policy Making and the Reinvention of Politics", in M. A Hajer and H. Wagenaar (eds.), Deliberative Policy Analysis. Understanding Governance in the Network Society. Cambridge, Cambridge University Press.
Hajer Maarten A. (1997).The Politics of Environmental Discourse. Oxford, Clarendon Press.
Hall, Peter. A (1993) "Policy Paradigms, Social Learning, and the State. The case of Economic Policymaking in Britain", Comparative Politics, 3 (25), 275-296.
Heath Dwight B. (2002). "Drinking patterns: an important (qualitative?) complement to epidemiological research for practical use", paper presented at the at the 28th Annual Meeting of the Kettil Bruun Society Social and Epidemiolgical Research on Alcohol, Paris, France, June.
Holder, Harold, D. (1994) "Public Health Approach to the Reduction of Alcohol Problems", Substance Abuse, vol 15 (2), 123-138.
Holder, Harold D., Kuhlhorn, Eckart, Nordlund, Sturla, Österberg, Esa, Romelsijlö Ander & Trygve Ugland (1998). European Integration and Nordic Alcohol Policie. Aldershot: Ashgate Publishing Ltd.
Howarth, David (2000). Discourse. Buckingham, Philadelphia: Open University Press.
I.C.A.P. (1999). www.icap.org/philosophy.htlm
Jellinek, E. M. (1952) "Phases of Alcohol Addiction", Quarterly Journal of Studies on Alcohol, 13 (4), 673-684.
Jenson, Jane (1989). "Paradigms and Political Discourse: Protective Legislation in France and the United States Before 1914", Canadian Journal of Political Science, XXII, 2, 235-258.
Jobert, Bruno (éd.) (1994). Le tournant néo-libéral en Europe. Idées et recettes dans les pratiques gouvernementales. Paris: L'Harmattan.
Jobert, Bruno et Pierre Muller (1987). L'Etat en action. Politiques publiques et corporatisme. Paris: PUF.

Katcher, Brian S. (1993). "The post-repeal eclipse in knowledge about the harmful effect of alcohol", Addiction, 88, 729-744.

Kenis Patrick et Volker Schneider (1991). Policy Netwotks and Policy Analysis. Scrutinizing a New Analytical Toolbox", in Bernd Marin (ed.). Policy networks: empirical evidence and theoretical considerations. Köln: Max-Plack Institut füt Gesellshaftforshung,

Kiissling-Naef Ingrid et Sandro Cattacin (1997). "Introduction: Agir étatique subsidiaire dans les sociétés modernes", Revue Suisse de Science Politique 3 (3), 17-33.

Laclau, Ernesto et Chantal Mouffe (1985). Hegemony and Socialist Strategy. Toward a Radical Democratic Politics. London, New-York: Verso.

Lee Bacci, Carole (1999). Women, Policy and Politics. The construction of policy problems. London, Sage publication.

Lemmens, Paul (1997). "Buying Research", Addiction, 92 (9), 1077-1079

Levine H. G. (1978). "The discovery of Addiction", Journal of Studies on Alcohol, vol. 39, (1), 143-174.

Levine H. G. (1984). "The Alcohol Problem in America: from Temperance to Alcoholism", British Journal of Addiction, 79, 109-119.

Lewis Jenny, M. (1999). "The Durabiliy of Ideas in Health Policy Making", in Braun, D. & Busch A. (eds). Public Policy and Political Ideas. Cheltenham: Edward Elgar, 152-167.

Lukes, Steven (1973). Power. A Radical View. London: Mac Millan Press

Luhmann, Niklas. (1982). The Differentiation of Society. New York, Columbia University Press.

Makela, Klaus & al. (1996). Alcoholics Anonymous as a Mutual Help Movement. A Study in Eight Societies. Madison: The University of Wisconsin Press.

Makela, Klaus, Robin Room, Eric Single, Pekka Sulkunen, Brendan Walsh (éd), (1981). Alcohol, Society and the State, Vol. 1: a Comparative Study of Alcohol Control. Toronto: Addiction Research Foundation.

Marin, Bernd (1991). "What is "Half-Knowledge" Sufficient to Know For - and When? Theoretical Comment on Policymakers' Uses of Social Science", Knowledge: Creation, Diffusion, Utilization 3(1), 34-60

Mosher, James F. et Jernigan, David H. (1989). "New direction in alcohol policy", Annual Review of Public Health, 10, 245-279.

Mitchell Allan (1987). "The unsung villain: alcoholism and the emergence of public welfare in France, 1870-1914", Contemporary Drug Problems, XII, 3, 447-471.

Mosher J. F., et D. H. Jernigan (1989). "New Direction in Alcohol Policy", Annual Review of Public Health, 10, 245-279.

Moran, Charles-Albert (2000). Le droit néo-moderne des politiques publiques. Paris: LGDJ.

Morand, Charles-Albert (1991). L'Etat propulsif. Paris: Publisud.

Muller, Pierre & Yves Surel (1998). L'analyse des politiques publiques. [public policy analysis] Paris: Montchrestien, Clefs Politiques.

Nozick, Robert (1974). Anarchy, State and Utopia. New York: Basic Books.

O'Connor, J. (1973). The Fiscal Crisis of the State. New York, St Martin Press .

Offe Klaus (1997). "Les nouveaux mouvements sociaux: un défi aux limites de la politique institutionnelle", in Klaus Offe, Les démocraties modernes à l'épreuves. Paris: L'Harmattan, logiques sociales, 98-132.

OMS (1993). European Alcohol Action Plan, Regional Office for Europe, Copenhague.

Papadopoulos, Yannis (1995). Complexité sociale et politiques publiques. Paris: Montchestien.

Petersen, Alan and Debohra Lupton (1996). The new public Health. Health and self in the age of risk. Sydney: Sage.

Pierson, Paul (1994). Dismantling the Welfare State? Reagan, Tatcher, and the Politics of Retrenchment. Cambridge: Cambridge University Press.

Polanyi, Karl (1983). La grande transformation. Paris: Gallimard.

Rae J. (1993). "The case for Collaboration", Addiction, 88, 11-12.

Rawls, John (1993). Justice et démocratie. Paris: Seuil.

Rehm, J. and al. (1996)." On the emerging paradigm of Drinkin Pattern and their social and health consequences", Addiction, 91, 1615-1622

Roberts, James S. (1985). "Alcohol, public policy and the Left: the socialist debate in early twentieth century Europe", Contemporary Drug Problems, XIII (2), 309-330.

Roberts, James S. (1984). Drink, Temperance and the Working Clas in Nineteeth-Century Germany. Boston: George Allan & Unwin.

Rosenqvist P. & J.P. Takala (1985). "Two experiences with lay board: the emergence of state organised treatment for alcoholic in Sweden and Finland", paper presented at the 31th International Institute on the Prevention and Treatment of Alcoholism, Rome.

Rosanvallon, Pierre (1989). Le liberalisme économique. Histoire de l'idée de marché. Paris: Seuil, Point.

Rosanvallon, Pierre (1981). La crise de l'Etat-providence. Paris: Seuil, Essais.

Room, Robin (1999). "Governing Images in Public Discourse about Problematic Drinking", paper presented at the NAD Symposium, Knowledge and Expertise in Alcohol and Drug Policy, Bergen, Norway, 23-25 septembre 1999.

Room, Robin (1998). "Controlled drinking as a moral achievement and a social program", paper presented at the conference Alcohol Policy and the Welfare State in Consumer Society", Lillehammer, Norway, 14-18 january 1998.

Room, Robin (1996). "The cultural framing of addiction", paper presented at a conference on Addiction and Culture, Claremont Graduate School.

Room, Robin (1983). "Sociological Asopect of the Disease Concept of Alcoholism", Research Advance in Alcohol and Drug Problems, vol 7, New York and London: Plenum Press, 47-91.

Rush B. (1872). Sermon to gentlemen upon temperance. Philadelphia

Sabatier, Paul (1998). "The Advocacy Coalition Framework: Revision and Relevance for Europe". Journal of European Public Policy, 5, (1), 98-130.

Sabatier, P. A & H. C. Jenkins-Smith (eds.) (1993). Policy Change and Learning. Boulder, Welstview.

Schneider, Volker (1992). "The structure of policy networks", European Journal of Political Research, 21, 109-129.

Spode H. (1997). "From the brandy plague" to the alcohol question": emergence and victory of the paradigm of alcoholism in central Europe. 18th until early XXth century". Paper presented at the 21th Annual Alcohol Epidemiology Symposium, Porto.

Stockwell T., Single E. Hawks D & J. Rehm (1997). "Sharpening the focus of alcohol policy from aggregate consumption to harm and risk reduction", Addiction Research, 5 (1), 1-9.

Sulkunen, Pekka, Sutton, Caroline, Tirgestedt, Christoffer & Katariina Warpenius (2000). Broken Spirits. Power and Ideas in Nordic Alcohol Control. Helsinki: NAD Publication N 39.

Sulkunen, Pekka & Katariina Warpenius (2000). "Reforming the self and the other: the temperance movement and the duality of modern subjectivity", Critical Public Health, 10 (4), 421-438.

Weir R. B. (1984). "Obsessed with moderation: the drink trades and the drink question (1870-1930)". Britsh Journal of Addiction, 79, pp: 93-107.

Willke, Helmut (1991). "Trois types de structures juridiques prgrammes conditionnels, programmes finalisés et programmes relationnels", in Charles-Albert Morand, L'Etat propulsif. Paris: Publisud, 65-80.

Willke, Helmut (1992). Ironie des Staates. [Irony of State]. Frankfurt: Suhrkamp.

1

H. D. HOLDER

COMMUNITY ACTION FROM AN INTERNATIONAL PERSPECTIVE

Key Words: Alcohol policy, community studies, community-based prevention programs, legal and regulatory issues

Abstract. At the community level, traditional prevention efforts have emphasized programs such as public media campaigns, alcoholism recovery efforts, and school education. For the most part, local prevention strategies have been program-based, not policy-based. However, alcohol policies can be implemented at a community level. Thus, a local alcohol policy is any established process, priority, or structure that purposefully alters local social, economic, or physical environments to reduce alcohol problems. Examples include making a priority of drinking and driving enforcement by the local police; using local zoning laws and land regulations to control hours of sale or location and density of alcohol outlets, mandating server training for bars, pubs, and restaurants; setting a written policy for responsible alcoholic beverage service by a retail licensed establishment; or allocating enforcement resources to prevent alcohol sales to underage persons. Therefore, local policy takes many forms that relate to alcohol use and thereby to alcohol problems, not simply restricting the retail sale of alcohol. This paper explores a number of community prevention efforts across the world in terms of (a) the wide range of actions, priorities, and structures that constitute local alcohol policy and (b) their effectiveness at the local level to reduce alcohol problems. The studies presented are community-wide, as opposed to targeting high-risk groups in their focus, seek to bring about community-level system change, use local news media targeted at key community leaders in the pursuit of policy change, and mobilize the entire community in the pursuit of such change.

1. INTRODUCTION

Prevention of alcohol problems at the community level across the world has typically utilized programs such as public media campaigns, alcoholism recovery efforts, and school education. For the most part, local prevention strategies have been program-based, not policy-based. A program strategy generally refers to organized efforts to reduce alcohol problems by training or educating clients or the general public. Individual prevention approaches typically view communities as catchment areas of people. From this catchment area perspective, the community is viewed largely as a collection of target groups with adverse behaviors and associated risks, and prevention operates largely through educational and treatment efforts to reduce the problems with alcohol. The strategy is thus to find and treat or serve those most at risk. No particular structural change is proposed and those outside the targeted groups are not considered.

On the other hand, local public policy seeks to prevent alcohol problems through structural change, i.e., a regulation, law, or enforcement priority. Thus, a local alcohol policy is any established process, priority, or structure that purposefully alters local social, economic, or physical environments to reduce alcohol problems. Examples include making a priority of drinking and driving enforcement by the local police; using local zoning laws and land regulations to control hours of sale or

R. Müller and H. Klingemann (eds.),
From Science to Action? 100 Years Later - Alcohol Policies Revisited, 101–112.

location and density of alcohol outlets, mandating server training for bars, pubs, and restaurants; setting a written policy for responsible alcoholic beverage service by a retail licensed establishment; or allocating enforcement resources to prevent alcohol sales to underage persons.

Thus, rather than attempt to reduce alcohol-related problems through the education and treatment of problem drinkers alone, local efforts can be directed toward affecting policy makers in positions to implement zoning restrictions governing outlet densities. More broadly, collective risk is thus reduced through interventions affecting community processes that influence alcohol use. In alcohol policies at the local level, the community is targeted, not individuals, for compelling reasons. First, substance use occurs largely within community contexts. That is, particularly in the case of alcohol, communities provide structures (e.g., zoning and control of alcohol establishments and their location) through which alcohol is typically obtained. Second, many of the costs associated with alcohol are borne collectively at the community level, for example, through traffic crashes, property damage, and alcohol-related violence.

2. ALCOHOL POLICIES AT THE LOCAL LEVEL

Many alcohol policy approaches (which usually are environmental strategies) have demonstrated evidence of potential effectiveness. Evidence has been collected for policies related to retail price, availability of alcohol, location and type of alcohol outlets including hours and days of sale, retail and social access to alcohol by young people, and enforcement and sanctions against high-risk alcohol use, e.g., drinking and driving. See Edwards et al. (1994) for a review. Many such policies have local analogs. Thus, policy at the local level can have a base of science on which to rest. This is not to imply that all policies are locally tested, only the potential for the policy to be effective may have been demonstrated.

Local policy takes many forms that relate to alcohol use and thereby to alcohol problems, not simply restricting the retail sale of alcohol. One important example of local alcohol policy is enforcement of laws concerning drinking and driving. Many competing demands are made on local police for enforcement priorities. The priority police give to drinking and driving deterrence can be expressed to the community by the level of attention and resources the police commit to drinking and driving deterrence. This type of administrative (not regulatory) decision is an example of a local policy that can be very effective. Another example of local policy is reflected in the alcohol serving practices of bars and restaurants and the sales of alcohol to underage persons by off-premise establishments. Alcohol serving practices reflect policy, whether the policy is written or not, for an establishment. A wide definition of alcohol policy goes well beyond the direct regulation of retail sales of alcohol by the government.

Local policy projects (such as those described here) differ from more traditional approaches in that they attempt to seek policy change, seek to bring about system-level, community-level change, use the media to target policy makers, and seek to mobilize the broader community to pursue desired changed. While applying policy at the community level has always been promising, only recently have there been systematic attempts to evaluate such efforts (Holder et al. 1997b; Casswell & Gilmore 1989). For this reason local policy makers find themselves attempting to implement policy changes in the absence of a scientific basis supporting such change.

Community policy projects use a systems approach to reduce alcohol problems by changing the community structures that provide the context in which alcohol consumption occurs. These system changes are achieved by local alcohol policies. Even if the control or licensing of alcohol production and sale is at the state or national level, policies at the local level can be used to control the number and site of retail outlets, the enforcement of laws regarding drinking driving and serving to intoxication, and various other aspects of drinking likely to affect alcohol use and problems.

3. EXAMPLES AND RESULTS OF COMMUNITY ALCOHOL POLICY PROJECTS INTERNATIONALLY

The studies presented here generally meet a number of criteria to qualify for inclusion. First, they are community-wide, as opposed to targeting high-risk groups, in their focus. Second, they seek to bring about community level system change. Third, to the extent that they use media strategically, such use is targeted at key community leaders in the pursuit of policy change. Fourth, they seek to mobilize the entire community in the pursuit of such change.

New Zealand

During the early 1980s, the Community Action Project (CAP) in New Zealand was targeted at increasing support among the general public for public policies limiting alcohol consumption as well as promoting attitudes and behavior supportive of moderate alcohol use (Casswell & Gilmore 1989). A mass media campaign intervention was designed to influence drinking behavior at the individual level among young males and a print media campaign was used to enhance media advocacy promoting support for restrictions on alcohol advertising and availability (Stewart & Casswell 1993). The community-action intervention was led by a full-time project organizer in each of the two communities. These project organizers worked with local community organizations, particularly local government sectors, in support of project goals. Work with the police and the licensing authorities attempted to restrict alcohol availability via the licensing process. Issues pertaining to alcohol were negotiated with local city councils, including the use of bylaws and placing conditions on leased property such as sports grounds. The project organizers used media advocacy techniques throughout the project, including capitalizing on the controversy engendered by the paid media campaigns (which were prevented from full publication and broadcast following criticism by the vested interest groups concerned). Norms about target social behaviors were significantly changed in communities exposed to both media and community organizations compared with the other two conditions. These were concerned with alcohol's effect on fitness and its use to quench thirst and also with the provision of alcoholic and non-alcoholic drinks when entertaining (Casswell & Gilmore 1989).

United States

The Rhode Island Community Alcohol Abuse/Injury Prevention Project (Putnam, Rocket & Campbell 1993) was directed toward reducing alcohol-related injuries. In particular, the intervention resulted in a 27% *increase* in alcohol-related assault arrest rates (reflecting increased enforcement) while emergency room visits declined 9% for injury, 21% for assault, and 10% for motor vehicle crashes with no comparable decline in the control community. However, follow-up data indicated that the increased enforcement brought about by the project was not maintained after the project ended (Stout et al. 1993).

Finland

The Lahti Project was to decrease alcohol-related harm by increasing awareness of alcohol consequences and lowering high-risk drinking (Holmila 1995, 1997). The evaluation, utilizing data from Lahti and two comparison communities before and after the intervention, found that the project had increased local newspaper attention to alcohol issues, public perception of alcohol as a social problem, and knowledge of alcohol content and the limits for risky drinking. There was a decline in self-reported heavy drinking (Holmila 1997).

United States

The Saving Lives Project was conducted in six communities in Massachusetts and was designed to reduce alcohol-impaired driving and related problems such as speeding (Hingson et al. 1996). Results of the evaluation indicated that during the five years that the program was in operation, cities that received the Saving Lives intervention produced a 25% greater decline in fatal crashes than the rest of Massachusetts, i.e., a 42% reduction in fatal auto crashes within the experimental communities, a 47% reduction in the number of fatally injured drivers who were positive for alcohol as well as a 5% decline in visible crash injuries and an 8% decline in 16 to 25-year-old crash injuries. In addition, there was a decline in self-reported driving after drinking (specifically among youth) as well as observed speeding. The greatest fatal and injury crash reductions occurred in the 16 to 25-year-old age group.

Australia

The COMPARI Project was designed to reduce alcohol-related injury by focusing on the general context of alcohol use in the community and not solely on alcoholics or heavy drinkers. The analyses failed to demonstrate an impact, possibly due to the short length of the follow-up period. On the other hand, the project was highly valued by the community. After completion of the university-managed demonstration project, the project was transferred to local control. It currently operates under a contract awarded by the government and is the only non-metropolitan alcohol and drug program undertaking community-wide activities in Western Australia (Midford et al. 1999).

Australia

The Surfers Paradise project was designed to reduce violence and disorder associated with the high concentration of licensed establishments in the resort town of Surfers Paradise in Queensland, Australia (Homel et al. 1997). The project used a full-time community organizer who formed a steering committee to oversee a number of activities focused on increasing safety in and around licensed establishments. The project involved three major strategies: (1) the creation of a Community Forum, including the development of task groups and implementation of a safety audit; (2) the development and implementation of risk assessments, Model House Policies, and a Code of Practice; and (3) improvement in the external regulation of licensed premises by police and liquor licensing inspectors (see Homel et al. 1997). The Surfers Paradise project and its replications in three North Queensland cities, Cairns, Townsville, and Mackay (Hauritz et al. 1998), resulted in significant improvements in police effectiveness, highlighting the need for mechanisms that can maintain gains achieved from community action projects (Homel et al. 1997).

United States

The Communities Mobilizing for Change on Alcohol (CMCA) was designed to reduce the accessibility of alcohol to youth under the legal drinking age of 21. The project was composed of five core components: (1) influences on community policies and practices, (2) community policies, (3) youth alcohol access, (4) youth alcohol consumption, and (5) youth alcohol problems. The CMCA project recruited 15 communities in Minnesota and western Wisconsin. Interventions included decoy operations with alcohol outlets (in which police typically have underage buyers purchase alcohol at selected outlets), citizen monitoring of outlets selling to youth, keg registration (which requires that purchasers of kegs of alcohol provide identifying information thus establishing liability for resulting problems at parties where minors are drinking), developing alcohol-free events for youth, shortening hours of sale for alcohol, responsible beverage service training, and developing educational programs for youth and adults. Merchant survey data revealed that they increased checking for age identification, reduced their likelihood of sales to minors, and reported more care in controlling sales to youth (Wagenaar et al. 1996). The study, using young looking purchasers, confirmed that alcohol merchants increased age identification checks and reduced their propensity to sell to minors. The telephone survey of 18 to 20-year-olds indicated that they were less likely to consume alcohol themselves and less likely to provide it to other underage persons (Wagenaar et al. 2000). Finally, the project found a statistically significant net decline (intervention compared to control communities) in drinking and driving arrests among 18 to 20-year-olds and disorderly conduct violations among 15 to 17-year-olds (Wagenaar, Murray & Toomey 2000).

United States

The Community Trials Project (Holder et al. 1997a) was a five-component community-level intervention conducted in three experimental communities matched to three comparisons selected for geographical and cultural diversity. The five interacting components included: (1) a "Community Knowledge, Values, and Mobilization" component to develop community organization and support for the goals and strategies of the project; (2) a "Responsible Beverage Service Practices" component to reduce the risk of intoxicated and/or underage customers in bars and restaurants; (3) a "Reduction of Underage Drinking" component to reduce underage access; (4) a "Risk of Drinking and Driving" component to increase enforcement efficiency regarding Driving While Impaired and reduce drinking and driving; and (5) an "Access to Alcohol" component to reduce overall availability of alcohol. As a result of this prevention project alcohol-involved traffic crashes were estimated (via time-series analysis with matched comparison communities) to have dropped by about 10% annually, drink/drive crashes with arrests dropped by 6%, alcohol-involved assault injuries appearing in the Emergency Room of local hospitals declined by 2%, and severe assault cases requiring hospitalization dropped by 43% in comparison to control communities (Holder et al. 2000).

New Zealand

The Waikato Rural Drink Driving Project was begun in 1996 as a community-action effort to implement strategies to reduce drink driving crashes in the Te Awamutu Police District. A major strategy developed and implemented as a part of this project was to increase police enforcement of drink driving in the district through adaptation of Compulsive Breath Testing (CBT) and mobile patrols to better fit the rural setting. The results of this local action project included: a reduction in fatal traffic crashes from 22% to 14%, alcohol positive breath test results by the police decreased sixfold, i.e., from 1 in 35 tests to 1 in 216 tests, prosecutions for drink driving increased by 23%, and local news coverage of drink driving and enforcement increased.

3. OBSERVATIONS FROM LOCAL ALCOHOL POLICY EFFORTS ACROSS THE GLOBE

Community action is essential for increasing local awareness, changing attitudes regarding alcohol use and problems, and increasing support for local alcohol policies (Casswell 1995; Holmila 1997; Holder et al. 2000; Midford et al. 1999). The most local alcohol policy projects internationally have focused on specific issues, such as underage drinking (Wagenaar et al. 1996), drinking and driving (Hingson et al. 1996; Holder et al. 2000; Voas, Holder & Gruenewald 1997), violence in and around licensed premises (Hauritz et al. 1998; Homel et al. 1997) or alcohol injuries (Putnam et al. 1993). None of these projects decreased overall alcohol consumption or sales, suggesting that community policy approaches may not be useful strategies for decreasing overall alcohol consumption, at least in the short-term, but have high potential to decrease alcohol problems.

Community Mobilization is Essential

Community mobilization in support of alcohol policies to reduce alcohol-related problems typically have the following methods in common:

- a full or part-time person serves as a community organizer
- the community organizer (and often others on the project) working with local government, businesses, police, etc., to support prevention policies and strategies.
- usually local committees are formed to develop or refine policies/interventions and support their implementation.
- media advocacy or the use of local news about alcohol issues and public policy as a key strategy.

As part of community action, the process of developing and sustaining alcohol policy approaches encourages local organizations and citizens to participate in and support policies. In this way, community action can result in powerful effects by developing a collection of strategies that work together synergistically

Media Advocacy Plays Important Role

Media advocacy as the purposeful use of local news to support policy initiatives has become an increasingly popular tool in local efforts. This approach complements health and community-action campaigns and is based on the view that public health problems are the result of social, economic, and political conditions. As noted by Wallack and Dorfman (1996), the two main goals of media advocacy are to gain access to the media to tell an important local story and to frame that story so that it focuses on the policy issues rather than the unhealthy behavior of individuals. By having newspaper or TV editors and reporters "tell the story" rather than paying for counter-advertising, or preparing PSAs, program staff time and resources can be more efficiently used.

Media advocacy is usually undertaken as a component of a multi-faceted, community-action initiative (see Stewart & Casswell 1993) or in connection with regulatory changes, law enforcement, community mobilization, and monitoring of high-risk behavior (Treno et al. 1996; Treno & Holder 1997; Holder & Treno 1997). Jernigan and Wright's (1996) volume provides case studies of media advocacy, and Stewart and Casswell (1993) provide outcomes from the New Zealand Community

Action Project (CAP) carried out in the early 1980s. In the New Zealand study there were positive effects in intervention communities, in comparison with the reference communities. For example, an increase in media coverage of alcohol-related material focusing on moderation and alcohol policy was evident.

Mechanisms for Change at the Local Level

Community-action projects support interventions whose effects can span several years. Effects can occur immediately and over the long term. Sometimes it is not possible to measure ultimate impacts during the timeframe of the project. Therefore, it is important to monitor proximal or mediating outcomes and link these in an overall causal model to long-term public health goals. For example, increased enforcement of laws against drink driving and increased local news attention to police enforcement has been linked to increases of perceived risk of arrest, which, in turn, has been linked to decreases in drinking and driving and subsequent automobile crashes (Voas, Holder & Gruenewald 1997; Hingson et al. 1996). Merchant training, enforcement of rules and regulations, and local news coverage of policy when used in combination appeared to be instrumental in reducing underage purchases (Wagenaar et al. 2000; Grube 1997). Similarly, both training and enforcement may be necessary in order to reduce service to intoxicated patrons (McKnight & Streff 1994; Saltz 1997). Finally, decreases in alcohol outlet densities have been linked recently to decreases in automobile crashes (Gruenewald & Johnson under review) suggesting that community efforts to limit such densities may produce desired outcomes in terms of crashes and resulting injuries and deaths.

4. "GOOD AND BAD NEWS" FROM LOCAL-BASED ALCOHOL POLICY EFFORTS

Enacting policy at the community level has a number of advantages. First, local citizens are close to where alcohol problems are experienced personally. The community must deal with drinking drivers and injuries and deaths from crashes involving alcohol-impaired drivers. It must provide hospital services and emergency medical services, conduct autopsies, and work with personal rehabilitation and recovery. Alcohol problems are personal experiences for community members, and efforts to prevent or reduce future problems are also a personal matter. Parent groups can be formed around a concern about underage drinking. Such groups can be mobilized to create public pressure against retail alcohol sales to underage persons and against access to alcohol at youthful social events. The consequences of such a policy, if it constrains local retailers or establishes priorities for local police enforcement, are experienced locally. When local policy advocates advance policy positions, they also encounter those who may oppose such policies (also members of the community) who may have vested interests in information dissemination, selling alcohol, and treatment. This means that policy can create, in a local forum, debate between opposing community groups and individuals and thus draw news media attention to such issues.

Funds to support extensive or expensive community alcohol programs are either limited or nonexistent in many countries today. If the implementation of an alcohol policy and its maintenance can be of low or no cost, then local leadership, especially elected officials who have a number of competing demands for tax revenue, may be especially receptive. Local leaders wish to show that they are finding solutions to problems that require little local funds. Low-cost approaches help leaders win elections, increasing their power and influence, and make a real contribution to the community. A policy can be shown to the community to (a) have the potential to reduce alcohol problems, (b) be inexpensive to implement and maintain, and (c) have local citizen support (even if there is special interest opposition, e.g., local alcohol wholesalers). These three elements are especially attractive to local leaders.

Many strategic alcohol policies have generated evidence of effectiveness (often at the national or state/provincial level) that can be presented to local citizens. Evidence of potential effectiveness within a real community appeals to both citizens and their leaders. In current times, prevention programs are increasingly being asked to demonstrate that they work or have benefit. The research base for many alcohol policies demonstrates what can and cannot work (see Edwards et al. 1994).

There are also problems and difficulties for alcohol policy at the local level. First, local alcohol policies are rarely highly visible, lacking lapel pins, balloons, posters, brochures, PSAs, etc. Policies, by their very nature, do not usually naturally generate public spectacles or celebrations. However, news media coverage prompted by media advocacy strategies (Treno et al. 1996) can stimulate public attention to the need for and support of specific policies. Public activities that bring attention to alcohol problems have a valuable place in a spectrum of prevention strategies, but they are almost certainly never sufficient. However, public activities such as an "Alcohol Awareness Week" produce personally satisfying experiences for citizens and leaders. Such programs generate enthusiasm and public recognition. Policies generally are not guaranteed to provide immediate personal satisfaction to their advocates in the way that a campaign or visible service program can.

Second, local alcohol policies generate controversy. Such controversies occurred in each of the three experimental communities of the U.S. community trial. Unless the local citizens who are supporting and leading efforts to implement special policies are prepared for opposition, the enthusiasm of local groups can be reduced. As opposition grows in response to a local alcohol policy, for example to restrictions on new alcohol outlets, local volunteers can feel torn between wanting to be "good neighbors" and wanting to reduce alcohol problems in the community. This conflict can arise in cases of local restrictions on alcohol retail outlets, stores, or bars and restaurants, and opposition by retailers.

Third, a program that provides services or educational materials is more easily grasped than are proposed changes in local zoning requirements that establish minimum distances between alcohol outlets. Community leaders may require more convincing before they appreciate the importance of local policies although policies were as easily understood and appreciated by community representatives as were prevention programs or services.

Fourth, policies often take time to work. Increased enforcement of laws prohibiting alcohol sales to minors coupled with manager/clerk training are unlikely to immediately reduce youthful drinking. As a result, local advocates will not necessarily personally experience a quick success. The potential long-term effectiveness of a policy can be difficult for people to accept.

5. OBSERVATIONS

This review of community approaches to the prevention of alcohol problems at the local level can draw important conclusions. The case studies reviewed here demonstrate the potential of a well-defined, theory-driven, community-action approach to reduce local alcohol problems. Each of these examples, and other local efforts not discussed here, show that local initiatives can be efficacious. Alcohol problems are best considered in terms of the community systems that produce them.

Community-action projects are just that—projects that seek to address the total community system and are not naturally limited to a specific target group or service group. These are not projects in which a local program to provide services to a specific target group happens to be located in a community. Most community-based prevention efforts involve the delivery of prevention "services" to individuals such as students or high-risk youth or heavy drinking individuals. These service-based prevention efforts require an organizational structure, philosophy, and resources very different from the organizational base of policy-based interventions. Policy-based interventions require the community prevention coalition to be thoughtful, strategic, and purposeful. The community efforts described here involved local leadership in designing, implementing, and supporting alcohol policies to reduce problems across the community in total, not only a specific target group. Local alcohol policy requires a different perspective than do service programs.

Local alcohol policy strategies have the greatest potential to be effective when prior scientific evidence is utilized. Many of the international local projects described here implemented a series of interventions that prior research had indicated were likely to reduce alcohol-related problems. In local prevention efforts, community members want to learn what science revealed about what prevention alternatives worked. Members understood the utility of project data collection for mid-course correction of intervention efforts and the import of science.

Media advocacy is essential to local community action which refers to the strategic use of media to advance policy goals (Wallack 1990; Holder & Treno 1997). Without skillful media work, it is very difficult (perhaps impossible) to create policy-driven structural changes within a community.

Policies can be self-sustaining because they can have a longer life, once implemented, than services that must be maintained and, thus, funded each year. A policy of required training for alcoholic beverage servers in bars and restaurants through an existing adult education system has a potentially longer period of effectiveness than does a professionally planned public education campaign which must be funded and implemented each year. Even when the potential effectiveness of a policy decays over time due to lower compliance or lowered regulation or enforcement, policies can continue to have sustaining effect, even without reinforcement. One illustration of this comes from the U.S. minimum drinking age set at 21 for all states. O'Malley and Wagenaar (1991) found that the effects on drinking and driving resulting from the increased minimum age were more sustained in states with previous higher drinking ages than in states with lower ages (18 to 19).

In the final analysis, complementary system strategies that seek to restructure the total alcohol environment are more likely to be effective than single intervention strategies. Prevention strategies with the natural capacity for long-term institutionalization are to be favored over interventions that are only in place for the life of the special project.

6. ACKNOWLEDGEMENTS

Preparation of this report was supported by the National Institute on Alcohol Abuse and Alcoholism, Center Grant AA06282 to the Prevention Research Center, Pacific Institute for Research and Evaluation.

7. REFERENCES

Casswell, S. (1995). Public discourse on alcohol: implications for public policy. In H.D. Holder, G. Edwards (Eds.), *Alcohol and public policy: evidence and issues* (pp. 190-212). Oxford: Oxford University Press.

Casswell, S., & Gilmore, L. (1989). An evaluated community action project on alcohol. *Journal of Studies on Alcohol, 50*, 339-346.

Edwards, G., Anderson, P., Babor, T.F., Cassell, S., Ferrence, R., Giesbrecht, N., Godfrey, C., Holder, H.D., Lemmens, P., Mäkelä, K., Midanik, L.T., Norström, T., Österberg, E., Romelsjö, A., Room, R., Simpura, J., Skog, O.-J. (1994). *Alcohol policy and the public good*. New York: Oxford University Press.

Grube, J.W. (1997). Preventing sales of alcohol to minors: results from a community trial. *Addiction, 92*(Supple. 2), S251-260.

Gruenewald, P.J., & Johnson, F.W. (under review). Drinking, driving and crashing: a traffic flow model of alcohol-related motor vehicle accidents.

Hauritz, M., Homel, R., McIlwain, G., Burrows, T., Townsley, M. (1998). Reducing violence in licensed venues through community safety action projects: the Queensland experience. *Contemporary Drug Problems*, *25*(Fall), 511-551.

Hingson, R., McGovern, T., Howland, J. Heeren, T., Winter, M., Zakocs, R. (1996). Reducing alcohol-impaired driving in Massachusetts: the Saving Lives Program. *American Journal of Public Health, 86*(6), 791-797.

Holder, H.D., Gruenewald, P.J., Ponicki, W.R., Grube, J.W., Saltz, R.F., Voas, R.B., Reynolds, R., Davis, J., Sanchez, L., Gaumont, G., Roeper, P., Treno, A.J. (November 8, 2000). Effect of community-based interventions on high-risk drinking and alcohol-related injuries. *The Journal of the American Medical Association*, *284*(18), 2341-2347.

Holder, H.D., Saltz, R.F., Grube, J.W., Voas, R.B., Gruenewald, P.J., Treno, A.J. (1997a). A community prevention trial to reduce alcohol-involved accidental injury and death: overview. *Addiction, 92*(Supple. 2), S155-71.

Holder, H.D., Saltz, R.F., Grube, J.W., Treno, A.J., Reynolds, R.I., Voas, R.B., Gruenewald, P.J. (1997b). Summing up: lessons from a comprehensive community prevention trial. *Addiction, 92*(Supple. 2), S293-S301.

Holder, H.D., & Treno, A.J. (1997). Media advocacy in community prevention: news as a means to advance policy change. *Addiction*, *92*(Supple. 2), S189-S199.

Holmila, M. (1997). *Community prevention of alcohol problems*. London: MacMillan Press, Ltd.

Holmila, M. (1995). Community action on alcohol: experiences of the Lahti Project in Finland. *Health Promotion International, 10*(4), 283-291.

Homel, R., Hauritz, M., Worthley, R., McIlwain, G., Carvolth, R. (1997). Preventing alcohol-relating crime through community action: the Surfers Paradise Safety Action Project. In R. Homel (Ed.),

Policing for prevention: reducing crime, public intoxication, and injury, crime prevention studies, Vol. 7 (pp. 35-90). New York: Criminal Justice Press.

Jernigan, D., & Wright, P.A. (1996). Media advocacy: lessons from community experience. *Journal of Public Health Policy, 17*(3), 306-329.

McKnight, A. J., & Streff, F.M. (1994). The effect of enforcement upon service of alcohol to intoxicated patrons of bars and restaurants. *Accident Analysis and Prevention, 26*, 79-88.

Midford, R., Boots, K., Masters, L., Chikritzhs, T. (1999). *Time series analysis of outcome measures from a community alcohol harm reduction project in Australia.* Paper presented at the Kettil Bruun Society Thematic Meeting Fourth Symposium on Community Action Research and the Prevention of Alcohol and Other Drug Problems, New Zealand.

O'Malley P.M., Wagenaar A.C. (1991). Effects of minimum drinking age laws on alcohol use, related behaviors, and traffic crash involvement among American youth: 1976-1987. *Journal of Studies on Alcohol, 52*, 478-491.

Partnerships Project - New Zealand Police. (1996). *Doing something about rural drink drive: the Waikato experience.* Waikato: Alcohol Advisory Council of New Zealand.

Putnam, S.L., Rockett, I.R.H., Campbell, M.K. (1993). Methodological issues in community-based alcohol-related injury prevention projects: attribution of program effects. In T.K. Greenfield, R. Zimmerman (Eds.), *Experiences with community action projects: new research in the prevention of alcohol and other drug problems* (pp. 31-39). Rockville: Center for Substance Abuse Prevention.

Saltz, R.F. (1997). Prevention where alcohol is sold and consumed: server intervention and responsible beverage service. In M. Plant, E. Singer, T. Stockwell (Eds.), *Alcohol: minimising the harm* (pp. 72-84). London: Free Association Books, Ltd.

Stewart, L., & Casswell, S. (1993). Media advocacy for alcohol policy support: results from the New Zealand Community Action Project. *Health Promotion International, 8*(3), 167-175.

Stout, R.L., Rose, J.S., Speare, M.C., Buka, S.L., Laforge, R.G., Campbell, M.K., Waters, W.J. (1993). Sustaining interventions in communities: the Rhode Island community-based prevention trial. In T.K. Greenfield, R. Zimmerman (Eds.), *Experiences with community action projects: new research in the prevention of alcohol and other drug problems* (pp. 253-261). Rockville: U.S. Department of Health and Human Services.

Treno, A.J., Breed, L., Holder, H.D., Roeper, P., Thomas, B.A., Gruenewald, P.J. (1996). Evaluation of media advocacy efforts within a community trial to reduce alcohol-involved injury: preliminary newspaper results. *Evaluation Review, 20*, 404-423.

Treno, A.J., & Holder, H.D. (1997). Community mobilization: evaluation of an environmental approach to local action. *Addiction, 92*(Supple. 2), S173-S187.

Voas, R.B., Holder, H.D., Gruenewald, P.J. (1997). The effect of drinking and driving interventions on alcohol-involved traffic crashes within a comprehensive community trial. *Addiction, 92*(Supple. 2), S221-S236.

Wagenaar, A.C., Murray, D.M., Gehan, J.P., Woofson, M., Forster, J., Toomey, T., Perry, C., Jones-Webb, R. (2000). Communities mobilizing for change on alcohol: outcomes from a randomized community trials. *Journal of Studies on Alcohol, 61*, 85-94.

Wagenaar, A.C., Murray, D.M., Toomey, T.L. (2000). Communities Mobilizing for Change on Alcohol (CMCA): effects of a randomized trial on arrests and traffic crashes. *Addiction, 95*, 209-217.

Wagenaar, A.C., Toomey, T.L., Murray, D.M., Short, B.J., Wolfson, M., Jones-Webb, R. (1996). Sources of alcohol for underage drinkers. *Journal of Studies on Alcohol, 57*(3), 325-333.

Wallack, L., & Dorfman, L. (1996) Media advocacy: a strategy for advancing policy and promoting health. *Health Education Quarterly, 23*, 293-317.

Wallack, L. (1990). Two approaches to health promotion in the mass media. *World Health Forum, 11*, 143-164.

8. AFFILIATION

Prevention Research Center
1995 University Avenue, Suite 450
Berkeley, California 94704, USA
Phone: 510 883 5725; Fax: 510 644 0594; email: holder@prev.org

M. KUO, J.-L. HEEB, G. GMEL & J. REHM

DOES PRICE MATTER? THE EFFECT OF DECREASED PRICE ON SPIRITS CONSUMPTION IN SWITZERLAND

Key words: alcohol consumption, spirit consumption, taxation, price changes, longitudinal study

This article originally appeared in Alcoholism: Clinical and Experimental Research, Vol. 27, No. 4, 2003: pp. 720-725, and is reprinted with permission of the publisher.

Background. On July 1st, 1999, the spirits market in Switzerland was reformed based on the World Trade Organization (WTO) agreement. The tax reform, in addition to increased competition, has resulted in a 30-50% decrease in price for foreign spirits (liquor). The purpose of the present study is to examine whether decreased prices due to the tax reform and the liberalized spirits market in Switzerland have had an effect on spirits consumption, and whether the effect differs by demographic and other correlates.
Methods. The present study uses data from a longitudinal study on changes in alcohol consumption in Switzerland's resident population. The baseline survey was conducted three months before the tax reform and the follow-up was conducted 28 months after the tax reform. A randomly selected sample of 4007 residents aged 15 years or older participated in the baseline survey and 73% in the follow-up survey. The data were obtained by computer-assisted telephone interview, including detailed questions on alcohol consumption, drinking habits, problem drinking, purchase of spirits and socio-demographic characteristics.
Results. Consumption of spirits increased after the price of spirits decreased. The increase in spirits consumption was consistent across sub-groups, with the exception of the group aged 60 or older. Moreover, the increase in spirits consumption persisted even after adjustment for significant correlates of spirits consumption. Apart from age, there was no evidence that the increase in spirits consumption differed between sub-groups as defined by sex, region, working status, education, smoking, drinking frequency, or average number of drinks.
Conclusions. The findings demonstrate that younger people are more affected by price than older persons. This study demonstrated that price should be considered an effective policy to reduce alcohol misuse and alcohol-related problems, especially among the younger population.

1. INTRODUCTION

On July 1st, 1999, the spirits (liquor) market in Switzerland was reformed based on the World Trade Organization (WTO) agreement to eliminate discrimination of taxes on foreign beverages. Before the changes, the tax rate for domestic spirits was CHF 26- per litre of pure alcohol, and the tax rate for foreign spirits ranged between CHF 32- and CHF 58- per litre of pure alcohol. In addition, only a very limited number of importers were allowed to import bottled spirits into Switzerland.

R. Müller and H. Klingemann (eds.),
From Science to Action? 100 Years Later - Alcohol Policies Revisited, 113–123.

According to the new regulation, a uniform tax rate of CHF 29- per litre of pure alcohol was introduced for both domestic and foreign spirits and every company is now allowed to import bottled spirits. The tax reform led to increased competition among importers, and therefore had an indirect effect of reducing former high profit margins of importers. Both aspects of tax reform and higher competition resulted in a 30-50% decrease in the retail price of foreign spirits. The industry did not increase the prices for domestic spirits, however, to avoid the loss of customers. The tax reform affected the price of foreign spirits only; the price of wine and beer did not change. The share of imported spirits accounted for 53% of the total spirits sales in 1998 (Schweizerische Fachstelle für Alkohol- und andere Drogenprobleme (SFA), 1999) prior to the reform, and then accounted for 58% after the reform in 2000 (Schweizerische Fachstelle für Alkohol- und andere Drogenprobleme (SFA), 2001). The marked decrease in the price of imported beverages within a short period of time allowed us to examine the impact of this policy change on spirits consumption.

Changes in price, such as the sudden decrease in the prices of imported spirits in Switzerland, are commonly referred to as "natural experiments". "Natural experiments" potentially allow control through a quasi-experimental study design, which is often lacking in other designs of social epidemiology (Cook and Campbell, 1979). In the present case, observed changes in consumption are more likely to be related to the price decrease rather than to other confounding predictors because of the suddenness of the intervention. In the last two decades, similar "natural experiments" on the impacts of alcohol policies have mainly resulted from the privatisation and deregulation of alcohol monopolies in the European Union (Nordic Studies on Alcohol and Drugs, 1999) and in North America (Her et al., 1998, 1999; Wagenaar et al., 1999). As a consequence, the alcohol distribution system enlarged, which typically results in changes in both economic and structural availability (Gruenewald, 1993). Therefore, it has been difficult to distinguish the economic effects from the structural effects evidenced in previous research.

Most often, empirical research on price effects has been conducted with aggregated rather than individual data. Series of sales data, for instance, have been analyzed by time series methods (Rehm and Gmel, 2001). Since these methods require many measurement points and the data used usually rests on annual statistics, they are generally useful to evidence long-term trends rather than short term economic impacts.

Previous studies have found the association between price and consumption. In general, as the price of alcohol increases, consumption decreases (Clements and Selvanathan, 1991; Levy and Sheflin, 1983; Österberg, 1995). However, the level of effect on consumption varies by age group, drinking level and type of alcohol (Coate and Grossman, 1988; Edwards et al., 1994; Manning et al., 1995) and the findings are not conclusive.

The critical lack of recent research on price effects at the individual level has been widely observed (Chaloupka et al., 1998; Godfrey, 1997; Her et al., 1999). To establish an effective alcohol policy, new studies on price effects in modern societies are required to adjust for changes in the societal environment (Plant et al., 1997; Rehm et al., 2000). In addition, studies at the aggregate level can provide no evidence for sub-groups (Cook and Campbell, 1979; Morgenstern, 1998; Rehm and

Strack, 1994); for instance, only individual-level studies are able to differentiate the responsiveness to price change among different types of drinkers.

The purpose of the present study is to investigate whether decreased prices due to tax reform and the liberalized market of spirits in Switzerland have increased spirits consumption over time, and whether this effect differs by demographic and other correlates. One strength of the study is its longitudinal design, which allows us to examine the overall price effect, as well as the effects on study subgroups.

2. METHOD

2.1. Study design and participants

The present study used data from a longitudinal study on changes in alcohol consumption in Switzerland's resident population. The sampling design involved a stratified two-stage probability sample, with oversampling of smaller French- and Italian-speaking regions. Oversampling was done to increase the sample sizes of those regions so that statistical tests would have sufficient power to test regional differences. At the baseline survey, 5595 households were randomly selected based on the Swiss telephone registry. (In Switzerland, most of the households have only one distinct telephone line). Within each household, a target person aged 15 or older was randomly chosen to participate in the study. A total of 4007 subjects participated in the baseline survey, with a response rate of 71.6 % (non-response included neutral losses—telephone number of holiday dwellings, automatic responders and faxes, non-valid number and refusal). The first two follow-up telephone interview surveys were conducted in autumn 1999 and spring 2000. Due to budget constraints, only a subsample (54%) of the original sample was re-contacted during these follow-ups. The final follow-up with the entire sample was conducted in autumn 2001. In the final follow-up, all 4007 subjects were re-contacted, and 73% of them (2923) participated in the follow-up telephone interviews. The present study was restricted to data from the baseline and final follow-up surveys.

The attrition rate between baseline and follow-up was 27.1%. Drop-outs (1084) were due to refusals (323), unable to reach the subjects (761), which included unable to update address despite of enormous efforts (417), health reasons including mortality (186), and time constraints for conducting the follow-up (158). Time constraints arose because it was necessary to conduct the follow-up surveys within a two-month period to avoid reports of atypical drinking occasions due to the Christmas holiday season. Interviews were conducted from October 10 through December 21, 1999. We examined the rate of attrition by demographics and other correlates. The results showed that attrition did not vary by sex, region, working status, education, or consumption ("having 3 or more glasses a typical day"). However, attrition varied significantly by age (attrition is higher in the group aged less than 30 years old and the group aged 60 or older), and smoking status (attrition is higher for smokers). Therefore, these correlates will be included in the multiple regression model to examine the increase in spirits consumption over time, to adjust for potential bias due to attrition (Muthén and Muthén, 2000).

2.2. Procedure

The baseline survey was conducted three months before the tax reform which began on July 1, 1999, and follow-up was conducted 28 months after the tax reform. The data were obtained by computer-assisted telephone interview. Respondents who were unable to speak German, French or Italian, or who could not participate for health reasons, were not interviewed (less than 3% of the sample contacted). A closed-ended questionnaire was used in the interview. The questionnaire included detailed questions on alcohol consumption, drinking habits, problem drinking, the purchase of spirits, and socio-demographic characteristics, and involved items developed at the Swiss Institute for the Prevention of Alcohol and Drug Problems for the Swiss Health Survey (Bundesamt für Statistik (BFS), 1994, 1998) and the Alcohol Research Group, Berkeley (Greenfield, 2000).

2.3. Measures

Spirits consumption (outcome variable). Spirits consumption was measured by a graduated frequency instrument (Greenfield, 2000; Midanik, 1994). Respondents were first asked if they drank spirits during the past seven days. If they did, they were asked to indicate the number of days they consumed spirits and number of drinks they had on the reported days. The response categories for the drinking quantity were *11 or more, 9-10, 7-8, 5-6, 3-4 and 1-2 drinks.* A drink is defined as 3 cl (centilitre) of spirits. Respondents who reported no weekly consumption were asked about consumption occasions for each drinking quantity during the past six months. The same response categories for drinking quantity were asked of subjects who reported drinking on a weekly basis. The response categories for consumption occasion during the past six months included *once a week, twice or three times a month, once a month, less often than once a month* and *never*. Estimated volume of spirits consumption was obtained by turning quantities and related frequencies into grams of pure alcohol per day (Rehm, 1998).

Demographic correlates. Include sex, age (categorized into 15-29, 30-59 and 60 or older), region (categorized into German-, French- and Italian-speaking), working status (Yes versus No) and education (dichotomized as more than high school versus other).

Other correlates. Include smoking (Yes versus No), having 6 glasses or more (monthly or more versus less than monthly) of any alcohol, having 3 or more glasses of any drink per typical day (Yes versus No).

2.4. Data analysis

Weighting based on stratification by linguistic regions and the number of persons in the household was used throughout the analysis. Both unweighted and weighted mean spirits consumption is presented at baseline and the final follow-up.

To examine the impact of attrition, we imputed missing data at follow-up based on the total alcohol consumption at baseline and the final follow-up, the spirits consumption at baseline and follow-up, sex, age, linguistic regions and smoking status using hot deck imputation by means of PRELIS (Jöreskog and Sörbom, 1993). The hot deck imputation of missing values for a respondent searches for other respondents that have the same response patterns over the variables. If a matching respondent is found, the corresponding value is "donated" to the respondent with the missing value. The results showed there were no differences in total alcohol consumption and spirits consumption between imputed mean and non-imputed mean in general, and among subgroups at follow-up. Therefore we presented the results using non-imputed means.

We examined the mean spirit consumption levels at baseline and follow-up within subgroups of each correlate, which are presented in Table 1. We further examined the differences of the time trends across correlates using Generalized Estimating Equations (GEE) (Liang and Zeger, 1986; Zeger et al., 1988). Time was coded 0 for baseline and 1 for the follow up. In addition, the interaction effect between time and each of the correlates was examined to test whether the effect of time on spirit consumption varied by each of the correlates.

The GEE is used to fit the regression models to handle correlated outcomes due to repeated measures of the same subject over time. The GEE approach estimates regression parameters by dealing with them only as they affect the marginal means. GEE can also handle correlated data with missing observations that produce a variable number of repeated observations across subjects.

A final multiple regression model (Table 2) describes the effect of time after controlling for all covariates (sex, age, age X time, smoking, having ≥6 drinks, average number of drinks), which significantly predicted spirit consumption in the previous regression models or varied significantly by attrition in order to adjust for potential confounding and potential bias due to attrition.

3. RESULTS

Overall, more women than men participated in the study (57 % women versus 43 % men). The sample thus consists of a slightly higher percentage of women compared with the Swiss resident population (51% women and 48% men) (Bundesamt für Statistik (BFS), 2001). Among the subjects, 19% were less than 30 years old, 54% were between 30 to 59, and 27% were 60 years or older. The age distribution in our sample approximates the Swiss resident population (22%, 54% and 24% respectively). The sample distributions of three linguistic regions - German-, French- and Italian-speaking are 48%, 25% and 28% respectively. Due to the oversampling of smaller French and Italian-speaking regions in the study design (in order to have sufficient power to test the regional difference), our sample consists of a greater proportion of French- and Italian- speaking persons compared to the Swiss resident population (64%, 19% and 8% respectively). About 57% of the subjects reported employment and 32% had more than a high school education at the time of the study. Thirty-three percent of the subjects reported smoking, 10% reported having 6 drinks monthly or more frequently, and 27% of the subjects reported having 3 or more drinks per typical day.

Table 1. Mean Spirits Consumption at Baseline and Follow-up by Correlates

	Unweighted				Weighted			
	Baseline		Final Follow-up		Baseline		Final Follow-up	
	n	Mean (Std)	*n*	Mean (Std)	Weighted *n*	Mean (Std)	Weighted *n*	Mean (Std)
Total	4007	**0.695**(1.991)	2923	**0.885** (2.251)	4007	**0.711** (1.948)	2966	**0.980** (2.345)
Sex[1]								
Male	1706	**1.002** (2.464)	1227	**1.230** (2.480)	1834	**0.936** (2.428)	1325	**1.217** (2.445)
Female	2301	**0.467** (1.511)	1696	**0.636** (2.034)	2173	**0.521** (1.471)	1641	**0.788** (2.253)
Age[1]								
<30	763	**0.925** (2.380)	519	**1.386** (2.799)	973	**0.934** (2.433)	683	**1.551** (3.246)
30-59	2152	**0.623** (1.510)	1656	**0.859** (2.195)	2162	**0.619** (1.417)	1675	**0.870** (2.212)
60 or more[2]	1092	**0.676** (2.461)	748	**0.594** (1.857)	872	**0.691** (2.402)	608	**0.639** (1.712)
Region								
German	1905	**0.707** (1.859)	1378	**0.881** (2.145)	2811	**0.716** (2.246)	2085	**0.953** (2.709)
French	991	**0.720** (2.275)	702	**0.931** (2.456)	955	**0.706** (2.168)	693	**1.083** (2.660)
Italian	1111	**0.651** (1.939)	843	**0.853** (2.242)	241	**0.668** (0.919)	188	**0.893** (1.084)
Working								
Yes	2304	**0.833** (2.159)	1802	**1.000** (2.377)	2446	**0.806** (2.160)	1944	**1.023** (2.456)
No	1374	**0.629** (1.897)	1121	**0.700** (2.018)	1255	**0.698** (1.764)	1022	**0.898** (2.152)
Education								
High	1288	**0.860** (2.280)	1029	**0.932** (2.262)	1143	**0.932** (2.367)	932	**1.024** (2.337)
Low	2371	**0.700** (1.934)	1877	**0.860** (2.247)	2546	**0.695** (1.799)	2024	**0.959** (2.355)
Smoking[1]								
Yes	1338	**0.895** (2.369)	930	**1.183** (2.858)	1331	**0.961** (2.453)	930	**1.314** (3.074)
No	2668	**0.594** (1.764)	1993	**0.746** (1.887)	2675	**0.587** (1.623)	2036	**0.827** (1.892)
≥ 6 Drinks[1]								
≥ monthly	415	**1.988** (3.736)	280	**1.874** (3.648)	429	**1.895** (3.543)	302	**2.050** (3.863)
< monthly	3592	**0.545** (1.612)	2643	**0.780** (2.021)	3578	**0.569** (1.611)	2664	**0.858** (2.088)
Ave No. drinks/d[1]								
3 or more	1071	**1.392** (2.809)	771	**1.513** (2.955)	1171	**1.337** (2.704)	871	**1.563** (3.111)
Less than 3	2936	**0.441** (1.514)	2152	**0.660** (1.888)	2836	**0.452** (1.514)	2094	**0.737** (1.952)

1. The differences of spirits consumption within the subgroups of the correlate were significant (p<0.01)
2. The spirits consumption increased significantly (p <0.01) for all subgroups at follow-up except for the group of aged 60 or more.

3.1. Spirits consumption and changes over time

Mean spirits consumption at baseline and follow-up by each demographic and other correlates is presented in Table 1. Overall, the mean spirits consumption significantly increased at follow-up. In addition, spirits consumption also increased at follow-up for most of the subgroup, with the exception of the group aged 60 or older.

Among the correlates, sex, age, smoking, heavy drinking frequency and average number of drinks were significantly related to spirits consumption overall. Men showed significantly higher spirits consumption than women; those aged 15-29 reported higher spirits consumption than those aged 30-59 or those aged 60 or older; and those who smoke evidenced higher spirits consumption. As expected, those who had 6 or more drinks monthly or more, and those who had 3 or more drinks in a typical day showed higher spirits consumption at both baseline and follow-up.

We examined the interactions of time and each correlate to assess whether the effect of time on spirits consumption varied by the subgroups of each correlate. The results showed that the increase of spirits consumption did not vary significantly by the subgroups of each correlate, with the exception of age. Among the three age subgroups, subjects aged 15-29 and 30-59 experienced significantly larger increases in spirits consumption, when compared to the subjects aged 60 or older.

A final multiple regression analysis was conducted to assess whether spirits consumption increased at follow-up after adjusting for sex, age, smoking, having 6 or more drinks monthly or more and having 3 or more drinks in a typical day (Table 2). The effect of time remains significant after adjusting for all of the significant covariates.

Table 2. Multiple regression model predicting spirits consumption over time

	Unweighted			Weighted		
	Test of the effect *p*-value[1]	Coefficient	*p*-value	Test of the effect *p*-value[1]	Coefficient	*p*-value
Intercept(baseline)		**0.429 (0.067)**	<0.0001		**0.469 (0.090)**	<0.0001
Follow-up	**<0.0001**	**-0.076 (0.086)**	0.3778	**0.0001**	**-0.045 (0.116)**	0.6964
Male	**<0.0001**	**0.301 (0.064)**	<0.0001	**0.0358**	**0.160 (0.076)**	0.0358
Age	**<0.0001**			**<0.0001**		
age 60 or more		reference			reference	
age 31-59		**-0.017 (0.111)**	0.8766		**0.012 (0.136)**	0.9277
age 15-29		**-0.289 (0.085)**	0.0007		**-0.285 (0.115)**	0.0132
Age * Time	**0.004**			**0.0022**		
Follow-up* age 60 or more		reference			reference	
Follow-up* age15-29		**0.571 (0.165)**	0.0005		**0.687 (0.199)**	0.0006
Follow-up* age30-59		**0.327 (0.101)**	0.0011		**0.304 (0.135)**	0.0236
Smoking	**0.0086**	**0.172 (0.066)**	0.0086	**0.0186**	**0.211 (0.090)**	0.0186
Have ≥6 drinks, ≥monthly	**<0.0001**	**0.812 (0.159)**	<0.0001	**<0.0001**	**0.806 (0.180)**	<0.0001
Average drinks/day, ≥3 drinks	**<0.0001**	**0.580 (0.076)**	<0.0001	**<0.0001**	**0.559 (0.098)**	<0.0001
R^2	**7%**			**7%**		

1. The *p*-value is derived from Wald chi-square statistics (Wald, 1943).

4. CONCLUSION

The present study is a longitudinal study that examined whether an increase in spirits consumption at the 28-month follow-up is related to the decreased price of spirits due to the Swiss tax reform and market competition. We found the increase in spirits consumption to be consistent among the subgroups except the group of aged 60 or older. Moreover, the increase in spirits consumption persists even after we adjust for significant correlates of spirits consumption. Other than age, we did not find spirits consumption to increase differently within subgroups of each correlate.

The present study allowed us to examine the effect of price on consumption at the individual level. In general, previous studies have shown that increased prices result in decreased consumption, while the present study showed the opposite effect: decreased prices resulted in increased consumption. We found only significant differences in price responsiveness by age, in that the younger age group responded more to the price change than the older age category. Those who are aged 60 or older did not respond to the price changes at all. Our finding is consistent with previous studies in that young people are more affected by the price of alcohol (Kenkel, 1993; Chaloupka and Wechsler, 1996; Godfrey, 1997). On the other hand, drinking habits for older people are more stable and therefore they are less likely to be affected by the price (Gmel et al., 1999).

Previous studies of price effects on types of drinkers are not conclusive. Studies on youth showed alcohol consumption is inversely related to monetary price, and frequent and heavy drinkers are more responsive to price (Coate and Grossman, 1988; Grossman et al., 1987; Laixuthai and Chaloupka, 1993). Chaloupka and Wechsler (1996) found an insignificant effect of price on alcohol consumption in a study of male college students and a relatively small effect on underage drinkers and female college students. However, another study has shown both light and heavy drinkers are less price-elastic than moderate drinkers (Manning et al., 1995). The present study found that all types of drinkers are affected by price and we did not find the effect of price to differ by type of drinkers. It is important to note, however, that these effects were tested linearly. According to Skog (1985) drinkers changed their consumption proportionally. Thus, our findings indicated that the increase in spirits consumption was relatively higher in moderate drinkers compared to heavy drinkers.

The present study demonstrated that a reduction in the price of spirits increased spirits consumption and this effect remains 28 months after the intervention. Although our study did not find that heavier drinkers were more affected by price than other type of drinkers, all types of drinkers were affected by the price. In addition, our study found younger age groups were more affected by price than older age groups. Since younger people are more likely to engage in alcohol-related problems such as motor vehicle accidents, property damage, physical injuries, unwanted sexual advances and encounters with police (Perkins, 2002; Wechsler et al., 2000), the present study demonstrated that the price of alcohol should be considered an effective policy strategy to reduce alcohol misuse and alcohol-related problems, especially among the younger population.

5. CAVEATS

The results of the present study should be interpreted with the following caveats. First, the present study is subject to the limitation of self-report survey. However, methodological reviews of such surveys have been determined to be generally valid when measuring consumption and examining alcohol responses, especially when comparing relative volume rather than absolute volume (Cooper et al., 1981; Midanik, 1988). Second, the present study is subject to the limitation of longitudinal studies where attrition is considered a common problem. Potential bias may have been introduced through attrition. However, several procedures were used to examine potential bias from attrition and found no effects on the results. For example, the imputation for missing observation at follow-up was performed and no significant difference in spirits consumption was found between imputed and non-imputed results, and the results were therefore presented using non-imputed data. In addition, we examined the correlates associated with attrition and found only age and smoking status were associated with attrition. We further included the significant correlates associated with attrition in the multiple regression model served to adjust results for potential bias. In all instances, the effect of increased spirits consumption remained persistent and has therefore been found to be robust.

6. ACKNOWLEDGEMENTS

This work was done at the Addiction Research Institute, Zurich University, and the Swiss Institute for Prevention of Alcohol and Drug Problems, Lausanne. The survey was founded by Swiss Alcohol Board and the analyses were supported by National Institute on Alcohol Abuse and Alcoholism (US) 1 R01 AA13346-01A1.

7. REFERENCES

Bundesamt für Statistik (BFS) (1994). *Swiss Health Survey - Initial Findings*. Neuchâtel: Bundesamt für Statistik.

Bundesamt für Statistik (BFS) (1998). *Swiss Health Survey - Initial Findings*. Neuchâtel: Bundesamt für Statistik.

Bundesamt für Statistik (BFS) (2001). *Statistisches Jahrbuch der Schweiz 2001*. Zürich: Verlag Neue Zürcher Zeitung.

Chaloupka, F. J., Grossman, M., & Saffer, H. (1998). The effects of price on the consequences of alcohol use and abuse. In M. Galanter (Ed.), *The Consequences of Alcoholism* (Vol. Vol. 14, pp. 331-346). New York, NY: Plenum Press.

Chaloupka, F. J., & Wechsler, H. (1996). Binge drinking in college: the impact of price, availability, and alcohol control policies. *Contemporary Economic Policy, 14* (4), 112-124.

Clements, K. W., & Selvanathan, S. (1991). The economic determinants of alcohol consumption. *Australian Journal of Agricultural Economics, 35*, 209-231.

Coate, D., & Grossman, M. (1988). Effects of alcoholic beverage prices and legal drinking ages on youth alcohol use. *Journal of Law and Economics, 31* (1), 145-171.

Cook, T. D., & Campbell, D. T. (1979). *Quasi-Experimentation: Design and Analysis Issues for Field Settings*. Chicago: Rand-McNally.

Cooper, A. M., Sobell, M. B., Sobell, L. C., & Maisto, S. A. (1981). Validity of alcoholic's self-reports: duration data. *International Journal of the Addictions, 16* (3), 401-406.

Edwards, G., Anderson, P., Babor, T. F., Casswell, S., Ferrence, R. G., Giesbrecht, N., et al. (1994). *Alcohol Policy and the Public Good*. New York: Oxford University Press.

Gmel, G., Truan, P., & François, Y. (1999). Alcoholic beverage preferences and self-reported problems in Switzerland. *Substance Use and Misuse, 34* (12), 1619-1645.

Godfrey, C. (1997). Can tax be used to minimise harm? A health economist's perspective. In M. A. Plant, E. Single & T. Stockwell (Eds.), *Alcohol: Minimising the Harm. What Work's?* (pp. 29-42). London: Free Association Books.

Greenfield, T. K. (2000). Ways of measuring drinking patterns and the difference they make: experience with graduated frequencies. *Journal of Substance Abuse, 12* (1-2), 33-49.

Grossman, M., Coate, D., & Arluck, G. M. (1987). Price sensitivity of alcoholic beverages in the United States: Youth alcohol consumption. In H. Holder (Ed.), *Advances Abuse Prevention: Strategies for States and Communities*. Greenwich CT: JAI.

Gruenewald, P. J. (1993). Alcohol availability and the ecology of drinkign behaviour. *Alcohol Health and Research World, 17* (2), 39-45.

Her, M., Giesbrecht, N., Room, R., & Rehm, J. (1998). Implications of privatizing/deregulating alcohol retail sales: Projections of alcohol consumption in Ontario. *Journal of Substance Abuse, 10* (4), 355-373.

Her, M., Giesbrecht, N., Room, R., & Rehm, J. (1999). Privatizing alcohol sales and alcohol consumption: evidence and implications. *Addiction, 94* (8), 1125-1139.

Jöreskog, K. G., & Sörbom, D. (1993). *PRELIS 2 User's Reference Guide*. Chicago, IL: SSI.

Kenkel, D. S. (1993). Prohibition versus taxation: reconsidering the legal drinking age. *Contemporary Policy Issues, 11* (3), 48-57.

Laixuthai, A., & Chaloupka, F. J. (1993). Youth alcohol use and public policy. *Contemporary Policy Issues, 11* (4), 70-81.

Levy, D., & Sheflin, N. (1983). New evidence on controlling alcohol use through price. *Journal of Studies on Alcohol, 44* (6), 929-937.

Liang, K. Y., & Zeger, S. L. (1986). Longitudinal data analysis using generalized linear models. *Biometrika, 73*, 13-22.

Manning, W. G., Blumberg, L., & Moulton, L. H. (1995). The demand for alcohol: the differential response to price. *Journal of Health Economics, 14* (2), 123-148.

Midanik, L. T. (1988). Validity of self-reported alcohol use: a literature review and assessment. *British Journal of Addiction, 83* (9), 1019-1030.

Midanik, L. T. (1994). Comparing usual quantity/frequency and graduated frequency scales to assess yearly alcohol consumption: results from the 1990 US National Alcohol Survey. *Addiction, 89* (4), 407-412.

Morgenstern, H. (1998). Ecologic studies. In K. J. Rothman & S. Greenland (Eds.), *Modern Epidemiology* (2nd ed., pp. 459-480). Philadelphia, PA: Lippincott-Raven Publishers.

Muthén, B. O., & Muthén, L. K. (2000). Development of heavy drinking and alcohol-related problems from ages 18 to 37 in a U.S. national sample. *Journal of Studies on Alcohol, 61* (2), 290-300.

Nordic Studies on Alcohol and Drugs (1999). *Alcohol and the EU: On Policies, Drinking Patterns, Harm and Benefits* (Vol. 16, English Suppl.). Helsinki: National Research and Development Centre of Welfare and Health.

Österberg, E. (1995). Do alcohol prices affect consumption and related problems? In H. Holder & E. Griffith (Eds.), *Alcohol and Public Policy* (pp. 145-163). Oxford: Oxford University Press.

Perkins, H. W. (2002). Surveying the damage: a review of research on consequences of alcohol misuse in college populations. *Journal of Studies on Alcohol, Suppl. 14*, 91-100.

Plant, M. A., Single, E., & Stockwell, T. (Eds.) (1997). *Alcohol: Minimising the Harm. What Works?* London: Free Association Books Ltd.

Rehm, J. (1998). Measuring quantity, frequency and volume of drinking. *Alcoholism, Clinical and Experimental Research, 22* (2 Suppl), 4S-14S.

Rehm, J., & Gmel, G. (2001). Aggregate time-series regression in the field of alcohol. *Addiction, 96* (7), 945-954.

Rehm, J., Gmel, G., & Her, M. (2000). Alcohol consumption, time-series methodology and disease outcomes. *Addiction, 95* (3), 352-353.

Rehm, J., & Strack, F. (1994). Kontrolltechniken [Control techniques]. In T. Hermann & W. Tack (Eds.), *Methodologische Grundlagen der Psychologie* [Methodology to Control for Inferring Causality] (Vol. Enzyklopädie der Psychologie, Themenbereich B, Serie 1, Band 1, pp. 508-555). Göttingen: Hogreve.

Schweizerische Fachstelle für Alkohol- und andere Drogenprobleme (SFA) (1999). *Zahlen und Fakten zu Alkohol und anderen Drogen* [Data and Facts about Alcohol and Other Drugs]. Lausanne: Schweizerische Fachstelle für Alkohol- und andere Drogenprobleme (SFA).

Schweizerische Fachstelle für Alkohol- und andere Drogenprobleme (SFA) (2001). *Zahlen und Fakten zu Alkohol und anderen Drogen* [Data and Facts about Alcohol and Other Drugs]. Lausanne: Schweizerische Fachstelle für Alkohol- und andere Drogenprobleme (SFA).

Skog, O.-J. (1985). The collectivity of drinking cultures: a theory of the distribution of alcohol consumption. *British Journal of Addiction, 80*, 83-99.

Wagenaar, A. C., Maynard, A., Moskalewicz, J., West, D. S., Romanus, G., Giesbrecht, N., et al. (1999). Comments on Her et al.'s "Privatizing alcohol sales and consumption evidence and implications". *Addiction, 94* (8), 1141-1153.

Wald, A. (1943). Test of statistical hypotheses concerning general parameters when the number of observations is large. *Transactions of the American Mathematical Society, 54*, 426-482.

Wechsler, H., Kuo, M., Lee, H., & Dowdall, G. W. (2000). Environmental correlates of underage alcohol use and related problems of college students. *American Journal of Preventive Medicine, 19* (1), 24-29.

Zeger, S. L., Liang, K. Y., & Albert, P. S. (1988). Models for longitudinal data: a generalized estimating equation approach. *Biometrics, 44*, 1049-1060.

8. AFFILIATION

Meichun Kuo: Addiction Research Institute, Zurich University, Switzerland & Department of Health and Social Behavior, Harvard School of Public Health

Jean-Luc Heeb: Swiss Institute for Alcohol and Drug Problems, Lausanne, Switzerland

Gerhard Gmel: Swiss Institute for Alcohol and Drug Problems, Lausanne, Switzerland

Jürgen Rehm: Addiction Research Institute, Zurich University, Switzerland & Centre for Addiction and Mental Health, Toronto, Canada & Public Health Sciences, University of Toronto, Canada

M. CRAPLET

POLICIES AND POLITICS IN FRANCE

"From apéritif to digestif"

Abstract. French alcohol policy has had many ups and downs since its inception after the defeat of France by Prussia in 1870 and the Commune rebellion, depending upon the political climate of the times. Only courageous politicians have succeeded in setting a coherent policy, for example during the 1950s. Some years later, due to the work of the demographist Sully Ledermann regarding the general consumption model, some physicians, led by Pierre Fouquet, developed a comprehensive approach to the problem resulting in a large interest in alcohol studies under the name "alcoologie".
The resistance of a wine producing country, blinded by a passion for alcohol, meant that it took a century for alcohol policy to develop from specific measures – such as legislation on public drunkenness and a ban on absinthe – to a public health approach, which included alcohol problems amongst other addictions. However progress continues to be undermined by the French attitude to alcohol. After the political changes in 2002 the French are once again experiencing the political vulnerability of its alcohol policy.

Key words. Alcohol policy, France, history, politics

A POLITICAL FEAR AT THE END OF THE NINETEENTH CENTURY

Alcohol prevention began in France in the very political climate following the French defeat by Prussia in 1870 and the events surrounding the Commune. Even though this rebellion was confined to the population of Paris, the bourgeoisie took fright as they relived the memory of the great French Revolution. After the defeat of the Communards, the conservatives pinpointed public drunkenness as being responsible for the troubles and for the spirit of sedition. It was easy for them to take up the theses of the alienist doctors of the period who had caricatured the role of alcohol on mental health in their theories of degeneracy.

It was in this context that an anti-alcohol league, a non-governmental organization, was created in 1872 by well-known men from the world of science and politics, amongst whom were Louis Pasteur and Claude Bernard. The first success of this League was to achieve the passing of a law against public drunkenness in 1873. In its first long campaign the League then targeted a very popular Franco Swiss aperitif: absinthe.

From 1870 to 1914, publications, demonstrations and petitions were organised in order to sensitise political leaders and inform public opinion on the dangers of this drink. Despite these efforts, the ban on absinthe was not introduced until the outbreak of the First World War through a decree issued the day after the declaration of war and confirmed by law in 1915.

R. Müller and H. Klingemann (eds.),
From Science to Action? 100 Years Later - Alcohol Policies Revisited, 125–130.

THE ALCOHOLIC WEAPONS OF THE TROOPS

Thus, absinthe with all its folklore disappeared. However wine became more established and it benefited from the events of the First World War. In 1914 the wine producers from the South of France had presented the army with large quantities of wine and, from the following year, the Ministry of War placed orders for even larger quantities. Wine, called "pinard" in the trenches (an epithet still in use today) was thus discovered by large numbers of soldiers from the Northern parts of France where they did not as yet have the wine drinking habit. A few years after his victory at the battle of Verdun, Marshall Pétain, gave a memorable eulogy in praise of wine. The most famous poets such as Apollinaire also extolled its praises, particularly champagne and its superiority over German beer. As he glorified the frontline Appolinaire wrote *"where the artillery uncork the sparkling bottles" (où l'artillerie débouche ses bouteilles crémantes)* [1].

The victory of 1918 brought in a period of the glorification of wine during the "roaring twenties" or, as we say in French *Les années 20* ou les *années VIN*, playing on words with the number "20" and the word "vin". Well-known personalities in the medical world appeared as "doctors – friends of wine" with texts such as *Wine – my Doctor*. The National League against Alcoholism was not very active during this period.

WAR PROHIBITION AND NATIONAL EXCESS

We can therefore see that during this first period in the prevention of alcoholism – that of the struggle against a social evil – internal and external political events greatly influenced this process. This was also the case during the Second World War. As in 1870, similar discussions arose pointing to alcohol as one of the causes for the defeat of the French army in 1940. In France, depending on the argument, wine can either be responsible for defeat or for victory. Once again, control measures were introduced by the French State (the Government of Occupation). It is impossible to evaluate the effect of these measures because it was the conditions caused by the occupation of France by the German army that led to a drop in wine consumption. These restrictions in supply were the cause of a considerable decline in alcohol related deaths. However, soon after 1945, the reconstruction of France was accompanied by a progressive "re alcoholisation" that led to a record level of consumption in 1957. Fortunately, the resulting problems provoked a reaction. The National League against Alcoholism was transformed in a new National Committee, Comité National de Défense Contre l'Alcoolisme (CNDCA).

For some years, France then had a coherent alcohol policy underpinned by a new "inter-ministerial" committee answerable to the Prime Minister, the "Haut Comité d'Etudes et d'Information sur l'Alcoolisme" (HCEIA). It was set up by two brave politicians. The Left Wing Pierre Mendès-France began the work in 1954 and this work was continued by the Right Wing Michel Debré in 1959. This shows that the problem crossed the political divide. Mendes France is still remembered for having provided schoolchildren with a glass of milk each morning. He had shocked public opinion by drinking this same glass of milk during public meetings.

At the same time, a demographist, Sully Ledermann published the study which led to the general consumption model. This was based on research undertaken in the public Institut National d'Etudes Démographiques. Ledermann gave a strong warning, saying that alcohol producers, retailers, and the French Treasury, had made a "long term investment in alcoholism" [2]. In spite of this clear statement, the French went on hiding their heads in the sand (or in their wine cellars) and the policy recommendations of Ledermann were only implemented in Northern Europe (North of the English Channel!), and were known in France only through Nordic publications. No one is a prophet in his own country.

THE CONCEPT OF ALCOHOLOGY: A COLLABORATION BETWEEN FRANCE AND SWITZERLAND

The sixties were noted for the start of specialised clinical work begun in particular by Pierre Fouquet, the founder of alcohology, a title which he had taken from Switzerland. In November 1966 Pierre Fouquet aroused interest in the concept of "alcohologie" – a word quoted in Mark Keller dictionary [3] – and proposed the use of this word in his first article on this topic: "Eloge de l'alcoolisme et naissance de l'alcoologie" [4]. Fouquet's vision of alcohology [5] was that of a discipline gathering together alcohol studies from all research fields in order to build a comprehensive and coherent approach to alcohol policy in France. Fouquet explained why he had adopted this term which had been introduced the previous year in Switzerland by a worker in the anti-alcoholism field called Gilbert Collette, a lawyer from Belgium – Vive la Francophonie! Collette had just founded a centre in Lausanne called the "Centre International d'Alcoologie" and a review called *Études et Informations* subtitled *Alcool, Alcoolisation, Alcoolisme.* Colette had himself borrowed the term from a doctor from Lausanne called Edouard Ceresole who had used it as early as 1923 in a communication addressed to the Vaudoise Society of Medicine. In a previous paper [6], I followed the origin of the word back even further, to a certain Robert Koppe, a German doctor practising in Moscow who had invented the German word "Alkohologie" in 1903. The history of this word which has jumped frontiers is quite interesting. I have tried to demonstrate in other papers [7] how the concept of alcohology is always pertinent in those countries where alcohol is the object of national passion.

THEORETICAL AND POLITICAL ISOLATION: NGOS ON THE FRONTLINE

Lets go back to the French situation at ground level. So France benefited from an official agency, had statistical data and intervention concepts in the field of prevention and care. Despite these measures, we see little coherence and little continuity in alcohol policy throughout the seventies and eighties. Progress was for a long time kept confidential in a country behoven to its passion for alcohol [8] and which was more interested in the commercialisation of the products of the vine and by the evaluation of its merits through the "good" ways of drinking.

It seemed that there could not be any change in the situation and that the French population was condemned to the highest consumption in the world and to a reduction in life expectancy. Alone private organisations such as the Association Nationale de Prévention de l'Alcoolisme (ANPA) – born out of the anti-alcohol League founded in 1872, through the Comité National de Défense Contre l'Alcoolisme (CNDCA) – kept the flame burning in the care for alcoholics and in prevention work. In order to fill the gap between needs and resources, local authorities used the efforts of these voluntary organisations, involved in prevention and rehabilitation, to carry out this unpopular task which was a cause of embarrassment to the authorities. Thus, the politicians were able to continue to focus all their attention on their supporters… the producers and the drinkers.

"LA DOUCE FRANCE" IN A CHANGING WORLD [9]

Changes began to appear through modernisation and internationalisation. Average consumption decreased from 19 litres of pure alcohol per capita per year in 1960 to 11 litres in 1998. Consumption has decreased especially with regard to daily consumption, and there has been a shift from national beverages (especially wine) to international drinks such as beers and spirits. We can also observe a reduction in the differences between regions, as the rural world moves into the modern age.

- The most important changes concern the patterns of consumption: alcohol is no longer drunk at every meal or even everyday. As in Northern Europe, it is becoming the drink of parties, football matches and rock concerts. It is less used as a food, but more and more as a drug for its psychoactive effect. Alcohol is drunk less during working hours and more during leisure time.
- As a result, we can observe a decrease in the medical complications of excessive drinking – chronic alcohol-related somatic diseases such as liver cirrhosis – but an increase in social harm due to binge drinking and addiction.
- Young people and urban citizens are the actors in these changes because they are refusing the traditional drinks of their parents and of their ancestors from rural backgrounds; this is why we can think that they will create new patterns.

A CONCEPT STUCK IN THE GULLET

In spite of some success (or perhaps because of it), the inter-ministerial committee (HCEIA) was dismantled after thirty years. It first passed to the administration of the Minister of Health (or the State Department depending on the weight given to health concerns by the different governments) and then was diluted in a "Haut Comité de la Santé Publique" (HCSP) which had at that time to deal with the increase in the consumption of illegal drugs and the problems of HIV/Aids. This most unfortunate situation provided the public authorities with an historical opportunity to put aside alcohol problems when faced with seemingly more urgent needs. Again NGOs were left alone to deal with the alcohol problem.

However, at the beginning of the nineties, the Loi Evin - dealing with advertising of alcohol – finally put the question of alcohol back on the political agenda of the policy makers in France and even in Europe, because of the consequences in the international media, particularly during the retransmission of international sporting events. This internationalisation of the issues was first taken on board by NGOs and led to the creation of European specialist organisations such as Eurocare where ANPA could voice French concerns when France itself was unwilling to face up to the fatality of alcoholism. An example of the French public agencies' contempt for the international field, is the fact that it was only in 1998 that the French Ministry of Health became involved in the work of the expert group "Alcohol and Health" set up by the European Commission (DGV).

Changes only appeared recently. During the last years, politicians have, at last, allowed the experts to define a new health policy in which the problems linked to alcohol consumption finally found their rightful place amongst other addictions. "But politicians as well as the general public still need to "digest" a very simple fact: 'alcohol is a drug'". France has still to face this terrible novelty – 45 years after the same position was taken by WHO. This is what I called "a concept stuck in the gullet" (in French we say "difficile à avaler" *hard to swallow* or "difficile à digérer", *hard to digest*).

Nevertheless, "the new French alcohol policy has arrived", as we say about the Beaujolais Nouveau. In several official reports, alcohol is considered as another "hard drug". This change appeared also through the work of another public agency "Mission Interministérielle de Lutte contre la Drogue et la Toxicomanie" (MILDT). This agency introduced the concept of addiction with a new word, "addictologie" [10]: French scientists are enamoured with new words.

HOPES AND RISKS OF COMPREHENSIVE POLICIES

It is true that most alcoholics experience at least one other addiction, for example to tobacco, tranquillisers, cannabis. It is true that alcohol is a gateway to other drugs for many young people. Nevertheless, this comprehensive approach may have some awkward side effects: public health interest in tobacco or psychoactive drugs misuse and public concern for cannabis or other illegal drugs may mask the most important problem: alcohol abuse. This was the risk I foresaw some years ago in the new alcohol policy [11]. Another risk appeared recently in the new political situation in France.

It is of interest to note that during the presidential election campaign of 2002 the approach to the problem became once again political: for whilst the drug problem is now considered a normal medical topic, it is still not considered a normal political topic [12]. The previous French Government and Prime Minister, who gave impetus to the new policy of including alcohol amongst other drugs, adopted fresh attitudes such as harm reduction and aired the question of the legalisation of cannabis. They lacked boldness in disseminating this information and using it in their campaign. New men are now in charge. Unfortunately indications are that alcohol consumption will benefit from the new political majority, using French traditional references to "art de vivre" which are always linked to alcohol. Another bad news is that the new right wing leaders stress the problems arising from illegal drugs and place their hopes more on repression than on education. The wheel of history sometimes turns in a backward direction.

Affiliation:
Assocation Nationale de Prévention de l'Alcoolism (ANPA)
20, Rue Saint Fiacre
FR-75002 Paris
France
Phone: + 33 1 42 33 51 04; Fax: + 33 1 45 08 17 02;
e-mail: mcraplet@anpa.asso.fr

REFERENCES

1. Apollinaire, G. Le vigneron champenois in La tête étoilée in *Calligrammes*.
2. Ledermann, S. (1964). *Alcool, Alcoolisation, Alcoolisme,* Tome II. Paris: PUF.
3. Keller, M. & Mc Cormick, M. (1968). *A dictionary of words about alcohol.* New Brunswick, New Jersey: Rutgers Center of Alcohol Studies.
4. Fouquet, P. (1967). Eloge de l'alcoolisme et naissance de l'alcoologie. *Alcool ou Santé*, *82* (2), 3-11.
5. Conversation with Dr Pierre Fouquet (1999). *British Journal of Addiction, 83,* 7-10.
6. Craplet, M. (1999). Alcoologie: mot français d'origine étrangère. *Alcoologie, 21* (HS), 133-142.
7. Craplet, M. (2000). Eloge de l'alcoologie et naissance de l'addictologie? *Alcoologie et addictologie*, *22* (3), 185-193. L'outil alcoologie. *Alcoologie*, *22* (2 Supp), 86S-88S.
8. Craplet, M. (2000). *Passion alcool*. Paris: Odile Jacob.
9. High Committee on Public Health (1999). *Health in France*. Paris: John Libbey Eurotext.
10. Favre, J.-D. (2000). Editorial. *Alcoologie et addictologie*, 3-4.
11. Craplet, M. (2001). Alcohol problems: is there a specifically French view? *Addiction*, *96,* 805-807, Editorial.
12. Craplet, M. (2003). *Parler d'alcool*. Paris: Editions de la Martinière.

H. SCHMID

DRUNKENNESS AND PREFERENCE FOR SPIRITS IN DIFFERENT COUNTRIES

Key words: alcohol, drunkenness, spirits, adolescents, international

Objective. International studies show a rise in drunkenness over the last years among young people. In this study the number of drunkenness occasions among 15-year old students in 22 countries is reported. The cross-national association between drunkenness and the preference for spirits is described. Variation between countries is examined on the basis of their drinking cultures.
Method. Data on alcohol use were taken from the 1998 World Health Organization (WHO) collaborative, cross-national survey on Health Behaviour of School-aged Children (HBSC). The multi-national representative sample consisted of 10,951 male and 11,451 female (drinking) students.
Results. The lifetime prevalence of drunkenness was 57.1% for males and 50.4% for females. The number of drunkenness occasions showed a significant variation in the 22 countries. The correlation between drunkenness and preference for spirits was positive in 21 countries and strong (Spearman's rho > .40) in some eastern countries. Geographic location turned out to be an important country level association with drunkenness and its predictors. Southern European countries showed moderate relations, whereas strong relations were found in Scandinavia, the Baltic countries and Russia.
Conclusions. Cultural differences in alcohol use exist and the use of spirits influences drunkenness. Regulation and restriction of spirits access to young people may be important to prevent drunkenness.

1. INTRODUCTION

The three most frequent forms of mortality among adolescents, i.e. accidental deaths, homicides, and suicides, are associated with alcohol use (Edwards et al., 1994; Sells and Blum, 1996; World Health Organisation, 2000; Zador et al., 2000). When the purpose of alcohol consumption is to get intoxicated, strong health effects can be expected for young people. Intoxication can easily occur in young adolescents even with the intake of a relative small amount of alcohol (Midanik, 1999; Windle et al., 1996).

Epidemiological data describing the trends of the prevalence of drunkenness show a considerable rise in drunkenness and high prevalence of drunkenness in general. The European School Survey Project on Alcohol and Other Drugs (ESPAD) reports that in the large majority of the 30 included countries, more than half of the 15-year-old students have been drunk at least once in their life (Hibell et al., 2000). Moreover, when looking at changes between the survey years 1995 and 1999, in none of the included countries figures have decreased and in about one third figures have risen. The high prevalence of drunkenness as well as the tendency towards more drunkenness holds for many countries and may be an indicator of a global trend.

Young people show a clear preference for certain types of beverages. Alcohol consumption among adolescent boys and girls is largely dominated by beer (Hibell et al., 2000; Nic Gabhainn and François, 2000). Wine and spirits are less likely to be

R. Müller and H. Klingemann (eds.),
From Science to Action? 100 Years Later - Alcohol Policies Revisited, 131–140.

drunk. However, recently girls also tend to drink alcopops and premixed drinks where spirits are mixed with lemonade (Hibell et al., 2000; Janin Jacquat et al., 2001). The most effective way of getting drunk is by the intake of spirits. High prevalence of drunkenness may therefore by hypothesized to covary with a preference for spirits.

Studies underline that alcohol consumption is not cross-culturally stable and that patterns of drinking differ (Rehm and Gmel, 2000). Across countries one may expect a considerable variation in the number of occasions in which drunkenness occurs, a high variation in the frequency of beer, wine and spirits intake and a high variation in the extent to which drunkenness is determined by a specific beverage.

The research question can be broken down into three parts:

1. Does the number of adolescent drunkenness occasions differ between countries?
2. What is the distribution of the adolescent beverage preference for beer, wine and spirits in different countries?
3. Is there a link between a specific beverage preference of adolescents and drunkenness and does this link vary between countries?

Our study focuses on 15-year-olds and examines relations for male and female students separately. Both genders differ substantially in their use of alcohol and in their attitudes towards alcohol (Schmid, 1998; Shope et al., 1996) and early adolescence is a critical time for acquiring new patterns of behavior especially in the field of alcohol use (Lintonen et al., 2000). If this pattern translates more and more in terms of the search for drunkenness by young people, especially by the use of spirits, detrimental effects on health can be expected and effective policy initiatives should be taken.

2. METHOD

2.1. Sample

The 1998 Health Behavior in School-Aged Children Study (HBSC) is a study of nationally representative samples of adolescents in 29 countries and regions (Currie, 1998). In each country, a cluster sample design was used with school classes as sampling units. Schools and classes within schools were selected to be representative by age level and regional geography. Three age groups of young people were sampled. Age group levels were "designed to represent the onset of adolescence – age 11; the challenge of physical and emotional changes – age 13; and the middle years when very important life and career decisions are beginning to be made – age 15." (Currie, 1998). Recommended sample sizes for each country were 1536 students per age group. Sample sizes assured a 95% confidence interval of +/- 3% for prevalence estimates, with a design effect of no more than 1.44 in any country (Currie, 1998).

The present analysis is based on 10,951 male and 11,451 female (drinking) students aged 15 years from 22 countries. We restricted our analysis to 15 year olds because of the high prevalence of drinking in this group (81% of male and 79% of female students drink alcohol) and because this may be a critical time in the course of a human life for intervention programs addressing the use of substances in general (Evans et al., 1978). The 22 countries included were Austria, Belgium (Flemish sample), Canada, Czech republic, Denmark, Estonia, Finland, France (Regions: Toulouse Midi-Pyrénées, Nancy-Metz Lorraine), Germany (Federal state of Nordrhein-Westfalen), Greece, Greenland (total population), Hungary, Latvia, Lithuania, Norway, Poland, Rep. of Ireland, Russia, Slovak republic, Sweden, Switzerland and USA. Countries excluded were Israel, because it did not have a self-weighting national sample; England, because another question format was used for the frequency of alcohol intake; Belgium (French sample), Northern Ireland, Scotland, as well as Wales because of missing data and Portugal because of outliers in spirits consumption.

We combined geographic regions where alcohol consumption may be seen as cross-culturally stable in order to represent the data. Southern European countries included France and Greece; Germanic countries included Germany, Belgium (Flanders), Austria, and Switzerland; Central European Countries included Poland, Czech Republic, Slovak Republic and Hungary and Baltic countries & Russia included Russia, Estonia, Latvia, and Lithuania. Subsequently, North American Countries, including Canada and the USA. The Republic of Ireland is the only country on the Island and Scandinavian Countries, included Greenland, Finland, Sweden, Norway and Denmark (Figure 1).

Figure 1. Countries and geographic regions covered in the 1998 Health Behavior in School aged Children study (HBSC)

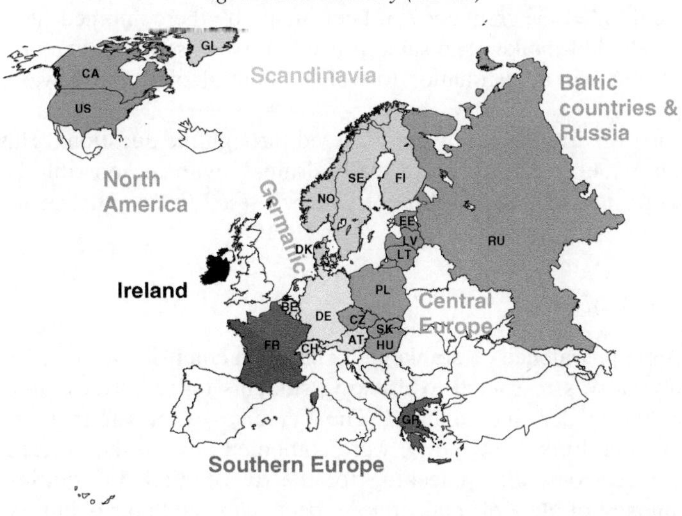

2.2. *Measures*

Data include students indications of their own alcohol use. Full descriptions of the questionnaire items assessed during 1998 and their development were published elsewhere (Currie, 1998; Delgrande et al., 1999a; Delgrande et al., 1999b; King et al., 1999). National questionnaires are translations and adaptations of the international standard version, with independent re-translation back to English, to guarantee a minimum of comparability. The overall goal of the HBSC is to "gain insights into and to increase our understanding of health behaviors, lifestyles and context in young people" (Currie, 1998). This occurs in part by identifying characteristics of youth that influence their health and well-being. Major categories of variables addressed in the survey include: demographics; general health and well-being; family and peer relationships; school environments; exercise and leisure time activities; diet; substance use; and sexual behavior. This study describes alcohol use with a special focus on drunkenness.

Data on alcohol use. Self-reports on alcohol use were collected through questions about the frequency of alcohol intake and the frequency of drunkenness derived from a previous version of the HBSC questionnaire (King et al., 1996).

Frequency of alcohol intake was addressed by three questions about the frequency of the consumption of beer, wine, and spirits separately: "At present, how often do you drink anything alcoholic, such as beer, wine or liquors? Try to include even those times when you only drink a small amount" with the possible answers: *never* (0), *less than once a month* (1), *every month but not every week* (2), *every week but not every day* (3), *every day* (4). Students who never drank any alcoholic beverages were excluded from further analysis. For the drinking students we took the mean of their frequency of beer, wine or spirits consumption as combined measure for the frequency of alcohol intake.

In order to calculate to which extent the alcohol intake was due to a specific beverage, we divided the frequency of beer intake by the combined measure for the frequency of alcohol intake. The same procedure was used for wine and for spirits. As result we obtained an estimation to which extent alcohol intake was due to beer, wine and spirits.

Self-reports on drunkenness were gathered through the question: "Have you ever had so much alcohol that you were really drunk?" with the possible answers: *No, never* (0), *Yes, once* (1), *Yes, 2-3 times* (2), *Yes, 4-10 times* (3), *Yes, more than 10 times* (4).

2.3. *Statistical Analysis*

The lifetime prevalence of drunkenness between countries were given in percent. Further analyses was restricted to drinking students only. All descriptive statistics were given by gender and country. The percentages of lifetime prevalence of drunkenness (non-drinkes excluded) were computed next to the ordered number of drunkenness occasions, after checking for the distribution. In addition, the mean relative frequency of alcohol intake due to beer, wine and spirits in percentage was calculated. As a measure of association between drunkenness and preference for beer, wine and spirits respectively we computed Spearman correlation coefficients.

3. RESULTS

A total of 30,247 students in 22 countries, 14,685 males (48.6%) and 15,562 females (51.4%), received the questionnaires and 28,158 (93.2%) completed all questions about alcohol use.

All further analysis on drunkenness was restricted to drinking students. Of the males 10,951 (80.8%) had drunk alcohol before and of the females 11,451 (78.6%) were drinkers.

Table 1 gives a description of the individual level data by country. The mean lifetime prevalence of drunkenness was 57.1% for males and 50.4% for females. The relative number of drinking students varies from 66.2% in the USA to 92.3% in Denmark for males and from 64.3% in Switzerland to 91.2% in Denmark for females. For male drinking students the prevalence of drunkenness is 65.0% and for female students it is 58.6%. This prevalence again shows important variation between the countries with 47.5% in Greece up to 85.1% in Denmark among males and 42.3% in Belgium (Flanders) up to 92.5% in Greenland among females. The frequency of drunkenness, measured on a five point scale, provides more information than the lifetime prevalence itself. E.g. more than 10 drunkenness occasions occur for 4.9% of male students in Greece and for 33.7% in Denmark. For female students these figures vary between 2.0% in Belgium and 26.6% in Denmark. The distribution of drunkenness does significantly vary from a normal distribution (males: Kolmogorov-Smirnov: .209; df=10951; p<.001; females: Kolmogorov-Smirnov: .242; df=11451; p<.001).

The frequency of beer intake divided by the combined measure for the frequency of alcohol intake results in the extent to which intake is due to beer consumption. In the majority of the countries beer is the preferred beverage among young people. In the countries Greenland, Sweden, Lithuania, Poland, Belgium (Flanders) and Switzerland more than 50% of the alcohol intake among males is due to beer. Regarding females, only Poland has a comparable large domination of beer. There are remarkable differences between male and female students in the beverage they prefer. In every country beer is the most preferred beverage among males. In Finland, Rep. of Ireland, USA, Russia, Estonia, Latvia, Lithuania, Czech republic, Slovak republic, Hungary, Germany and Austria female students prefer wine to beer. In Greenland, Denmark, Canada, and Hungary we find more than one third of the alcohol intake attributable to the consumption of spirits among males and females. Other countries are the USA with high spirit domination among males and Austria among females.

After Fisher z transformation the mean correlation between drunkenness and the preference for beer, wine and spirits is near zero for beer, negative for wine and positive for spirits domination (Figure 2). Countries with a high correlation (Spearman's rho > .40) between drunkenness and the domination of spirits are Russia, Lithuania and Poland for both genders.

Table 1. Description of data on drunkenness and preference of an alcoholic beverage for 15 year olds from the 1998 Health Behavior in School aged Children study (HBSC)

Geographic Localization	Country	Acronym	Prevalence of ever had been drunk Males %	Prevalence of ever had been drunk Females %	Prevalence of drinkers Males %	Prevalence of drinkers Females %	Prevalence of ever had been drunk (non-drinkers excluded) Males %	Prevalence of ever had been drunk (non-drinkers excluded) Females %	Number of Drinkers Males N	Number of Drinkers Females N
Scandinavia	Greenland	GL	78.1	81.8	76.1	81.2	84.6	92.5	149	147
	Finland	FI	61.0	69.1	79.2	79.6	74.5	83.9	553	578
	Sweden	SE	50.3	52.7	70.4	73.3	65.3	67.5	334	320
	Norway	NO	46.9	54.4	66.4	73.0	66.1	69.6	516	546
	Denmark	DK	79.7	75.1	92.3	91.2	85.1	81.1	643	688
North America	Canada	CA	55.2	55.4	79.8	78.6	67.8	68.1	882	978
	USA	US	47.1	44.2	66.2	65.7	66.3	61.3	516	635
Ireland	Rep. of Ireland	IE	54.0	42.8	81.3	71.2	63.3	53.9	528	466
Baltic countries & Russia	Russia	RU	51.3	46.1	84.8	89.7	58.4	50.2	519	637
	Estonia	EE	60.0	39.7	83.6	83.6	70.2	46.0	188	250
	Latvia	LV	70.5	45.7	91.5	86.9	75.4	52.1	422	601
	Lithuania	LT	58.8	45.7	85.5	86.5	65.1	50.4	464	601
Central Europe	Poland	PL	57.5	41.5	84.3	79.1	66.4	50.6	737	575
	Czech republic	CZ	55.6	42.0	90.0	83.9	59.6	46.0	502	494
	Slovak republic	SK	62.2	49.9	81.6	75.0	72.1	60.7	387	239
	Hungary	HU	57.2	40.3	73.4	64.5	73.7	54.3	232	258
Germanic	Germany	DE	54.1	49.2	84.2	85.2	61.7	56.5	639	646
	Belgium (Flanders)	BE	49.0	37.5	86.0	82.7	54.6	42.3	641	605
	Austria	AT	62.4	58.1	83.1	79.2	72.4	68.6	492	583
	Switzerland	CH	39.2	31.5	73.1	64.3	50.1	45.3	647	572
Southern Europe	France	FR	41.1	35.5	76.8	68.6	53.0	48.8	413	408
	Greece	GR	44.6	42.8	92.2	88.0	47.5	47.9	547	624
Total			**57.1**	**50.4**	**80.8**	**78.6**	**65.0**	**58.6**	**10951**	**11451**

Table 1 (continued)

Frequency of drunkenness (non-drinkers excluded)										Alcohol intake due to ... (non-drinkers excluded)						Correlation between drunkenness and preference for ... (non-drinkers excluded)					
Males					Females					Males			Females			Males			Females		
0 'never' in %	1 'once' in %	2 '2-3 times' in %	3 '4-10 times' in %	4 'more' in %	0 'never' in %	1 'once' in %	2 '2-3 times' in %	3 '4-10 times' in %	4 'more' in %	Beer in %	Wine in %	Spirits in %	Beer in %	Wine in %	Spirits in %	Beer Spearman rho	Wine Spearman rho	Spirits Spearman rho	Beer Spearman rho	Wine Spearman rho	Spirits Spearman rho
15.4	18.1	24.2	16.1	26.2	7.5	21.8	26.5	19.7	24.5	53.0	14.0	33.0	48.3	15.8	35.9	-0.14	0.06	0.23	0.12	-0.08	-0.01
25.5	9.6	23.0	17.4	24.6	16.1	12.5	23.9	24.7	22.8	43.7	27.0	29.2	32.2	35.4	32.4	0.10	-0.21	0.24	0.13	-0.25	0.24
34.7	12.3	20.1	13.8	19.2	32.5	13.4	19.4	19.1	15.6	49.6	21.1	29.2	41.1	27.0	31.9	-0.15	0.07	0.29	-0.14	-0.01	0.26
33.9	13.4	19.6	14.3	18.8	30.4	15.6	20.9	17.4	15.8	46.6	24.2	29.1	42.3	27.1	30.6	-0.02	-0.11	0.27	0.02	-0.16	0.26
14.9	9.5	20.2	21.6	33.7	18.9	12.5	21.8	20.2	26.6	49.4	16.7	33.9	41.1	21.8	37.2	-0.07	0.07	0.14	0.13	-0.10	0.03
32.2	15.4	18.3	13.4	20.7	31.9	15.4	20.7	15.1	16.9	43.8	23.9	32.3	37.7	27.7	34.6	0.15	-0.21	0.23	0.21	-0.29	0.24
33.7	17.2	18.0	11.8	19.2	38.7	21.3	18.4	10.1	11.5	37.6	30.5	31.9	26.3	43.9	29.8	0.17	-0.26	0.31	0.30	-0.38	0.25
36.7	13.6	16.3	14.2	19.1	46.1	15.9	19.3	11.6	7.1	48.6	24.9	26.6	31.9	36.4	31.6	0.06	-0.21	0.32	0.14	-0.28	0.32
41.6	20.6	22.5	7.7	7.5	49.8	22.6	17.1	6.9	3.6	48.9	36.2	15.0	43.0	45.9	11.1	-0.07	-0.30	0.50	0.03	-0.39	0.48
29.8	18.6	23.4	14.9	13.3	54.0	19.2	18.4	5.2	3.2	47.8	29.5	22.7	33.1	47.8	19.1	-0.15	-0.18	0.39	0.12	-0.26	0.37
24.6	23.9	23.2	13.7	14.5	47.9	25.8	19.5	3.7	3.2	47.6	29.3	23.2	35.3	40.6	24.1	-0.06	-0.13	0.25	-0.03	-0.10	0.20
34.9	25.9	24.4	9.3	5.6	49.6	26.0	17.8	3.7	3.0	52.5	36.2	11.4	40.1	52.6	7.3	-0.02	-0.23	0.46	0.12	-0.33	0.43
33.6	20.4	23.3	10.3	12.3	49.4	25.4	17.2	4.9	3.1	61.9	19.5	18.6	61.1	25.8	13.0	-0.34	0.10	0.49	-0.16	-0.09	0.51
40.4	19.5	24.1	9.2	6.8	54.0	20.9	17.4	4.9	2.8	48.5	30.0	21.5	36.9	43.7	19.4	0.04	-0.11	0.22	0.07	-0.19	0.28
27.9	13.7	20.7	26.4	11.4	39.3	20.5	22.6	15.5	2.1	40.9	37.1	22.0	25.9	50.7	23.4	0.09	-0.25	0.29	0.19	-0.22	0.22
26.3	15.9	28.0	11.2	18.5	45.7	21.3	20.5	7.0	5.4	36.3	31.4	32.3	25.3	35.6	39.1	0.06	-0.23	0.28	0.08	-0.15	0.24
38.3	20.7	18.6	9.9	12.5	43.5	20.3	21.1	7.6	7.6	47.0	30.5	22.5	33.0	44.6	22.4	0.03	-0.20	0.30	0.26	-0.37	0.25
45.4	17.6	20.0	8.9	8.1	57.7	16.7	18.5	5.1	2.0	52.1	27.0	20.9	48.2	34.6	17.2	-0.03	-0.14	0.32	0.04	-0.18	0.27
27.6	14.4	24.2	16.7	17.1	31.4	24.2	20.1	13.7	10.6	42.0	31.4	26.6	22.3	44.2	33.5	0.10	-0.02	0.09	0.30	-0.10	0.03
49.9	16.7	15.5	9.4	8.5	54.7	21.5	13.8	6.3	3.7	49.5	24.4	26.1	48.4	28.3	23.3	-0.02	-0.02	0.21	0.11	-0.13	0.16
47.0	15.7	18.6	10.4	8.2	51.2	20.8	16.9	8.1	2.9	45.2	30.3	24.5	43.9	25.1	31.0	0.03	-0.17	0.37	0.08	-0.16	0.23
52.5	21.9	15.7	4.9	4.9	52.1	24.4	17.5	3.8	2.2	46.7	29.0	24.2	46.2	25.4	28.4	-0.10	-0.12	0.28	-0.05	-0.12	0.26
35.0	**17.0**	**20.5**	**12.6**	**14.9**	**41.4**	**19.8**	**19.3**	**10.4**	**9.1**	**47.6**	**27.2**	**25.1**	**38.7**	**35.4**	**25.8**	**-0.02**	**-0.13**	**0.31**	**0.09**	**-0.20**	**0.26**

Figure 2. Mean correlation between drunkenness and preference for beer, wine and sprits by gender after Fisher z transformation

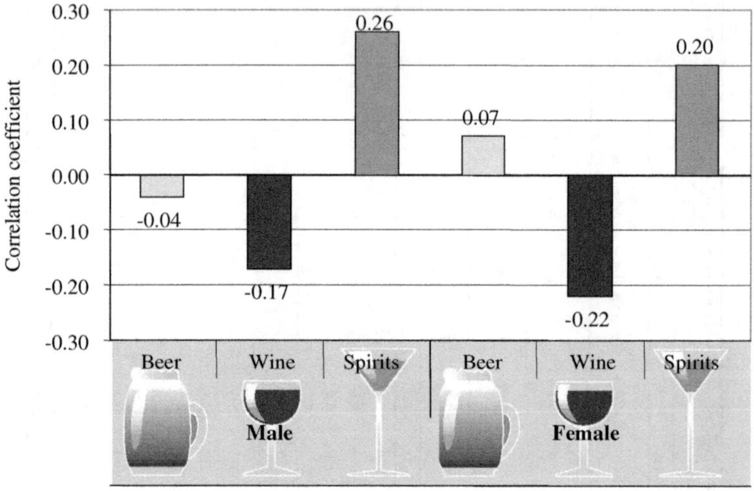

4. DISCUSSION

Drunkenness among young people is a major public health concern. Epidemiological studies show dramatic increases in the prevalence of drunkenness since at least the mid nineties. On the basis of a representative sample from 22 countries with 10,951 male and 11,451 female drinking students aged 15 years the present study shows a high prevalence of drunkenness, with a mean value of 65.0% in males and 58.6% in females for drinking students only and of 57.1% in males and 50.4% in females for the whole sample. In addition, countries vary considerably in the prevalence of adolescent drunkenness (research question 1). In every country beer is the most preferred beverage for males, while females prefer wine over beer in 12 out of 22 countries. In Greenland, Denmark, Canada, and Hungary more than one third of the alcohol intake by both genders is attributable to the consumption of spirits (research question 2). The association between drunkenness and domination of spirits is positive, underlining the fact, that spirits play an important role in the occurrence of drunkenness.

The extent to which alcohol intake is due to spirits relate to drunkenness. It is more likely for students to having been drunk, when the alcohol intake is highly due to spirits (research question 3). The link between drunkenness and spirits preference varies considerably.

Within the present study, clusters of countries may be differentiated according to their tradition in alcohol use. There are European countries representing Mediterranean, wine-producing countries (e.g. France and Greece). For both genders, low numbers of drunkenness occasions were observed in Southern European countries. Another cluster of countries may be defined as representing the

Nordic drinking tradition (e.g. Finland, Norway, Sweden). In the population of young people, relatively low proportions of wine intake can be observed. However, these countries can also be characterized by a high proportion of young people who get drunk. Compared to the other countries, the Baltic countries and Russia with a more or less spirits-oriented drinking culture, are found to have strong relations between sprits intake and drunkenness. The countries of Central Europe (e.g. Poland, Czech republic, Slovak republic, Hungary) and Germanic Countries (Germany, Belgium (Flanders), Austria, Switzerland) with combined traditions can be characterised by a high proportion of 15 year old male and female beer drinkers. In addition, countries outside of Europe (Canada, USA) are participating in the study, which also represent particular aspects of distinct drinking cultures. However, these countries show no clear pattern of alcohol use in young people.

The extent to which alcohol intake can be attributed to spirits is an important mediator for the prevention of drunkenness. Drunkenness itself can be addressed by preventive action, e.g. by mass media campaigns. Given the significant relation with a preference for spirits, we may have identified variables that may be more sensible and better defined targets for preventive action and policy measures. E.g. advertising restriction on spirits, the regulation of availability of spirits to youth, and high taxation on spirits may be expected to reduce drunkenness in young people.

The high prevalence of drunkenness as well as the trend towards more drunkenness – especially by the use of spirits – can be observed in many countries. Detrimental effects on health can be expected and effective policy initiatives should be taken. Knowledge of the variation in policy and preventive measures that exist between countries should be combined with data on alcohol use, health and health behavior of national representative samples of young people. Future research should bring together more data on an individual and a structural level and first attempts have already been undertaken (cf. Schmid et al., in press).

5. ACKNOWLEDGEMENTS

HBSC is a WHO/EURO collaborative study. International Coordinator of the 1997/98 study: Candace Currie, University of Edinburgh, Scotland; Data Bank Manager: Bente Wold, University of Bergen. This publication on the 1997/98 HBSC reports on data from the following countries (principal investigator(s) at that time): Austria (Wolfgang Dür); Belgium (Flanders) (Lea Maes); Canada (Will Boyce, Alan King); Czech republic (Ladislav Csémy); Denmark (Pernille Due, Bjørn E. Holstein); Estonia (Mai Maser); Finland (Jorma Tynjälä); France (Chriatiane Dressen); Germany (Klaus Hurrelmann); Greece (Anna Kokkevi); Greenland (Michael Pedersen); Hungary (Anna Aszmann); Latvia (Ieva Ranka); Lithuania (Apolinaras Zaborskis); Norway (Bente Wold); Poland (Barbara Woynarowska); Rep. of Ireland (Saoirse Nic Gabhainn); Russia (Alexander Komkov); Slovak republic (Miro Bronis); Sweden (Ulla Marklund); Switzerland (Béatrice Janin Jacquat); USA (Mary Overpeck).

6. REFERENCES

Currie, C. (1998). *Health behavior in school-aged children: research protocol for the 1997-98 survey.* Edinburgh, Scotland: WHO Coordinating Center for the Study of Health Behavior in School-Aged Children.

Delgrande, M., Kuntsche, E. N., & Schmid, H. (1999a). *Befragung zum Gesundheitsverhalten von 12- bis 15-jährigen SchülerInnen. Deskriptive Statistik der 1998 erhobenen Gesamtschweizer Daten.* Lausanne: Schweizerische Fachstelle für Alkohol- und andere Drogenprobleme.

Delgrande, M., Kuntsche, E. N., & Schmid, H. (1999b). *Enquête sur les comportements de santé chez les écoliers de 12 à 15 ans. Une statistique descriptive des données nationales de 1998*. Lausanne: Institut suisse de prévention de l'alcoolisme et autres toxicomanies.

Edwards, G., Anderson, P., Babor, T. F., & et al. (1994). *Alcohol Policy and the Public Good*. Oxford: Oxford University Press.

Evans, R., Rozelle, R., Mittelmark, M., Rozelle, R. M., Hansen, W. B., Bane, A. L., et al. (1978). Deterring the onset of smoking in children: Knowledge of immediate physiological effects and coping with peer pressure, media pressure, and parent modeling. *Journal of Applied Social Psychology, 8*(2), 126-135.

Hibell, B., Andersson, B., Ahström, S., Balakireva, O., Bjarnason, T., Kokkevi, A., et al. (2000). *The ESPAD Report - Alcohol and other drugs among students in 30 European countries*. Stockholm: The Swedish Council for Information on Alcohol and Other Drugs (CAN), The Pompidou Group at the Council of Europe.

Janin Jacquat, B., François, Y., & Schmid, H. (2001). Konsum psychoaktiver Substanzen. In H. Schmid, E. N. Kuntsche & M. Delgrande (Eds.), *Anpassen, ausweichen, auflehnen? Fakten und Hintergründe zur psychosozialen Gesundheit und zum Konsum psychoaktiver Substanzen von Schülerinnen und Schülern* (pp. 347-391). Bern: Haupt.

King, A., Boyce, W. F., & King, M. A. (1999). *Trends in the health of canadian youth - La sante des jeunes, tendances au Canada*. Ottawa: Health Canada.

King, A., Wold, B., Smith, C. T., & Harel, Y. (1996). *The health of youth: a cross-national survey*. Copenhagen: World Health Organization. Regional Publications. European Series No. 69.

Lintonen, T., Rimpela, M., Vikat, A., & Rimpela, A. (2000). The effect of societal changes on drunkenness trends in early adolescence. *Health Education Research, 15*(3), 261-269.

Midanik, L. T. (1999). Drunkenness, feeling the effects and 5+ measures. *Addiction, 94*(6), 887-897.

Nic Gabhainn, S., & François, Y. (2000). Substance use. In C. Currie, K. Hurrelmann, W. Settertobulte, R. Smith & J. Todd (Eds.), *Health and health behaviour among young people* (pp. 97-114). Copenhagen: World Health Organization, Regional Office for Europe.

Rehm, J., & Gmel, G. (2000). Gaps and needs in international alcohol epidemiology. *Journal of Substance Use, 5*, 6-13.

Schmid, H. (1998). Female and male students' intention to accept illicit drugs as a function of their risk perception and risk taking. *Swiss Journal of Psychology, 57*(1), 47-56.

Schmid, H., ter Bogt, T., Godeau, E., Hublet, A., Dias, S. F., & Fotiou, A. (in press). Drunkenness among young people. A cross-national comparison. *Journal of Studies on Alcohol.*

Sells, C. W., & Blum, R. W. (1996). Current Trends in Adolescent Health. In R. J. DiClemente, W. B. Hansen & L. E. Ponton (Eds.), *Handbook of adolescent health-risk behaviour* (pp. 5-34). New York: Plenum Press.

Shope, J. T., Waller, P. F., & Lang, S. W. (1996). Alcohol-related predictors of adolescent driving: gender differences in crashes and offences. *Accident Analysis And Prevention, 28*(6), 755-764.

Windle, M., Shope, J. T., & Bukstein, O. (1996). Alcohol Use. In R. J. DiClemente, W. B. Hansen & L. E. Ponton (Eds.), *Handbook of adolescent health-risk behaviour* (pp. 115-160). New York: Plenum Press.

World Health Organisation. (2000). *International Guide for Monitoring Alcohol Consumption and Related Harm* (No. WHO/MSD/MSB/00.4): Department of Mental Health an Substance Dependence Noncommunicable Diseases and Mental Health Cluster.

Zador, P. L., Krawchuk, S. A., & Voas, R. B. (2000). Alcohol-related risk of driver fatalities and driver improvement in fatal crashes in relation to driver age and gender: An update using 1996 data. *Journal of Studies on Alcohol, 61*, 387-395.

7. AFFILIATION

Swiss Institute for the Prevention of Alcohol and Drug Problems (SIPA),
P.O. Box 870
CH-1001 Lausanne, Switzerland
Phone: + 41 21 3212953; Fax: + 41 21 3212940; e-mail: hschmid@sfa-ispa.ch

H.GARRETSEN & I. VAN DE GOOR

TOWARDS EVIDENCE-BASED POLICY

Key words: evidence-based procedures, evaluation of care, prevention and policy, effectiveness

To what extent are addiction care, prevention and policy evidence-based? Are activities and programs based on research results? Are the activities undertaken effective? Are new activities evaluated and if so, in such a way that their effectiveness can be solidly assessed? This chapter addresses these questions. Among other it is stated that the clinical sector, the cure, is more evidence-based than the not-clinical sector, the care and the prevention sectors. In these sectors activities are insufficiently evidence-based. Possible explanations for this are discussed. A closer co-operation between researchers and addiction care and prevention organisations is recommended as is the establishment of academic workplaces (like academic hospitals) in this sector.

1. INTRODUCTION

In how far is alcohol policy evidence based? (Evidence-based procedures are procedures that make conscious, explicit, and judicious use of the best available evidence when making decisions (Sackett, Rosenberg, Muir Gray, Haynes, Richardson, 1996). Do we learn from history? Do we study the effects of alcohol policy measures, also measures taken in the past or taken in other countries, in cultures with similar or with different drinking habits? Do we take the results of such studies into account in discussing new policies?

In this contemplative contribution, it will be argued that alcohol policy is often not evidence based in the sense that measures taken are proven effective. Still, much knowledge is available with regard to many possible policy measures, like measures concerning the availability of alcohol, the effects of tax and price policies, prevention programs, and so on. Also, it is possible to learn a lot if alcohol policy measures are compared with measures taken in related fields such as drug policy. Much knowledge is already available. It is possible and necessary to expand and renew this knowledge constantly by accompanying alcohol related events/alcohol policy measures by research. Many alcohol- related events take place with respect to (governmental) rules and regulations an with respect to educational and other efforts. Different actors who consciously or unconsciously are responsible for these events can be distinguished, such as local, regional, and national governments, alcohol producers, and pressure groups. Of course, it is only possible to gather new evidence and to learn from events when they are studied/evaluated in a valid way. Quite often, however, this is not the case. There are many reasons for this, including methodological reasons. It is not always possible to develop an adequate research

R. Müller and H. Klingemann (eds.),
From Science to Action? 100 Years Later - Alcohol Policies Revisited, 141–151.

design. However, especially in cases where it is known beforehand that an event is coming up (planned governmental policy measures, for example), it is possible to undertake methodologically sound research.

This contribution will address the following three topics: which alcohol policy measures are often used and are they evidence based, how to evaluate policy measures in a sound way, and what reasons can be distinguished for the lack of evidence-based policy-making.

2. FREQUENTLY USED ALCOHOL POLICY MEASURES AND THE EVIDENCE FOR THEIR EFFECTIVENESS

Alcohol policy is not usually directed at preventing every use of alcohol. In contrast to tobacco use, not every use is harmful; moderate alcohol use can have positive (health) effects, too. In the western world, alcohol policy is often directed towards the prevention of heavy drinking and the prevention of alcohol related problems. These problems can take several forms – addiction problems, health problems, social problems, and so on. In general, in alcohol policy, three approaches can be distinguished: supply reduction, demand reduction, and harm reduction. In supply reduction, the aim is to influence the supply of alcohol and to decrease the availability of alcohol. Often used measures are, for instance, age limits (restricting the availability for a population subgroup), increasing taxes/prices (restricting the financial availability), and measures restricting the availability by limiting the number of outlets, the opening hours, etcetera. Demand reduction aims at influencing the demand side. Education is of importance here. Programmes often are aimed at drinking norms, beliefs, and attitudes. The harm reduction approach is not directed to drinking in itself but to the prevention of alcohol related problems. Examples are related to alcohol use in traffic, to the use of toughened glasses in bars, etcetera.

With regard to *supply reduction,* a rich body of literature is available. A breakthrough is the publication of the so-called purple book: "Alcohol control policies in public health perspective" (Bruun et al., 1975). In this publication, 11 leading scientists state that a substantial increase in mean consumption is very likely to be accompanied by an increase in the prevalence of heavy users. The reverse is true, too– a lowering of the total consumption of alcohol is likely to be accompanied by a reduction in the prevalence of heavy users. The degree of overall availability of alcohol in a society seems to have an independent effect on the general level of alcohol consumption. Changes in the overall consumption of alcoholic beverages have a bearing on the health of the people in any society. With these conclusions, the control of alcohol availability becomes a public health issue. A few years later, these conclusions formed the background for the comprehensive study "Alcohol, Society and the State" (Makela, Room, Single, Sulkunen, Walsh, 1981). This major collaborative enterprise contains an international discussion of the post-war experiences (1950-1975) with regard to alcohol control measures in seven societies. In this new study, nothing was found that would require a revision of the basic conclusions of the purple book. In the years to come, the development of a burgeoning literature on the effects of alcohol control measures can be seen. Scientists like Skog and Lemmens elaborated on the question of in how far it is true that, when the average consumption in a society increases, the percentage of heavy drinkers increases even more (Lemmens, 1991). The importance of the so-called public health approach is again stressed by Edwards et al. (1994). Total prohibition is the most extreme form of restricting the availability of alcohol. It is commonly believed that the perhaps best known prohibition, the prohibition in the United States from 1916 onwards, has failed. However, this is not the case: the per capita consumption did fall, as did the prevalence rates of alcohol related problems like alcoholic liver cirrhosis (Goldstein & Kalant, 1990). Of course, major "side effects" occurred around illegal trade and associated crimes. This situation is more or less comparable with the present situation around illegal drugs like heroin and cocaine in many western countries. Less extreme instances of measures concerning the availability of alcohol which have been shown to have an effect in at least some countries/cultures involve, for example, changes in age limits, number of outlets, and prices. It can be concluded that much evidence is available with regard to the effectiveness of measures restricting the availability of alcohol (an extensive overview is given by Room, 2000).

In *demand reduction,* education is very important. Education programmes aimed at behavioural change are often based on social psychological models. Social learning theories, for example, reflect on processes in which beliefs, attitudes, and behaviours are taken over or learned from the environment (Akers & Cochran, 1985). The problem behaviour theory tries to explain why youngsters show problem behaviour. It argues that certain individuals are predisposed to adopt a range of problem behaviours because of particular personalities and beliefs (Jessor & Jessor, 1975; Wright, 2000). In the theory of reasoned action and in the theory of planned behaviour attitudes towards drinking, beliefs about drinking-norms, and (in the case of the theory of planned behaviour) self-efficacy, play an important role. It argues that people's behaviour can be accurately predicted by their stated intention to act in a certain way (Ajzen, 1985; 1988; Wright, 2000). These last theories appear to be important: in many European countries one tries to prevent heavy drinking and alcohol related problems by influencing beliefs and attitudes. In recent years, more and more attention has been paid to self-efficacy, to correcting perceived social norms, and to peer-led approaches (Wright, 2000).

Education programmes in schools, which are often based on these models, are important. Much research with regard to the effectiveness of educational (school based) approaches has been carried out but there is little evidence for substantial and lasting effects (Room, 2000; Wright, 2000; Reuter, 2001). Next to school programmes, mass-media campaigns are prevalent, however, these campaigns are generally insufficient to effect changes in attitudes and behaviour. It must be stated that a lack of effectiveness does not always imply that a measure should not be implemented. For example, a lack of evidence with regard to the effectiveness of educational programmes on behaviour does not mean that these programmes are useless. People have the moral right to be educated, and education programmes can play an important role in supporting other activities which, generally speaking, cannot rely on public popularity (education campaigns in order to legitimate other activities). Furthermore, campaigns may play a role in extending the knowledge/familiarity with the treatment sector (Garretsen, 2001) Specific forms of influencing the demand are, for example, "deterrence", (sanctions or incentives for behaviour) and provision/encouraging of alternative activities (like offering cheaper soft drinks). With regard to deterrence, for instance, drinking-driving legislation has been shown to be effective in changing drivers' behaviour. With regard to the provision of alternatives, no lasting effects on drinking behaviour have been found (Room, 2000).

Harm reduction tries to achieve a significant reduction in levels of alcohol problems (an extensive overview is given in Plant, Single, & Stockwell, 1997). The term harm reduction has been used for quite a long time already with regard to the policy on illegal drugs. Harm reduction is not directed towards the use of drugs/alcohol but towards reducing (health) risks related to this use (Garretsen, 2001). Harm reduction is not in conflict with the reduction of overall consumption as a measure to prevent alcohol problems (Plant et al., 1997). Harm reduction measures include, for instance, servers-interventions and responsible beverage service, creating safer bars, and all kind of measures with regard to drinking and driving. It has been proven possible to achieve marked reductions in levels of alcohol related problems, especially in the field of alcohol-impaired driving (Plant et al., 1997; Room, 2000).

The question "which alcohol policy measures are often used and are they evidence based" can be answered in two ways:

First, it can be observed that some alcohol policy measures have been studied a lot and others hardly at all (Room, 2000). Often, it is not known whether measures are effective or not. Also it is often too easy to apply measures, proven to be effective in one particular situation, in other situations. It is questionable whether measures proven to be effective in one situation can be applied easily in other contexts. The effects of measures vary in different cultural and situational conditions. Also, major changes over time occur: new drinking customs, for instance, emerge all the time. It is and will be necessary to evaluate policy measures regulary with sound research. In the next section of this contribution, attention is paid to the question of how to evaluate policy measures.

Second, the question whether alcohol policy measures are evidence based can be answered by stating that popular alcohol policy measures are not the most effective ones. Room, for decades already a leading scientist in this field and involved in many major publications in this area (Bruun et al., 1975; Makela et al., 1981; Edwards et al., 1994) states that approaches which are most popular with the general public and with politicians (like education and providing alternatives for drinking) are not the most effective ones. On the other hand, the most effective approaches (like taxes and regulating availability) are not the most popular ones (Room, 2000). In the last section of this contribution, attention is paid to the question of which reasons can be distinguished for this lack of evidence-based policy-making.

3. HOW TO EVALUATE POLICY MEASURES IN A SOUND WAY?

Quite often, alcohol policy measures are not evaluated in a sound way. The effects of measures are often determined by interpreting statistics. For example, the effect of a change in drunk-driving legislation may be measured by comparing police statistics before and after the new legislation. However, in this way, it is not possible to conclude for sure that changes are actually caused by this legislation (only). Changes in statistics can also be due to changes in police-efforts, changes in norms and values, etcetera. As another example, the effects of (school) prevention programmes may be measured by asking those involved (implementers and recipients) whether they were satisfied and whether they will change their behaviour. Such outcomes don't provide "proof"; in most cases, the majority of recipients claim to be satisfied with a programme and actual changes in behaviour are not measured.

What, then, is the sound way to evaluate policy measures? Before trying to answer this question, it is, of course, necessary to define very carefully which intended effects must be measured. For some questions, a process-evaluation appears to be the proper thing to do. However, when alcohol policy measures are to be evaluated for their effects on drinking behaviour or for the prevalence of alcohol related problems, activities such as those mentioned above and cross-sectional studies in general do not produce (enough) solid evidence. Generally, a research design with at least a pre- and post- measurement and a control-situation is required to establish whether observed changes can actually be attributed to the policy measure or intervention carried out. In health care research, randomised controlled trials (RCT's) and meta-analyses (combining the results of various studies with the aid of statistical methods) are often considered standard. Although their results never offer absolute certainty, these methods probably yield the most conclusive proof of the effectiveness of care activities, interventions, and programmes (Cook, Guyatt, Laupacis, Sackett, 1992). Ideally, in an RCT, randomised, double-blind research takes place: the recipients of an intervention are randomly assigned to the experimental and the control groups, and neither the researcher nor subject knows who is in which group. This type of research design is often applied in pharmaceutical research. In other fields, there are occasional application problems with this type of design for which solutions are increasingly being found, however. Problems arise when interventions cannot be properly randomised or blinded and when interventions are not directed at individuals but at groups.

The evaluation of heroin provision in the Netherlands is a good example of an intervention that cannot be blinded: subjects can tell immediately whether they have been given heroin or a placebo. Still, it appeared possible to set up an adequate, slightly adapted design. Concerning the use of RCT in the evaluation of alcohol policy measures, the problem of the intervention being geared at collectives such as countries, neighbourhoods, or schools instead of individuals needs specific attention. In such situations, community intervention trials (CIT-s) are increasingly being executed in which, rather than individuals, collectives such as cities and schools are distributed over the experimental and control situations. There is a great deal of debate (especially in the public health field) about the methodological pros and cons of CIT-s (Susser, 1995; Murray, 1995; Koepsell, Diehr, Cheadle, Kristal, 1995; Koepsell et al., 1992; Sansor-Fisher et al., 1996; Mackenbach, 1998; Tones, 2000) However, where the effectiveness of community interventions is at stake the CIT is seen by many as a standard, among other reasons because of the lack of better alternatives.

Observational designs, qualitative methods, and triangulation, in which the combination of various data sources and methods is proposed, are discussed as alternative methods that might provide more and better insight than RCT and CIT (Susser, 1995; De Haes, 2000; 2001; Cuijpers and Van Gageldonk, 2000; Nutbeam, 1996; Wright, 2000; Maso and Smaling, 1998; Tones, 2000; Nutbeam, 1999). Combining sources and methods as is done in triangulation is especially attractive to improve understanding. However, in the case of effect evaluation, triangulation appears not to be the panacea for all problems. Especially when information from various sources is contradictory, it is difficult to decide what will serve as the golden standard in such cases. In addition, there is also the so-called "judicial review": this is an assessment of proof by a "jury" on the basis of evidence obtained by triangulation of data, methods, and researchers (Tones, 2000). However, it can not serve as the new standard, since this method is also troubled by difficulties in objectivity.

However, it would seem that, in many cases, the most reliable and useful effect evaluations of policy measures can be obtained by combining "quantitative" effect research, such as RCT/CIT, with (more qualitative oriented) process evaluations. Besides evaluating for solid outcomes, or quantitative effects, it is necessary to obtain information on context and the entire progress of the process. Replication, for that matter, is only possible if there is sufficient information about the activity itself, about what was done and how, who was reached in what way, whether everything went according to plan or whether some things were adjusted as things progressed, etc. Process evaluation can provide this information.

Conversely, it follows from the above that information about the course of an activity is necessary but not sufficient. Process evaluation is useful and can generate new insights, but, by itself, it generally does not produce enough valid information about the effectiveness of care or prevention programmes (Garretsen & Van de Goor, 2002).

Whether or not it is always advisable to go for RCT/CIT in combination with process evaluation depends on many factors. Alcohol policy may benefit a lot from more and better insight into the effectiveness, or the outcomes, of different policy measures. This means, therefore, that more solid evidence must be produced. This does not mean, however, that it is always necessary to reach for the heavy and expensive means of RCT-s/CIT-s. New activities, for example, may be accompanied, in certain cases, by only non-experimental, observational research first. If such research then indeed indicates positive results, a randomised controlled trial with process evaluation can be carried out afterwards to produce incontrovertible evidence[1].

It should be avoided that the execution of RCT-s/CIT-s becomes a dogma. If the most far-reaching and often most expensive kind of evaluation research is not too swiftly resorted to, this may actually augment the readiness of those involved to evaluate activities. This leads to the third question raised in this contribution: what reasons can be distinghuished for the lack of evidence-based policy- making?

4. REASONS FOR A LACK OF EVIDENCE-BASED POLICY-MAKING

Reasons vary depending on the measure to be taken and, perhaps even more important, on the actors involved. To ask whether a government applies measures proven effective or evaluates a new alcohol law is a totally different question than to ask whether a prevention worker does or does not evaluate a prevention programme. However, it seems possible to make some general observations. Different issues are important: the actual wish to work evidence based, the structure of policy-making, and means and expertise.

- Perhaps the "real" goal one tries to achieve is not to decrease heavy drinking or the prevalence of alcohol related problems. A tax increase, for example, can be presented as a measure to decrease heavy drinking but, in fact, the real goal can be higher incomes for the state.
- One may wish not to evaluate one's own activities because, for example, one may have anxieties about the results and even more about one's continued existence as an organisation. When organisations wish to evaluate their own outcomes, they often confine themselves to executing formal performance assessments such as benchmarking, or informal performance assessments such as customer feedback and the like (Kenis, 2000).
- Also one may genuinely feel that the effectiveness of one's own work cannot be influenced. Here, it is possible to refer to the experience of "limited strategic space", meaning that organisations are often constricted by legal or political barriers, the employment situation, etcetera: they do not always have the scope to do what they wish to do. Knowledge of the effectiveness of products may then be a source of frustration rather than an incentive for improvement (Joldersma, Mouwen, Otto, Geurts, 2000) This is even more true when one feels that one does not have alternatives available.
- One may prefer one's work to be ideology based and not science based. Kenis (2000), for example, indicates that non-profit organisations may have other priorities or a different rationale for their working procedures: they may have a feeling they are "doing good work", in a general sense without necessarily having the results to show it. Or, something may be seen as evil or dangerous which must be combatted, and toughness, then, does not need an empirical justification (Reuter, 2001). In general, meaures proven to be effective may be unused because they conflict with competing values and ideologies. For that matter, it is important to realise that acceptable strategies often are already in place (Room, 2000).
- Furthermore the structure of policy-making seems to be important (Reuter, 2001). At the nationwide level, for instance, policy-making can be very

fractioned; many actors/departments may be involved and the responsibility may be shared and not always clear.

- Means are important, too. It costs money to check whether evidence is already available and to evaluate activities. The availability of funds plays a role: amongst providers of prevention programmes, for instance, it is not common practice to spend part of the budget on the scientific basis of their work, nor are they often expected to do so. If they actually do feel a need for a scientific basis, it is often impossible to allocate sufficient funds to it.
- Finally, the lack of use of sufficient evidence-based procedures can be due to the lack of expertise on the part of the policy-makers, prevention workers etcetera. One may feel that the results of their work cannot be easily measured. Also, outcome evaluation requires specific expertise, as regards both the choice of research design and the implementation of the research results themselves. It is assumed that this might be one of the major reasons for the lack of a scientific basis (Garretsen & Van de Goor, 2002).

How to change this situation? The factors mentioned above are not easy to deal with. Still, it must be possible to promote a climate in which it is more stimulating to work evidence-based.

In general, it seems to be advisable to develop standards and protocols and to make knowledge readily available using electronic databases (like the Cochrane library on the field of medical problems). However, this is a necessary but not a sufficient precondition. Knowledge also needs to be translated into good practice, and is required for setting up one's own evaluation activities. Many policy-makers and prevention workers would benefit from closer contacts with researchers. Researchers, in turn, would also benefit from more intensive co-operation, as this would allow them to test theoretical concepts and hypotheses in practice and herewith adapt and refine these concepts and hypotheses. In certain situations, it is clear that evaluation research needs to be external and as independent as possible, and that closer alliances between policy-makers and researchers would be frowned upon. However, in many cases, improved communication between researchers and providers is to be recommended (Nutbeam, 1996; 1998). Stepping up personal contacts may be the best guarantee for a better scientific basis of (preventive) services. It must be made more attractive for policy-makers and prevention workers to work in evidence-based ways; they should be enabled to relate to research. Besides the subject of the research and the way in which researchers publish their research results, other kinds of communication may be helpful in achieving this: for example, joint meetings for policy-makers/prevention workers and researchers. This may help the first to feel more involved in research and allow researchers to get to know the gaps in knowledge. A tried and tested way to involve researchers and interventionists in structural co-operation is the establishment of academic workplaces, such as can be found in university hospitals. Not only with regard to addiction care but also with regard to alcohol-policy, a structural relation with universities would be beneficial.

Affiliations

Henk Garretsen is affiliated as professor and Ien van de Goor is affiliated as senior researcher at the Tranzo Research Group, Tilburg University and at the Addiction Research Institute, Universities of Maastricht, Nijmegen, Rotterdam and Tilburg.

NOTES

[1] A more extensive overview of the pros and cons of evaluation of policy measures and community interventions can be found in Garretsen, H.F.L.& Van de Goor, L.A.M. (2002) Evidence-based addiction care and prevention: Reducing the gap between research and practice (Paris, Presentation 28th Annual Alcohol Epidemiology Symposium Kettil Bruun Society).

REFERENCES

Ajzen, I. (1988). *Attitudes, personality and behavior.* Homewood: Dorsey Press.

Ajzen, I. (1985). From decisions to actions: A theory of planned behavior. In J. Kuhl, & J. Beckman (Eds), *In action-control: From cognition to behavior* (pp. 11-39). New York: Springer.

Akers, R.L., & Cochran, J.K. (1985). Adolescent marihuana use: A test of three theories of deviant behavior. *Deviant Behavior, 6*, 323-346.

Brouwer de Koning, J. (2001). De les van Rotterdam (The lesson from Rotterdam). *Mediator, 12*, 3.

Bruun, K., Edwards, G., Lumio, M., Makela, K., Pan, L., Popham, R.E., Room, R., Schmidt, W., Skog, O.J., Sulkunen, P., Osterberg, E. (1975). *Alcohol Control Policies in public health perspective.* Helsinki: The Finnish Foundation for Alcohol Studies/ WHO Europe, Addiction Research Foundation Ontario.

Cook, D.J., Guyatt, G.H., Laupacis, A., Sackett, D. (1992). Rules of evidence and clinical recommendations on the use of anti-thrombotic agents. *Chest, 102*, 305-311; *Chest, 105*, 647.

Cuijpers, P., van Gageldonk, A. (2000). Systematische review-studies en de onwil om effecten van drugpreventie aan te tonen (Systematic reviews and the reluctance to show effects of drug education). *Tijdschrift voor Gezondheidswetenschappen, 78*, 511-513.

Edwards, G., Anderson, P., Babor, T.F., Casswell, S., Ferrence, R., Giesbrecht, N., Godfrey, C., Holder, H., Lemmens, P., Makela, K., Midanik, L., Norstrom, T., Osterberg, E., Romelsjo, A., Room, R., Simpura, J., Skog, O.J. (1994). *Alcohol policy and the public good.* Oxford: University Press.

Garretsen, H.F.L. (2001). Going Dutch? Successes and problems of drugs policies in the Netherlands. *Eurohealth, 7*, 8-10.

Garretsen, H.F.L. (2001). Dutch Alcohol Policy Developments: The last decades and present state of affairs. *Medicine and Law, 20*, 301-311.

Garretsen, H.F.L. & Van de Goor, L.A.M. (2002). *Evidence-based addiction care and prevention: Reducing the gap between research and practice.* Paris: Presentation 28th Annual Alcohol Epidemiology Symposium Kettil Bruun Society.

Goldstein, A. & Kalant, H. (1990). Drug policy: Striking the right balance. *Science, 249*,1513-1521.

De Haes, W.F.M. (2001). Aan welke eisen moet een reviewstudie voldoen? Een Repliek (Which standards apply for review studies?). *Tijdschrift voorGezondheidswetenschappen, 79*, 58-59.

De Haes, W. (2000). Het nut van review-studies voor gedragsgerichte interventies: de casus van alcohol- en drugvoorlichting (The use of review studies for behavioural interventions: The case of alcohol and drug education), redactioneel. *Tijdschrift voor Gezondheidswetenschappen, 78*, 329-330.

Jessor, R. & Jessor, S. (1975). Adolescent development and the onset of drinking, a longitudinal study. *Journal of Studies on Alcohol, 36*, 27-51.

Joldersma, F., Mouwen, C.A.M., Otto, M.M., Geurts, J.L.A. (2000). *Strategisch Management voor non-profitorganisaties (Strategic management for non-profit organisations).* Assen: Van Gorcum.

Kenis, P. (2000). *Success and failure in the non-profit sector: How to judge?* Florence: Paper presented at the conference The new welfare mix in Europe: what role for the third sector?

Koepsell, T.D., Diehr, P.H., Cheadle, A., Kristal, A. (1995). Invited commentary: Symposium on community intervention trials. *American Journal of Epidemiology, 142*, 594-599.

Koepsell, T.D., Wagner, E.H., Cheadle, A.C., Patrick, D.L., Martin, D.C., Diehr, P.H., Perrin, E.B., Kristal, A.B., Allan-Andrilla, C.H., Dey, L.J. (1992). Selected methodological issues in evaluating community-based health promotion and disease prevention programs. *Annual Review on Public Health, 13*, 31-57.

Lemmens, P.H.H.M. (1991). *Measurement and Distribution of Alcohol Consumption* (dissertation). Maastricht: University of Maastricht.

Mackenbach, J.P. (1988). Beyond RCT? CIT! *Tijdschrift voor Gezondheidswetenschappen,76*, 279-281.

Makela, K., Room, R., Single, E., Sulkunen, P., Walsh, B. (1981). *Alcohol, Society and the State Part I and II.* Toronto: Addiction Research Foundation.

Maso, I., Smaling, A. (1998). *Kwalitatief onderzoek: praktijk en theorie (Qualitative research: theory and practice).* Amsterdam: Boom.

Murray, D.M. (1995). Design and analysis of community trials: Lessons from the Minnesota Heart Health Program. *American Journal of Epidemiology, 142*, 569-575.

Nutbeam, D. (1996). Achieving best practice in health promotion: Improving the fit between research and practice. *Health Education Research, 11*, 317-326.

Nutbeam,D. (1998). Evaluating health promotion-Progress, problems and solutions. *Health promotion international, 13*, 27-44.

Nutbeam, D. (1999). Evaluatie van oorzaak en gevolg in gezondheidsbevorderings-projecten, aanpassing van onderzoeksmethoden aan interventiemethoden (Evaluation of cause and effect in health promotion projects, adaptation of research methods to intervention methods). *Tijdschrift voor Gezondheidswetenschappen, 77*, 15-23.

Plant, M., Single, E. & Stockwell, T. (1997). *Alcohol, minimizing the harm: What works.* London/New York: Free Association Books.

Reuter, P. (2001). Editorail: Why does research have so little impact on American drug policy? *Addiction, 96*, 373 -376.

Room, R. (2001). *Preventing alcohol problems: Popular approaches are ineffective, effective approaches are political impossible*. Scheveningen: Presentation National conference on alcohol policy, The Netherlands.

Sackett, D.L., Rosenberg, W.M.C., Muir Gray, J.A., Brian Haynes, R.B., Scott Richardson, W. (1996). Editorial: Evidence-based medicine, what it is and what it isn't. *British Medical Journal, 312*, 71-2.

Sanson-Fisher, R., Redman, S., Hancock, L., Halpin, S., Clark, P., Schefield, M., Burton, R., Hensley, M., Gibberd, R., Reid, A., Walsh, R. (1996). Developing methodologies for evaluating community-wide health promotion. *Health Promotion International, 11*, 227-236.

Susser, M. (1995). Editorial: the Tribulations of trials-intervention in communities. *American Journal of Public Health, 85*, 156-158.

Tones, K. (2000). Evaluating health promotion: A tale of three errors. *Patient education and counselling, 39*, 227-236.

Wright, L. (2000). Evidence-based alcohol education in schools. In M. Plant, D. Cameron (Eds.), *The Alcohol Report* (pp. 206-234). London: Free Association books.

ROBIN ROOM

WHAT IF WE FOUND THE MAGIC BULLET?

Ideological and ethical constraints on biological alcohol research and its application

Key words: biomedical research, disease concept of alcoholism, abstinence goal, medications, liver transplants, patient compliance

Abstract. Funding for biomedical research on alcohol is justified in terms of the eventual development of pharmacotherapies for alcoholism treatment. Three medications have so far been approved: disulfiram, an aversive substance with a 50-year history, not much used now because of patient noncompliance; and naltrexone and acamprosate, which are now thought to be mildly effective. Ideological and practical limits on the development of medications include the focus on "alcoholism", rather than on reducing the harm from heavy drinking, and the requirement of abstinence as a goal. These constraints have been argued to limit the effectiveness of naltrexone, and have diverted attention from such substances as propylthiouracil with promise to prevent liver deterioration, and from the success of liver transplantation in reducing alcohol-related deaths. Patient compliance will be a problem with any medication that deters drinking, or takes the pleasure out of it, particularly when the treatment is coerced, as much alcohol treatment is, formally or informally. In light of this analysis, it is hard to imagine a medication (other than another psychoactive substance) which would be both politically acceptable and effective. There is a need for ethical consideration prior to the advent of such future developments as a preventive vaccine interrupting the action of alcohol on the brain. Refocusing on biomedical means of reducing health harms from alcohol would be a useful path forward.

THE RISE OF BIOMEDICAL RESEARCH FUNDING, AND ITS JUSTIFICATION

These are heady days for biological research in the alcohol field, particularly in the U.S. In 2001, well over half of NIAAA's research spending was in this category (Midanik, 2002). Nor is American investment in biological alcohol research limited to the federal government. The Gallo Center in the San Francisco area, originally funded with $6.5 million seed money from the cofounder of the world's biggest wine company, received $143 million from the state of California for a 1998-2003 "Manhattan project" studying the biological causes and treatment of alcoholism (Harper, 2001).

There is no doubt that biomedical research has contributed new knowledge and understanding of the biological side of alcohol issues. But the justification for the

R. Müller and H. Klingemann (eds.),
From Science to Action? 100 Years Later - Alcohol Policies Revisited, 153–162.

investment in research is not just in terms of improving the stock of human knowledge. The fundamental justification is in terms of a cure -- of medications or other physical interventions which will reduce problems of alcohol. "The goal posts are to have drugs that are in trials", as Kirk Wilhelmsen, a laboratory director at the Gallo Center, put it concerning the Center's goals for 2003. "I'm fully expecting ... to redefine alcoholism based on the underlying biological process and what it is about alcoholism that's inherited. If there's a gene that's involved, there's a molecule that's involved, and a drug that can be developed for that" (Harper, 2001). At the outset of the steepest rise in NIAAA's spending on neuroscience research, Enoch Gordis, its director, stated the rationale this way:

> Developing effective pharmacotherapies for alcoholism treatment is a top priority of alcohol research. Doing so depends on neuroscientists' continuing elucidation of how alcohol acts on the brain to produce the fundamental phenomena of alcoholism -- tolerance, withdrawal, impaired control over drinking, and craving -- and how these phenomena can be interrupted or controlled. (Gordis, 1996)

MEDICATIONS FOR ALCOHOL PROBLEMS: THE CURRENT SITUATION

In terms of medications for alcohol dependence, the cupboard presently is not quite bare, but it is not very full. Discussions of medications in current use for alcohol cases usually confine themselves to three: disulfiram (antabuse), naltrexone and acamprosate.

Disulfiram, which has been around for 50 years, is basically an aversive drug. By interfering with the process of metabolization of alcohol, it makes drinking uncomfortable and presumably something to be avoided. But the big problem with disulfiram is "patient compliance": that alcoholic patients do not continue taking it regularly. To some extent, this can be overcome by implanting the disulfiram tablet under the patient's skin. A comparative study of the cost-effectiveness of different treatments ranks "oral disulfiram" quite low in effectiveness, but "disulfiram implants" among the top four treatment modalities (Finney and Monahan, 1996). Chick (2001) comments that "this is seldom used now, partly because the active drug was often not detectable in blood after about 2 weeks". However, recent news reports on a famous English ex-soccer player's liver transplant noted that for more than a year prior to the operation he had had surgically implanted disulfiram tablets; his doctor reported that "he found the implant treatment that he has had a great help over the last year" (Wilson, 2002).

Naltrexone and acamprosate both came to fore as treatments for alcohol problems in the 1990s, with naltrexone promoted primarily by U.S. champions and acamprosate primarily by Europeans. By 1996, "the development of naltrexone in the United States and acamprosate in Europe" was being hailed as "an important convergence of neurosciences and clinical research" (Gordis, 1996).

Naltrexone has been thought to reduce the rewarding effects of drinking, and acamprosate to reduce craving or other cues for relapse (Chick, 2001). However, in a familiar pattern, the estimated effectiveness of each drug has tended to decline in the later studies (Kranzler & Van Kirk, 2001), and recent large controlled trails, finding no significant effect, have put the effectiveness of each of these drugs seriously in question (Chick et al., 2000 for acamprosate; Krystal et al., 2001 for naltrexone). A recent meta-analysis concluded that "naltrexone may be mildly effective for prevention of relapse to heavy drinking, and that acamprosate may be mildly effective for maintaining abstinence", although "the sizes of the effects were small". (Hopkins et al., 2002).

THE LIMITS OF WHAT "COUNTS" AND WHAT IS ACCEPTABLE

No doubt the enormous investment in biomedical research, particularly in the U.S., will bring some new candidate medications to the fore. But the experience of the recent past suggests that the search for a magic bullet is constrained not only by the fiendish complications of alcohol's actions in the body, but also by ideological and practical limits.

The focus on "alcoholism"

First, the main emphasis in the search for a magic bullet is on medications that will deal with "alcoholism", as much of this literature persists in calling it. In NIAAA-sponsored research meetings, one gets a sense of a hierarchy of prestige among the biomedical researchers. The highest prestige is given to studying the biology of "the fundamental phenomena of alcoholism -- tolerance, withdrawal, impaired control over drinking, and craving", as Gordis put it. Studying the biology of alcohol's effects on body systems or organs -- that is, studying the health effects of heavy drinking -- is accepted as part of the field, but is relegated to a second rank. Researchers on alcohol's health effects may be very distinguished in their role as heart or immune-system researchers, but in the alcohol field their work is regarded as secondary.

This makes great difficulties for biological researchers, because it means that they are trying to study a condition which is polymorphous and not fully reducible to the biological stratum. "Craving", for instance, sounds like something definable and measurable, but researchers have had great difficulty pinning down a concept which has long since escaped into general cultural use, and which functions mainly as an apparent explanation for the otherwise inexplicable (Room, forthcoming). Drummond et al. (2000) conclude that "opinion remains divided on the importance of craving, on one hand being seen as the key substrate of addiction, and on the other hand, a redundant epiphenomenon. The term 'craving' continues to be used in different ways to describe different phenomena".

Even more problematic for biological research is the main technical term for the object of study, alcohol dependence or the alcohol dependence syndrome. There are six criteria for this in the International Classification of Diseases (ICD-10). Two of them -- tolerance and withdrawal -- can be directly measured biologically in animal models and in humans. The other four criteria all have elements of human cognitions or desires built into them, so that they cannot be captured by physical measurement of humans, and any animal model is operating by hypothesized analogy rather than direct measurement. Furthermore, dependence is defined by satisfying any three of the six criteria, so that no case can be defined solely on direct biological measurement, and some cases will satisfy neither of the directly measurable criteria (Room, 1998).

The target for a magic bullet for "alcoholism" is thus in considerable part obscured from view at the level of biology. The focus on finding interventions for "alcoholism" also turns attention away from some outstanding accomplishments of biomedical research. These are interventions which diminish the health harms from drinking. In Sweden nowadays, between 500 and 550 people die each year from liver cirrhosis as the underlying cause, with alcohol involved in well over half of the cases (CAN 2002). But each year about 100 Swedes are saved from death by liver transplant operations, some of which are undoubtedly alcohol cases (I will return later to why there are not more). Liver transplant surgery, including surgery on alcohol cases, can legitimately be regarded as a triumph of biomedical research in reducing the harm from drinking.

The requirement of a goal of abstinence

The focus on medications for alcoholism/alcohol dependence carries with it, particularly in the United States, the requirement that abstinence be the goal of treatment. Efforts by psychologists and others to gain acceptance of controlled drinking as a goal have met determined resistance in the U.S. (Roizen, 1987), and NIAAA and most of the clinical world have long accepted abstinence as the formal outcome goal. Whether it is alcohol, nicotine or opiate addiction which involved, medical treatment is often conditioned on abstinence (Rehm et al., 2003).

This does not mean that treatment outcome is measured only in terms of continuous abstinence (imposing such a strict criterion would bring long-term success rates down to about 7% -- Room, 1980), but it does mean that a medication is only seen as suitable if it enforces or helps to sustain abstinence.

Naltrexone and the abstinence standard

Sinclair has argued strongly that it is this requirement of abstinence in conjunction with the medication which has rendered naltrexone relatively ineffective in many of the treatment trials. "We found that naltrexone was not effective in patients who were asked to abstain from alcohol but was effective [in preventing binges] in those not required to abstain" (Sinclair et al., 2002; see also Sinclair, 2001). However, the ideological commitment to the abstinence goal remains strong in the U.S. (Room, 2000), as in some other societies, and it is presently inconceivable that Sinclair's clinical paradigm will be widely adopted. Thus, to be acceptable as a magic bullet for alcoholism, a medication must enforce or reinforce abstinence.

Liver transplants and the abstinence standard

The same insistence on abstinence can be seen at work in present practice with regard to liver transplants. Common practice is to require 6 months abstinence prior to the transplant, a requirement which in one sample excluded over one-quarter of alcoholic liver disease (ALD) candidates from listing for transplant (Karman et al., 2001). Beyond this, lifetime abstinence is demanded after the transplant. However, studies comparing the survival records of alcoholic liver disease (ALD) with other liver disease transplant cases find similar survival rates, although from one-third to more than a half of ALD cases do at least some drinking, and quite a few of them some heavy drinking, after the transplant (Fireman & Rabkin, 2001; Pereira et al., 1997). But despite these results, the search continues in the literature for pre-transplant measures which will predict "alcoholism relapse" after transplant, presumably so that those with a high score on the measure can be denied a transplant (DiMartini et al., 1998). There are even articles in the medical literature explicitly supporting ALD patients getting a lower priority for liver transplants not on medical but on moral grounds (Glannon, 1998).

PTU, the alcoholism focus and the abstinence standard

It is my hypothesis that the combination of the devaluing of medications other than for alcoholism and of the requirement of an abstinence goal lies behind the failure of the field to pick up another promising medication. Propylthiouracil (PTU) is an established thyroid drug, an antioxidant, which was proposed as a treatment which would prevent further deterioration of the liver for those with alcoholic liver disease. A small randomized double-blind controlled study was successfully carried out (Orrego et al., 1979), followed by a full-blown longer trial, also showing good results (Orrego et al., 1994). The second full clinical trial required for the use of PTU for this purpose to be officially listed was considered in various quarters, including the U.S. Veterans Administration, but never carried out. The Addiction Research Foundation of Ontario, which had sponsored the trials, held a consensus conference of leading liver researchers in 1993. Those present agreed on the desirability of another trial, but none ever eventuated. And there the matter sits, apart from a couple more animal studies supporting the idea that PTU can prevent liver failure (e.g., Bruck et al., 1998).

As I sat in the 1993 conference, the issue of why PTU had never been picked up by NIAAA or other research agencies nagged at me. Part of the explanation may be that PTU helps the liver, rather than treating the alcoholism. But more important, I came to feel, was the fact that PTU was helpful for the livers of those who continued to drink (about 90% of those in the large trial drank at some time during the trial period), and perhaps particularly helpful for those with the most deteriorated livers. In the orthodox perspective of American alcohol treatment providers, this made PTU's action undesirable: that a drinker's liver was deteriorating is viewed by them as one of the main spurs to come into alcoholism treatment. In the larger society, also, there is sufficient moral opprobrium on heavy drinking that there would probably be little support for the idea of a medication which would allow the heavy drinker to continue drinking without dying.

If my analysis is correct, the PTU experience suggests that medications that would reduce the harm from drinking are unwelcome, since they tend to allow at least some drinking (even at a reduced level) to continue. Social attitudes about alcoholism not only require that medications for alcoholism enforce or reinforce abstinence, but also disfavour medications that would reduce the harm from continued drinking.

THE PROBLEM OF PATIENT COMPLIANCE, AND WHAT LIES BEHIND IT

As already noted, patient compliance is a big problem with disulfiram. It is not only with alcohol patients that doctors have trouble getting the patient to take the medication. But the problem is particularly pressing in alcohol treatment for a medication that deters drinking, or for that matter that takes the pleasure out of it. Even "motivated" clients in alcohol treatment are often of two minds, and subject to changes of mind, about leaving the life they have become used to. And many clients are not in treatment of their own choice. In a sample of those entering treatment in a California county, 41% of cases had received an ultimatum to enter treatment from at least one source (Polcin & Weisner, 1999).

One root of the problem of "patient compliance" in the alcohol field, then, is the fact that many patients are in treatment against their will. This is a situation which is outside the normative expectations of those attracted into the "helping professions". Normatively, for instance, the doctor gives advice to the patient, but must defer to the patient's wishes, and the treatment must be with the patient's informed consent. The medical and other professions deal with the disjunction between this normative frame of reference and the reality of alcohol treatment in various ways. At the level of the individual practitioner, one frequent solution is to escape the situation as soon as possible. Specialities involving coerced clients tend to have low status in the helping professions, and in some circumstances have chronic difficulties recruited competent practitioners.

A more noxious alternative is to impose on the unwilling clients punitive or dehumanizing regimes. In this regard, earlier generations of those committed to biologized solutions to alcohol problems have much to answer for, in the record of lobotomies and other psychosurgery (White, 1998:87-95). A recent report from St. Petersburg, Russia of a series of 335 operations on drug users between 1999 and 2002 in which part of the brain was removed demonstrate that this impulse for treating addiction has not yet entirely disappeared. When the operations were halted by the authorities, administrators of the institute conducting the operations appealed against the decision. "Until now we have had no complaints about the operation," said the institute's deputy director. "As with any medical procedure, we do not guarantee 100% success" (Walsh, 2002).

A common response of members of the helping professions to the coercion often built into the therapeutic situation is to ignore its reality as much as possible. The client's resistance to treatment is redefined as "denial", and denial, indeed, often gets built into the definition of the disorder (ASAM, 1990). But the result of this is considerable therapeutic frustration: "the addict's compulsive pursuit of disease over health defies many of the basic tenets of our profession and provokes conflict in us" (Sellers, 2002).

WOULD A MAGIC BULLET BE ACCEPTABLE?

In terms of the experience so far of medications and other biological interventions, then, it is hard to imagine a medication which would be both politically acceptable, at least in the United States, and effective. The medication would have to be directed against alcohol dependence or such crucial components as craving; it would have to enforce or work in conjunction with abstinence; and it would have to be attractive enough to the client that there would be sufficient compliance for it to be effective. It is hard to imagine a medication, other than another psychoactive substance, that would fit these requirements.

LOOKING TO THE FUTURE

By and large, the medications which have been in use so far would potentially have application to any person whose drinking it is desired to affect, though in practice they seem to have been used only on persons identified as having a problem with their drinking. However, we must expect in the future biological interventions and medications which are much more specifically targeted, on the basis of genetic testing and identification. A substantial part of the current biological research is directed towards research into genetic factors relevant to alcohol dependence, and sooner or later a genetically-specific medication or intervention will be put forward. Such a medication or intervention might be used not only for those who already have an alcohol problem but as a preventive measure for persons identified as genetically at high risk of such a problem.

Such developments will raise new and contentious issues about the ethics of treatment, and about the ethics of biological testing and identification in the first place, with the attendant risks of stigmatization and discrimination against those identified. The same sort of issues would also be raised if some kind of preventive "vaccine" is developed that interrupts the action of alcohol on the brain, as is being studied for cocaine. Hall and Carter (2002) have recently considered and discussed the substantial ethical issues which are raised by a cocaine vaccine. It is time to begin the public discussion of these issues now, before the medications arrive.

CONCLUSIONS

1. There has been a great increase in biological research on alcohol, but it has so far yielded a rather modest harvest of biological therapies.

2. In part, this has been because one specific area has been privileged: the search for cures for alcoholism/alcohol dependence, a condition which is defined in terms which are disjunctive and not directly measurable in biological terms. The privileging of the search for a breakthrough on alcoholism/alcohol dependence means that tangible advances in other parts of the biological arena, such as liver transplantation for alcoholic liver disease, draw too little attention.

3. In part, also, the search for and application of biological interventions to reduce alcohol problems have been handicapped by the insistence that abstinence is the only acceptable goal, and the only condition in which the interventions should be applied. With naltrexone, there is some evidence that a useful medication may be already on the scene, but we refuse to apply it in the terms on which it might best work.

4. Many clients coming to treatment for alcohol problems are coerced, and ambivalent at best about giving up drinking. Compliance with medication regimes is thus a special problem, particularly if the regime enforces abstinence. Compliance is likely to be more common with medications which reduce the harm from drinking without necessarily reducing the drinking. Such medications are within reach of reality, but are given little attention since they conflict with the abstinence standard for those in treatment.

5. New medications on the horizon, including those deriving from genetic research, will raise new ethical issues which need prior public discussion. However, so long as the present ideological constraints remain in place, they too are likely to have limited effectiveness.

6. A useful path forward would be to abandon the privileging of alcoholism/alcohol dependence as the main target for biological research and therapeutic intervention, and to turn the formidable talents of biological alcohol researchers loose on developing medications aimed specifically at reducing particular physical or psychological harms from drinking.

Centre for Social Research on Alcohol and Drugs
Stockholm University, Sveaplan
106 91 Stockholm, Sweden

NOTE

Revised from a paper presented at a conference hosted by the Swiss Institute for the Prevention of Alcohol and Drug Problems, AFrom Science to Action? 100 Years Later -- Alcohol Policies Revisited@, Bern,

Switzerland, 28-29 October, 2002.

REFERENCES

ASAM (1990) The definition of alcoholism. Approved by Board of Directors, American Society of Addiction Medicine, 25 February. http://www.asam.org/ppol/Definition%20of%20Alcoholism.htm

Bruck, R., Oren, R., Shirin, H., Aeed, H., Papa, M., Matas, Z., Zaidel, L., Avni, Y. & Halpern, Z. (1998) Hypothyroidism minimizes liver damage and improves survival in rats with thioacetamide induced fulminant hepatic failure. *Hepatology* 27:1013-20.

CAN (2002) *Drogutvecklingen i Sverige: Rapport 2002* (Drug developments in Sweden: Report for 2002). Stockholm: Centralförbundet för alkohol- och narkotikaupplysning, Report No. 68.

Chick, J. (2001) Pharmacological treatments. Pp. 541-555 in Nick Heather, Timothy J. Peters & Tim Stockwell, eds., *International Handbook of Alcohol Dependence and Problems*. Chichester, etc.: John Wiley & Sons.

Chick, J., Howlett, H., Morgan, M.Y. & Ritson, B. (2000) United Kingdom Multicentre Acamprosate Study (UKMAS): a 6-month prospective study of acamprosate versus placebo in preventing relapse after withdrawal from alcohol. *Alcohol and Alcoholism* 35:176-187.

DiMartini, A., Khera, G., Yates, W.R., Irish, W., Magill, J. & Fitzgerald, M.G. (1998) Use of a high-risk alcohol relapse scale in evaluating liver transplant candidates. *Psychosomatics* 39:218-219.

Drummond, D.C., Litten, R.Z., Lowman, C. & Hunt, W.A. (2000) Craving research: future directions. *Addiction* 95 (Supplement 2):S247-S255.

Finney, J.W. & Monahan, S.C. (1996) The cost-effectiveness of treatment for alcoholism: a second approximation. *Journal of Studies on Alcohol* 57:229-243.

Fireman, M. & Rabkin, J.M. (2001) Outcome of liver transplantation in patients with alcohol and other chemical dependence. *Psychosomatics* 42:172-173.

Glannon, W. (1998) Responsibility, alcoholism, and liver transplantation. *Journal of Medicine and Philosophy* 23:31-49.

Gordis, E. (1996) Neuroscience research and medications development B a commentary. In: "Neuroscience Research and Medications Development", *Alcohol Alert* No. 33. Rockville: NIAAA. http://ww.niaaa.nih.gov/publications/aa33.htm

Hall, W. & Carter, L. (2002) Ethical issues in using a cocaine vaccine to treat and prevent cocaine dependence. Brisbane: Office of Public Policy and Ethics, Institute of Molecular Bioscience, University of Queensland.

Harper, W. (2001) Strange brew: will there ever be a cure for alcoholism? And why is wine tycoon Ernest Gallo spending millions trying to find out? *East Bay Express,* August 1. http://www.eastbayexpress.com/issues/2001-08-01/feature.html/1/index.html

Hopkins, J.S., Grabutt, J.C., Poole, C.L., West, S.L. & Carey, T.S. (2002) Naltrexone and acamprosate: meta-analysis of two medical treatments for alcoholism. Presented at the annual meeting of the Research Society on Alcoholism, San Francisco, June 28-July 3. Abstract in *Alcoholism: Clinical and Experimental Research* 26(5) Supplement:130A.

Karman, J.F., Sileri, P., Kamuda, D., Cicalese, L, Ratselli, C., Wiley, T.E., Layden, T.J. & Benedetti, E. (2001) Risk factors for failure to meet listing requirements in liver transplant candidates with alcoholic cirrhosis. *Transplantation* 71:1210-1213.

Kranzler, H.R. & Van Kirk, H.R. (2001) Efficacy of naltrexone and acamprosate for alcoholism treatment: a meta-analysis. *Alcoholism: Clinical and Experimental Research* 25:1335-1341.

Krystal, J.H., Cramer, J.A., Krol, W.F., Kirk, G.F. & Rosenheck, R.A. (2001) Naltrexone in the treatment of alcohol dependence. *New England Journal of Medicine* 345:1734-1739.

Midanik, L. (2002) The biomedicalization of alcohol research in the U.S.: the new wave. Presented at the 28th annual meeting of the Kettil Bruun Society for Social and Epidemiological Research on Alcohol, Paris, France, June 2-7.

Orrego, H., Kalant, H. & Israel, Y. (1979) Effect of short-term therapy with propylthiouracil in patients with alcoholic liver disease. *Gastroenterology* 76:105-115. Orrego, H., Blake, J.E., Blendis, L.M., Compton, K.V., Volpe, R. & Israel, Y. (1994) Long-term treatment of alcoholic liver disease with propylthiouracil: Part 2. Influence of drop-out rates and of continued alcohol consumption in a clinical trial. *Journal of Hepatology* 20:343-349.

Pereira, S.P., Muiesan, P., Howard, L., Rela, M., Heaton, N. & Williams, R. (1997) Long-term survival and quality of life after liver transplantation for alcoholic liver disease. *Gut* 41:(Suppl. 3):A78.

Polcin, D.L. & Weisner, C. (1999) Factors associated with coercion in entering treatment for alcohol problems. *Drug and Alcohol Dependence* 54:63-68.

Rehm, J., Fischer, B., Hayden, E. & Room, R. (2003) Abstinence ideology and somatic treatment for addicts – ethical considerations. *Addiction Research and Theory* 11:287-293.

Roizen, R. (1987) The great controlled-drinking controversy. Pp. 245-279 in Marc Galanter (ed.), *Recent Developments in Alcoholism*, Vol. 5. New York: Plenum. http://www.roizen.com/ron/cont-dri.htm

Room, R. (1980) New curves in the course. *British Journal of Addiction* 75:351-360.

Room, R. (1998) Alcohol and drug disorders in the International Classification of Diseases: a shifting kaleidoscope, *Drug and Alcohol Review* 17:305-317.

Room, R. (2000) Rör inte helnykterhetsprincipen! Ny drabbingar i USA (Abstinence as the only treatment goal: new U.S. battles) *Nordisk Alkohol- och Narkotikatidskrift* 17:149-151. In English at: http://www.stakes.fi/nat/nat00/0300room.htm

Room, R. (forthcoming) The cultural framing of addiction. *Janus Head*, in press.

Sellers, B. (2002) Conflicting social forces impede addiction treatment. *Psychiatric News* 37(15): 12, August 2. http://pn.psychiatryonline.org/cgi/content/full/37/15/12

Sinclair, J.D. (2001) Evidence about the use of naltrexone and for different ways of using it in the treatment of alcoholism. *Alcohol and Alcoholism* 36:2-10.

Sinclair, J.D., Alho, H. & Shinderman, M. (2002) [letter to the editor] *New England Journal of Medicine* 346:1330.

Walsh, N.P. (2002) Russia bans brain surgery on drug addicts, *Guardian* (London) August 9. http://www.guardian.co.uk/international/story/0,3604,771463,00.html

White, W.L. (1998) *Slaying the Dragon: The History of Addiction Treatment and Recovery in America*. Bloomington, Ill.: Chestnut Health Systems.

Wilson, J. (2002) George Best doing well after liver transplant, doctors say, *Guardian* (London), August 1. http://www.guardian.co.uk/uk_news/story/0,3604,767216,00.html

NORMAN GIESBRECHT

SCIENCE, PUBLIC POLICY AND THE ALCOHOL INDUSTRY

Key words: Social Aspects Organizations, alcohol industry, prevention, alcohol policy

Abstract. Alcohol is associated with a wide range of problems with high social and economic costs, and drinking has a negative impact on abstainers, moderate drinkers and heavy drinkers. In light of this damage it is incumbent that the most effective prevention policies and interventions should be promoted by all private, non-governmental and governmental agencies involved in prevention. In recent years the alcohol industry -- through the social aspect organizations (SAOs) that they sponsor -- has taken an increasingly active role in prevention. This paper analyzes their perspectives on alcohol problems, intervention foci and prevention and policy initiatives that they support. SAOs support industry self-regulation of alcohol advertising, despite countless breaches of advertising codes, and individually oriented information or persuasion prevention campaigns found generally to be ineffective. Furthermore, the industry seeks to block other measures, such as increased taxation on alcohol, lower legal BAC levels for all drivers, and controls on outlet density, which have been shown to be effective in reducing drinking-related harm. It appears that the perspectives of the SAOs -- and those of their industry sponsors -- on prevention are not out-of-line with marketing and commercial agendas. It is concluded that to date these activities by the alcohol industries have not furthered effective prevention, and may have blocked progress in reducing drinking-related problems. If the alcohol industries are to have a role in prevention that is effective and evidence-based, a dramatic change in priorities is required along with clear guidelines as to their contribution.

1. THE CHALLENGE: REDUCING DRINKING-RELATED PROBLEMS

New evidence is emerging of the cost and scope of drinking-related problems. Some decades ago the popular press did not acknowledge problems related to drink that went

R. Müller and H. Klingemann (eds.),
From Science to Action? 100 Years Later - Alcohol Policies Revisited, 163–183.

much beyond the short list of public drunkenness, alcohol dependence and drinking and driving (McKenzie and Giesbrecht, 1981). However, alcohol consumption is associated with many acute or traumatic incidents, such as violence, property damage, alcoholic poisoning, and chronic conditions linked to alcohol, such as fetal alcohol effects and cancers (Corrao et al. 1999; Midanik et al., 1996). The estimated damage and economic impact are substantial (Single et al., 1998; WHO, 1999). Epidemiology, medicine and social science research continue to uncover a long litany of alcohol-related troubles, which range from chronic or acute troubles of the heaviest consumers to increased risks among drinkers whose consumption is considered moderate by most conventions (e.g., Room et al., 1995; US Secretary of Health and Human Services, 1997; World Health Organization, 1999; 2001). It has been noted that alcohol accounts "for 3.5% of the disability-adjusted life years (DALYs) lost in 1990, more than tobacco at 2.6%", the former taking into account the possible beneficial effects of moderate drinking for some consumers (Anderson, 2002a, p. 19, citing Murray and Lopez, 1996).

There has been an increased awareness of a wide range of problems associated with drinking; concurrently the evidence supporting the nature of the link is stronger (with regard to violence, see Room and Rossow, 2001; Leonard, 2001). Certain risks associated with drinking have dipped closer to the range of consumption of the social drinker (Room et al., 1995). Furthermore, some studies note that in the previous year most citizens will have experienced some personal disruption, inconvenience or serious risks due to the drinking-related behaviour of others, be it public disorder, threats, violence, or riding in a car where the driver was not fit to be behind the wheel (e.g., Allen et al., 1998). Alcohol-related damage thus also intrudes into the lives of those who are not drinkers or drink very little.

Given the extent of the problems faced in many jurisdictions, and the ongoing challenges to generate support for effective prevention initiatives, it would seem, in principle, that initiatives to contribute to the amelioration of drinking-related problems would be welcomed from a broad spectrum of organizations -- including the alcohol industry. This paper addresses several questions: Is there a role for the alcohol industry in the prevention of drinking-related harm? Will the participation of the alcohol industry reduce drinking-related problems? If there is a role, what are some options that would enhance effective control and prevention of drinking-related problems?

As a background, it is relevant first to consider industry marketing and promotion strategies, and alcohol policy agenda management activities. It is also important to understand the industry perspectives and initiatives with regard to the definition of drinking-related problems, views on alcohol policies and prevention, and how these prevention initiatives fit with what is know about effectiveness of various interventions. The concluding paragraphs consider alternatives to the current scene.

Several assumptions and caveats are offered at the outset in order to provide a context for the remarks that follow.

The alcohol industry has a legitimate role with regard to production and distribution of its products within the constraints of regional, national and international laws and regulations.

This role is a privilege, not an unfettered right, given that alcohol is a drug and is at least equal to tobacco, in terms of the damage and disruption related to its use.

In order to reduce message confusion to current consumers, abstainers, and policy makers, and to avoid confounding the policy-making process, the marketing of alcohol should be distinct and separate from the prevention of alcohol problems.

Although there are many factors that contribute to planning and implementing effective prevention, it would seem that the following are especially important: a common aim of reducing alcohol-related problems in the population, a sound epidemiological basis for assessing problems and the impacts of interventions, a willingness to prioritize interventions based on evidence from previous initiatives, and an effective organization to 'deliver' the intervention.

The focus of this paper is on prevention efforts by the alcohol industry. Many of the comments about the assumptions, foci and strategies of prevention also apply to initiatives by government and non-government organizations, but that topic is beyond the scope of this paper.

2. INDUSTRY ACTIVITIES

The alcohol industry[i] is not monolithic in the details of its agendas, activities or policies. However, promotion, distribution and sales to new and loyal customers alike, appear to be common high priority goals. The industry has demonstrated a combination of inventiveness and persistence on several fronts, including marketing, product diversification, industry integration and political connections and lobbying (e.g., Jernigan, 2000; Jackson et al., 2000). While what is culturally tolerated or legally allowed varies considerably by jurisdiction, it is possible to see marketing that includes T-shirts for toddlers with beer logos (WHO, 2001; Rutherford, 2002), names of alcoholic beverage producers on ski lift equipment, alcohol advertising on racing cars and other sports equipment, and advertising that appears to associate a beverage or drinking with violence, sexual adventures or high school graduation, to mention a few (e.g., The Globe, 2002). The elaboration of beverage labels, types, strength variations, size of containers and blending with juices and other non-alcoholic drinks appears to go hand-in-hand with the elaboration of marketing and promotion techniques.

Some sectors of the alcohol industry often justify extensive promotion by citing the need to retain market share (Advertising Association, 2000). However, given the large sums spent on advertising and promotion (Anderson, 2002a; Jernigan, 2002), it would seem that attracting new customers, including youth, retaining loyal customers and increasing consumption of the products advertised are equally important if not more basic goals (see Cooke et al., 2002; Gogek, 2003). While the self-regulatory industry guidelines (e.g., Beer Institute, n.d.; Distilled Spirits Council of the U.S., n.d.) state that youth are not a focus, the symbols, images and methods used by some sectors of the industry strongly suggest otherwise (Lieberman and Orlandi, 1987; Jernigan, 2001; WHO, 2001; Rutherford, 2002). The ubiquity and diversity of techniques used in the promotion of alcoholic beverages in many countries, including the developing world (Assunta, 2001-2002; Gunasekera, 2001; Jernigan, 2000; 2001) serve to normalize drinking and integrate it into many social activities. In contrast, the current levels of counter-advertising appear to be a modest token gesture by comparison (e.g., Saffer, 2002).

The alcohol industry has also been politically effective. It has a longstanding tradition of political activism at all levels of government. At national levels, it has succeeded in blocking some policy initiatives, watering down others, and getting topics off the agenda that were contrary to its goals (e.g., Ogborne and Giesbrecht, 1999; Greenfield et al., 1999; Rutherford, 2002; Gogek, 2003). At local levels, there are examples of the industry seeking to counter restrictions on density of outlets, to expand the types of venues that can be licensed, or to resist stronger enforcement of on-premise regulation, to mention a few (Mosher, 1999; Anderson, 2002a). In some instances the proposed policies that have been blocked would have reduced harm from alcohol through higher taxes on alcohol, or curtailed extensive promotion of alcohol in formats that are attractive to underage drinkers (e.g. Gogek, 2003).

However, it is at the international level where the influence of the alcohol industry arguably has the most significant negative implications for prevention and harm reduction. The industry has made various attempts to thwart the World Health Organization's promotion of effective alcohol controls as laid out in the European Alcohol Action Plan (e.g. Rutherford, 2002). Along with other commercially oriented forces within the European Union community, the alcohol industry has had a significant role in either promoting relaxation of controls on cross-border alcohol trade allowances or criticizing alcohol monopoly arrangements and controls on advertising (e.g., Grieshaber-Otto and Schacter, 2002; Holder et al., 1995).

Furthermore, the arrangements pertaining to the General Agreement on Trade in Services (GATS) seem to be tailor-made for the expansionist agenda of multi-national alcohol industries, offering to provide a broad range of conditions that member countries to the World Trade Organization must abide by. Most of them are oriented to facilitating rather than controlling alcohol sales, higher density of alcohol outlets, greater duty-free cross-border trade, and, by implication, an increase in alcohol-related problems, with narrow and few exceptions noted (Grieshaber-Otto and Schacter, 2002).

The general drift appears to be twofold: toward deregulation of controls and increasing normalization of alcohol use. Both are patterns that have been associated with increased drinking-related harm (Bruun et al., 1975; Edwards et al., 1994). Thus, on balance, the alcohol industry has been, and continues to be, very successful in facilitating and encouraging national and international conditions that are favourable to the trade and distribution of its products, and in developing new, exotic and attractive products (WHO 2001). It also often plays an effective role in blocking or undermining initiatives that counter its trade and marketing agenda (e.g. Hawks, 1992; CSPI, 1996; Ogborne and Giesbrecht, 1999), and in doing so contributes to thwarting the more effective prevention initiatives (Babor et al., in press).

3. EMERGENCE OF SOCIAL ASPECT ORGANIZATIONS

In recent decades the alcohol industry has increased and expanded its social marketing and public relations initiatives, with the sponsorship and development of social aspects organizations (SAOs) being a central feature of these changes.[ii] The stated goals of these organizations include: delivering better education to young people, discouraging drinking and driving, disseminating the sensible drinking idea for those who choose to drink; and developing and enhancing mechanisms for providing a level of self-regulation of industry marketing practices (Max and Willersdorf, 2001). More details can be found on their web pages[iii] and in other reports (Grant, 1998; Grant and Litvak, 1998; ICAP, n.d.-a; Leverton et al., 2000; Anderson, 2002a; 2002b; Rutherford, 2000).

Their structure varies but a basic model appears to be that a number of producer corporations provide funds, have representatives on the board and oversee the general direction of the SAO. The SAOs seek to demonstrate or illustrate 'socially responsible' use and attitudes to alcohol, promote the exchange of ideas (Grant 2000), collaborate on prevention groups and organizations (both government and NGOs), and fund research and analysis (Anderson 2002a, McCreanor et al., 2000; Rutherford, 2002). Related activities may include providing commentary or critiques of terms, perspectives and interventions (e.g., ICAP, 1997a; 1997b). Thus while some SAOs may aim to have an 'arms length' association with their benefactors (see the Society for Alcohol & Social Policy Initiative http://education.vsnl.comp/saspi/html), the prevention activity goals of the SAOs are generally in line with those of the alcohol producers who sponsor them. Furthermore, the SAOs develop a close working relationship with selected public health and research personnel through the development of consensus statements (Hannum, 1997) and use prestigious names to link to their meetings, events and summary statements (Casswell, 2000; Room, 2000; Anderson, 2002b). These strategies serve to legitimize their mission and goals in the eyes of policy makers, the public and the alcohol producers that sponsor them (Anderson, 2002a: 2002b).

4. PERSPECTIVES & ACTIONS

However, to look at the SAOs in isolation provides an incomplete picture. It is worth considering the match between the head office and marketplace activities of their sponsors, the alcohol producers, and the activities of the SAOs that these companies support. In the following sections I examine industry perspectives with regard to promotion of alcohol and drinking, alcohol-related problems, and priorities concerning prevention and alcohol policy. Of particular interest is what is emphasized versus what is downplayed or ignored. It is noteworthy that these perspectives, summarized below, are complementary with an agenda of increasing alcohol sales. Also, these orientations likely divert attention from prevention efforts that are most effective in controlling alcohol-related problems, especially at the aggregate level (Moser, 2000; Mosher, 2001).

4.1 Promotion of Alcohol & Drinking

While there is variation by jurisdiction, an underlying theme is that the alcohol industry maintains that it is a right, not a privilege, to promote and distribute its products as extensively as possible. In the United States, for example, almost any debate about constraints on alcohol promotion leads to the alcohol, marketing and broadcasting industries "wrapping themselves in the flag" by referring to constitutional issues (Giesbrecht, 2000).

The alcohol industry will resist minimum constraints on promotion of their products, but nevertheless deny that the billions spent on advertising have any impact in increasing sales (see Cooke et al., 2002). The industry uses extensive, varied and expensive methods to advertise its products (Advertising Association, 2000; WHO, 2001). In many instances there are symbols and imagery that many would consider culturally insensitive or offensive (Alaniz and Wilkes, 1998), or that may encourage risk-taking and be appealing to persons below the legal drinking age (Grube and Nygaard, 2001). Sectors of the alcohol industry sponsor numerous advertisements that are appear to be breaches of the codes they ascribe to or are held to by governments (for examples see Rutherford, 2002; The Globe, 2003, pp. 3-6; Jernigan, 2003).

In response to criticisms of some of industry advertising practices and as a way of avoiding government-imposed regulation, voluntary codes of conduct for advertising are proposed and frequently advocated by SAOs (e.g., The Amsterdam Group, 2001; ICAP, 2001). The threat of government-imposed regulation may stimulate industry initiatives to introduce or upgrade voluntary codes or promote them (ICAP, 2001, p. 8). While breach of these codes appear to be common (The Marin Institute, 1999; Federal Communications Commission, 1999), the umbrella alcohol trade organizations do not seem to have the political power or inclination to react effectively when infractions occur (Anderson 2002b, pp. 11-17). There are statements about number of complaints (e.g. The Portman Group, 2002, pp. 26-27) and their outcome. However critical evaluation appears not to be undertaken; for example, there is need for a systematic pre-post comparison of whether or not the introduction or promotion of self-regulation actually had an impact on reducing the total number of breaches. While there may be some interest in assessing if the codes actually make a difference in reducing the number and type of breaches, a thorough analysis has not been undertaken.[iv]

A typical response from SAOs is to defend responsible advertising codes and the notion of a self-regulated industry (e.g., The Amsterdam Group www.amsterdamgroup.org/topics/comcom_selfreg4.htlm; Portman Group www.portman-group.org.uk; also The Globe, 2002). Nevertheless in at least one instance a SAO supported document noted, "When self-regulation is shown not to be effective, governments should intervene with legislation or regulation" (International Center for Alcohol Policies, 2002, p. 2). To date there does not appear to be independent assessment of impact of these voluntary codes. Also there is no agreement as to what the criteria or threshold should be with regard to "ineffectiveness". It is unlikely that there will soon be industry or SAO consensus on when breaches are sufficiently numerous, persistent or blatant to consider self-regulation ineffective.

4.2 Alcohol-related Problems & Priorities

There is ongoing debate in the research literature about the underlying causes of alcohol problems, and the alcohol industry and the SAOs draw selectively from this literature. They note that alcohol-related problems have many causes, but particularly draw attention to personal and family factors (e.g., SASPI—http://education.vsnl.comp.saspi/).

A dominant focus is on the individual high-risk drinker and deviant consumer rather than the population as a whole. A typical industry perspective divides the drinking population into drinkers with problems (assumed to be the minority) and drinkers without problems (assumed to be the majority) (ICAP n.d). The same perspective says that efforts to prevent or reduce alcohol problems should focus primarily on those who are problem drinkers and not inconvenience or bother those – the majority -- who drink socially, responsibly and in moderation. Thus, the most important underlying causes of alcohol problems, according to this view, are not related to the socio-economic environment (Anderson, 2002a; 2002b).

There is also reluctance to accept a population-based strategy or an environmental perspective.[v] The former may be contrary to the view that most persons drink responsibly. The latter would quickly lead to considering the contexts of alcohol sales and consumption, such as real price, place of sales, product availability and promotion. It would invariably lead to considering the role of the industry in offering greater access to alcohol and the links between increased access and an increase in drinking rates or change in drinking patterns and a rise of drinking-related problems.

There is little reference to the large numbers of moderate drinkers who occasionally drink a lot and experience some problems, so that their contribution to the overall aggregate number of problems is significant (Edwards et al., 1994)[vi]. Furthermore, when the industry discusses heavy or problem drinkers, the proportion of alcohol consumed by those who drink the most is not central to such deliberations. Studies in Australia (Stockwell et al., 2002), Canada (Greenfield et al., 1996), and the US (Greenfield and Rogers, 1999) estimate that at least half of the alcohol in these societies is consumed in high-risk situations. Any effective effort to control drinking-related problems would have a significant positive impact (i.e., reduction) on the drinking of heavier consumers, and thus a negative impact on sales (Anderson, 2002a). The industry's vested interests in increasing sales combined with views on the causes and nature of alcohol problems – views that are promoted by the SAOs -- make it highly unlikely that the industry will support the most effective interventions.

The drinking problems labeled in their campaigns and initiatives are high profile ones that are currently popular, such as drinking and driving, binge drinking by youth, alcohol dependence and fetal alcohol effects (e.g. Century Council, n.d.). The greatest attention appears to be devoted to drinking and driving (e.g., Anglin et al., 2000), likely reflecting the extent of the problem, long-standing efforts to curtail it and public awareness of the extent and damage caused by drunk driving. While these problems are worthy of attention, it is also important to note what topics have a lower profile or are not mentioned. For example, alcohol-related cancers are typically not on the alcohol industry's agenda, although there are some exceptions (e.g., The Amsterdam Group, n.d.; The Portman Group, 2002, p. 13). In connection with discussion of binge drinking or underage consumption, it is uncommon to see reference to 'Spring Break' events for US college students—many of these events include a strong industry marketing presence and also involve heavy drinking by young adults, many who are underage. One is also not likely to find reference to drinking and other drug use or drinking and smoking in these documents.

These problems and associations evidently carry with them the potential for tarnishing industry images. In summary, the industry prevention initiatives place an emphasis on the individual, high risk and dependent drinkers and the more dramatic and high profile problems, such as drinking and driving. Despite the long-standing (e.g., Bruun et al., 1975) and new evidence (e.g. Ramstedt, 2003; Skog, 203) about the association between population consumption levels and drinking-related problems, this association is either dismissed or downplayed in industry-sponsored documents.

4.3 Alcohol Policy & Prevention

It is in the prevention arena where the alcohol industry, mainly through the SAOs, but also on a corporate basis, is particularly active. The strategies that are supported include promotion of counter-messages and law enforcement; however, a significant share of resources appears to be devoted to education and information campaigns, often in collaboration with police forces, liquor boards and others (Giesbrecht and MacKenzie, 2000).[vii] The support for prevention also includes direct funding of media and information campaigns – which typically contain the company logo or name -- and partial funding of groups that are involved in prevention activities, and sponsorship of research.

The education and information campaigns that the industry supports are not those that advocate for stronger and more effective control policies, but those that focus on personal decisions about drinking, including admonitions about the responsible use of alcohol (Burrows, 1990). These initiatives may encourage a more cautious approach to drinking or increased awareness about the risks of drinking. Some have the potential to inform users about risks of drinking or performing certain tasks, such as driving a motor vehicle, while under the influence of alcohol. They may raise public awareness, promote concern about certain alcohol-related problems, and even generate interest in community-based action.

However, relatively few of the industry-supported educational campaigns are evaluated so that continued support of many of them seems to be based on good intentions, optimism or logo promotion, rather than empirical evidence of their role in harm reduction.[viii] In general, evaluation of these types of informational programs, such as school-based campaigns, suggests that their impact in the desired direction is minimal, uncommon, equivocal and transitory (e.g., Foxcroft et al., 1997; 2003). Whether the industry-funded programs actually achieve their goals and reduce drinking-related problems is difficult to determine, since they are rarely, if ever, subjected to independent evaluation. Furthermore, while the industry through SAOs is involved in many prevention programs, the resources devoted to them are likely a fraction of the amount spent on alcohol advertising, promotion and lobbying (see Mosher, 2001), not to mention related promotional activities supporting its corporations, agenda and products.

While the list of prevention activities the industry or SAOs are involved in is extensive, there are other noteworthy prevention options that they avoid, criticize or block. For example a document on harm reduction and alcohol policies, lists the following areas considered to show promise: alcohol education, responsible serving of alcohol, measures aimed at ensuring quality control in the production of alcohol, reducing risks associated with intoxication, controlled drinking programs, and alternative transportation programs (International Center for Alcohol Policies, n.d.–c). It is noteworthy that a number of societal level interventions, that have been shown to reduce harm, are not mentioned – for example, alcohol taxation policies, controls on outlet density, minimum drinking age, and lower legal BAC levels, to mention a few (e.g. Edwards et al., 1994; Babor et al., in press).

Policies supported by SAOs are likely to be those that either do not impede or indeed support the industry's commercial agenda. Those opposed by SAOs are those that will strain commercial and marketing activities, but it turns out that a number of the more effective interventions are those that reduce harm through curtailing access to alcohol and reducing drinking rates (Babor et al., in press).

The alcohol industry is typically opposed to any policy that will restrict the promotion of alcohol (Burrows, 1990; Alexander, 1995). In general, policies that control access through pricing and taxation, effective management of retail outlets, controls on density of outlets, and aggressive marketing and advertising are not considered appropriate (Anderson, 2002a; 2002b, pp. 12-15). Indeed, there are numerous examples of where the industry has sought to block the passage of such policies, or compromise their potential impact (Greenfield et al., 1999; Ogborne and Giesbrecht, 1999; Giesbrecht, 2000; Mosher, 2001; Rutherford, 2002).

In specific arenas the industry also opposes other types of regulation, such as lowering the official blood alcohol concentration (BAC) for drinking and driving. The view by the industry and other organizations is that a lower legal BAC will have little positive impact, although a review of international studies (Mann et al., 2001) has shown that a lower BAC has potential to reduce deaths associated with drinking and driving. The industry argues instead that more attention needs to be directed at the chronic drinking-driver (see The Century Council www.centurycouncil.org) rather than to support environmentally based measures that can prevent drinking and driving from occurring in the first place.

Another example is in the taxation arena. The industry organizes or supports various efforts to block an increase in taxes and roll-back taxation legislation once implemented (e.g. Greenfield et al., 1999; Ogborne and Giesbrecht, 1999), despite the extensive evidence that higher prices through taxes control consumption and drinking-related harm, such as liver cirrhosis deaths, drinking and driving crashes, heavy drinking among youth and violence (Cook, 1981; Chaloupka, 1993; Österberg, 1995; Godfrey, 1997).

There are attempts to counter the research that has demonstrated a positive association between alcohol policies, per capita consumption and drinking-related damage (The Amsterdam Group, 2001; Anderson, 2002a). In general, industry perspectives on policy contradict the extensive international research demonstrating that a number of these controls will reduce drinking-related harm (e.g. Bruun et al., 1975; Moore and Gerstein, 1981; Moskowitz, 1989; Edwards et al., 1994; Holder and Edwards, 1995; Babor et al., in press; Giesbrecht and Greenfield, in press).

To summarize, the alcohol industry and SAOs are interested in prevention and they are interested in prevention of alcohol-related problems that deserve attention. However, the identification of the focus population, definition of the problem and prevention agendas favoured, insure that these activities will not compromise commercial agenda. Furthermore, such interventions may detract from considering the more effective interventions, including control or environmentally based strategies (e.g., Babor et al., in press).

5. INTERPRETATIONS

At the outset three questions were posed, and summary responses to them are provided in the following paragraphs.

5.1 The Alcohol Industry and Prevention

Is there a role for the alcohol industry in the prevention of alcohol-related harm? The primary legitimate function of the alcohol industry is to produce and sell its products. Public health advocates may be opposed to extensive efforts on the part of the industry to establish strong footholds in developing countries, but the industry thus far seems to have many national laws and major international trade agreements on its side. The SAOs offer a number of functions that are not contrary to these activities. Their unique value for the industry is to demonstrate to the policy makers and others interested in the alcohol arena, that SAOs are interested in dialogue and partnership on prevention. They also seek to influence perceptions of alcohol, the alcohol industry and prevention options. To the extent that these initiatives are successful they also potentially detract from closer analysis of the main agenda of the industry, and consideration of prevention options with the greatest potential.

The evidence is not convincing that the alcohol industry has a role in the prevention of drinking-related harm. There are several developments that point to this conclusion. The prevention activities of the SAOs include the social marketing of the alcohol producers, and their views, in the guise of prevention. Through the agendas that the SAOs promote and the nature of their involvement there is a blurring the distinction between marketing of alcohol and the prevention of drinking-related problems. In some cases prevention workers are dependent on the industry for funds, which creates a substantial imbalance given the political power and financial resources of the alcohol production industry. This makes it unlikely that those so sponsored will actively promote those interventions that their sponsors are opposed to. Finally, by seeking to block the more effective prevention measures, the activities by the alcohol industry and SAOs may not constitute a net gain for prevention.

The business of the alcohol industry is to produce and market alcohol. This should be their main function. It is not likely that in the foreseeable future the industry will sponsor or support prevention efforts that will curtail its marketing potential and distribution arrangements. However, it is highly unlikely that significant progress will be made in the prevention at important aggregate national or international levels without some constraint on marketing and distribution. Initiatives in the prevention arena undertaken by the industry, or sponsored by them, are compromised, confounded or influenced by their over-riding commercial and marketing goals.

Therefore, in the interests of public health and safety one can question whether the alcohol industry should be in the alcohol problem prevention business.

5.2 Industry Participation and Reduction of Drinking-Related Problems

Will industry participation in prevention activities contribute to reducing drinking-related problems? The alcohol industry's interest in prevention, as demonstrated by SAO activities, is overshadowed by other agenda, noted above, and therefore compromised. These initiatives divert attention and resources from the most effective strategies. They cloud a clear observation of the industry's marketing and distribution practices and compromise the potential of prevention partners to take a stand on policy agenda. Currently the alcohol industry devotes a very small share of its potential resources to prevention. However, this contribution appears to go a long way in framing alcohol problems and setting prevention agendas, including offering alternatives to controls and government regulations, and promoting a corporate image of caring about high-risk drinkers and certain alcohol-related problems. The industry is involved in prevention primarily on its own terms.

To date it appears that the industry's involvement in prevention provides, at best, mixed results. As noted above, it tends to favour the less effective programs, such as information dissemination and persuasion techniques. Also, independent or 'arms-length' evaluation of their prevention activities is uncommon. This leads to unevaluated initiatives being promoted. More effective policies may be blocked or discredited because they are perceived as running counter to industry retailing and marketing agendas.

5.3 Options for the Alcohol Industry in the Prevention Arena

If there is a role, what options are there with regard to the alcohol industry and prevention agendas? Several are outlined below, which are not necessarily mutually exclusive.[ix]

The first is having those local or national groups that receive funds from the industry develop clear and firm guidelines of the conditions for the arrangement, in the hope that their efforts are not compromised or image tarnished, and that this does not confound their ability to work with other prevention groups in the future (Mosher 2001).

A second is that the industry agrees to contribute to prevention through supporting taxation levels that at a minimum keep pace with cost of living indices so that alcohol does not become a bargain relative to other goods and services. This contribution would be a small step in the right direction, considering the burden to social, health, welfare and law enforcement services related to drinking.

A third option is finding a way of dealing with alcohol marketing and advertising. Currently there seems to be a large gap in some western countries, such as Canada and the United States, between government regulations and guidelines and industry practices. Self-regulatory arrangements have not made significant strides in closing this gap (Cooke et al., 2002; WHO, 2001; Anderson, 2002a). The industries involved in the sponsoring, production, advertising and promotion of alcohol need to come together with government, research and public health groups. The two sides need to agree upon standards for advertising, including not promoting alcohol to under-age youth, how these standards are operationalized and enforced, and swift, sure and effective responses to breaches. In turn, public health advocates need to acknowledge positive and negative developments when it comes to this question – for example, when standards are met, if there is improvement over time, and when there are breaches. This arrangement should be monitored on an annual basis and subsequent improvements made in the protocol to insure a more effective procedure. If the industry were prepared to enter into this type of arrangement, which includes powers of monitoring and enforcement, this would be a significant step toward countering the current situation where there is discontinuity between words and deeds when it comes to self-regulation and alcohol advertising.

A fourth option is that the industry agrees to participate in 'arms length' committees or groups that provide advice on alcohol issues but are not dominated by representatives from the alcohol industry (Babor et al., 1996; Babor, 2000; Giesbrecht, 2000). These committees should have diverse composition, including representatives from the major players who have a role in minimizing the risks of drinking for individuals, communities and wider jurisdictions. These groups should include representatives from public health and safety sectors, citizen non-government groups, retailers and producers, government representatives and researchers. The alcohol industry would have representation on this type of group, but not constitute the majority. While it is beyond the scope of this paper to define this type of group in more detail, one option would be that a national group might be an advisor to government on high priorities in research and prevention -- based on the most pressing drinking-related problems and evidence of the prevention initiatives known to have a strong positive track record (e.g. Babor et al., in press). Decisions or recommendations made by this type of group should be made by the majority and not by consensus, the latter giving any one participant veto power (Room, 2000). A group might be established on a trial basis and its experiences and progress assessed after a two to three year period.

These options are neither prohibitionist nor draconian: they do not prevent the industry from producing or marketing its products, but at the same time they offer a fairer and more responsible multi-sectorial planning on alcohol issues than currently exists. There is considerable public ambivalence about the alcohol industry.[x] This sense of unease about its goals in prevention arena will increase if the industry continues to focus on social marketing of prevention, primarily through the SAOs, which appear to be have thinly disguised roles of protecting and enhancing commercial agenda of their sponsors.

5.4 Setting priorities

Alcohol is involved in a wide range of problems that affect both drinkers and abstainers and impose a tremendous social and economic burden. In recent years, consumption levels seem to be rising in some countriesxi, and this could very likely give rise to a heavier burden of drinking-related harm (e.g., Ramstedt, 2003; Skog, 2003; Holder, 2003). In face of current and future drinking-related problems, governments and non-government agencies need to work together to plan, support and promote the most effective interventions and policies. While this paper has focused on the alcohol industry and the SAOs that it sponsors, it is incumbent upon regional, national and international groups to allocate their prevention resources to those interventions with the best track record and greatest potential to achieve widespread harm reduction. However, those policies and prevention efforts currently favoured by the alcohol industry typically do not meet these criteria.

The alcohol industry is therefore encouraged to facilitate the development of policies and practices that indicate changes in orientation and priority. Willingness to pursue the types of options noted above, and to allow for an assessment of their impact, will signal a welcome change in perspective. Another positive step would be a decline and eventual phasing out of efforts on the part of the industry to block or undermine the passage or implementation of the most effective interventions. A further step would involve the phasing out of industry sponsorship of prevention initiatives that have shown to be ineffective. Finally, it is hoped that in the near future the alcohol industry will focus its support for those policies and prevention initiatives that have the greatest potential in reducing the social and individual harm related to alcohol consumption.

ACKNOWLEDGEMENTS

This is a revised version of a paper presented at 100 Years Birthday Symposium 2002 "From Science to Action? 100 Years Later – Alcohol Policies Revisited" October 28-29, 2002 Bern, Switzerland. I wish to acknowledge the sponsors for providing travel support to participate in the symposium, and thank Lise Anglin, Paula Neves and Robert

Reynolds for their advise, and Karen Schwartz for contributions to editing and formatting. The views and opinions expressed are those of the author and are not necessarily indicative of the policies or positions of the Centre for Addiction and Mental Health.

NOTES

i The singular 'alcohol industry' is used to designate a collection of industries. There are differences in the orientation of the producers, suppliers, wholesalers and retailers on many of the issues noted above. However, since it is the producers who tend to sponsor the social aspects organizations, in this paper 'alcohol industry' refers primarily to alcohol producers.

ii According to Max and Willersdorf (2001) there is a long history of alcohol industry involvement in alcohol education and social policy. They note "in the late 1980s a number of major international drinks companies began to take a broader look at the way the alcohol industry responded to alcohol issues" (p. 278). They indicate that there were four such groups in 1989 and over 30 by 2001.

iii For example, see the following: The Amsterdam Group www.amsterdamgroup.org; The Century Council www.centurycouncil.org; the International Center for Alcohol Policies www.icap.org; The Portman Group www.portman-group.org; Society for Alcohol & Social Policy Initiative http://education.vsnl.comp/saspi/; Taiwan Beverage Alcohol Form www.tbaf.org.tw.

iv In response to a question about whether there is a consensus about advertising self-regulation, the following is noted: "In the absence of a systemic review of beverage alcohol self-regulation, it is difficult to say unequivocally that all systems work. However, in Europe, North America, and Australia where self-regulation is practiced most, the industry has shown that they can be quick to respond to complaints and are more willing participants in the process" (International Center for Alcohol Policies, n.d.-b).

v For example, in a recent report it was noted: "Evidence suggests that the prevalence of alcohol-related problems is not directly related to the average per capita consumption, but rather to problematic patterns of drinking. TAG therefore strongly advocates further development of pragmatic policies directed to the promotion of responsible drinking patterns as well as to the reduction of the harm done by alcohol abuse" (The Amsterdam Group, 2001).

vi An exception is found in a recent report by the International Center for Alcohol Policies (2003) in which, quoting a report on the workplace, it noted: "According to a report by the ILO, 'simply because their numbers are [high], moderate and occasional drinkers account for the largest proportion of alcohol-related problems in the workplace.'" (ILO, 2003).

vii For example, it is noted that "Education as the best form of prevention". "TPG [The Portman Group] believes that greater emphasis should be placed on preventing alcohol misuse through the dissemination of accurate and balanced information about alcohol. (The Portman Group, 2002, pp. 7-8).

viii Houghton (1998) provides a comparison of alcohol education programs sponsored by the alcoholic beverage industry in 1984 and 1996 and notes that while independent evaluation of these programs is being taken more seriously, there is still room for improvement.

ix See also guidelines proposed for public health and scientific bodies by Babor (2000).

x In the 1999 Ontario survey almost no one was willing to sue the alcohol companies, either for disease or accidents (more than 80% disagreed for both (Anglin et al., 2003) Yet in the 2003 survey, the majority of the total sample (64%) opposed industry self-regulation of alcohol advertising (Anglin et al., manuscript).

These sets of responses imply some ambivalence: i.e., not wishing to legally 'punish' the industry for certain drinking-related problems, but also not trusting it to undertake alcohol marketing in a responsible way.

[xi] The rate of sales in Canada increased from 7.18 litres of absolute alcohol per capita (aged 15+) in 1996 to 7.99 in 2000.

REFERENCES

Advertising Association (2000). Advertising and consumption: the research findings. Executive Brief 19th December 2000: Advertising Association website: **www.adassoc.org.uk/briefs/alc.html**.

Alaniz, M. L., & Wilkes, C. (1998). Pro-drinking messages and message environment for young adults: The case of alcohol industry advertising in African American, Mexican American, and Native American Communities. *Journal of Public Health Policy,* 19 (4), 447-472.

Allen, B., Anglin, L., & Giesbrecht, N. (1998). Effects of others' drinking as perceived by community members. *Canadian Journal of Public Health* 89(5), 337-341.

Alexander, B. (1995). The role of the alcohol beverage industry in preventing abuse. Paper presented at the 37th International Congress on Alcohol and Drug Dependence. ICAA Section on Alcohol Policy, San Diego, California, August, 1995.

The Amsterdam Group (n.d.) *Scientific developments – Alcohol and cancer.* www.amsterdamgroup.org/scientific/cancer.html

The Amsterdam Group (2001). *The Amsterdam Group – Report 2001. Executive summary -- Alcohol and society.* www.amsterdamgroup.org

Anderson, P. (2002a). The beverage alcohol industry's social aspects organizations: A public health warning. *TheGlobe*, Issue 3, 3-30.

Anderson, P. (2002b). The International Center for Alcohol Policies: a public health body or a marketing arm of the beverage alcohol industry? *The Globe,* Issue 1, 3-7.

Anglin, L., Johnson, S., Giesbrecht, N., & Greenfield, T. (2000) Alcohol policy content analysis: a comparison of public health and alcohol industry trade newsletters. *Drug and Alcohol Review,* 19, 203-212.

Anglin, L., Giesbrecht, N., Ialtomiteanu, A., McAllister, J., & Ogborne, A. (2003). Public perception of alcohol policy issues relating directly or indirectly to privatisation. *Canadian Journal of Public Health,* 94(3), 201-206.

Anglin, L, Giesbrecht, N., Grand, L., Ialomiteanu, A., Mann, R., & McAllister, J. (draft manuscript). Public opinion on current alcohol policy issues: Findings from a 2002 Ontario survey. *CAMH Research Document Series.* Toronto: Centre for Addiction and Mental Health.

Assunta, M. (2001-2002). Impact of alcohol consumption on Asia, *The Globe,* Special Issue 4, 4-8.

Babor, T.F. (2000). Partnerships, profits and public health. *Addiction*, 95, 190-191.

Babor, T.F., Edwards, G., & Stockwell, T. (1996). Science and the drinks industry: Cause for concern. *Addiction*, 91(1), 5-9.

Babor, T. , Caetano, R., Casswell, S., Edwards, G., Giesbrecht, N., Graham, K., Grube, J., Gruenewald, P., Hill, L., Holder, H., Romel, R., Österberg, E., Rehm, J., Room, R., & Rossow, R. (in press). *Alcohol, no ordinary commodity: Research and public policy.* Oxford: Oxford University Press.

Beer Institute (n.d.) . *Advertising & Marketing Code.*

Bruun, K., Edwards, G., Lumio, M., Makela, K.,. Pan, L., Popham, R.E., Room, R., Schmidt, W., Skog, O.-J., Sulkunen, P., & Őstenberg, E. (1975). *Alcohol control policies in public health perspective.* Helsinki: Finnish Foundation for Alcohol Studies, Volume 25

Burrows, S.J. (1990). Awareness and education vs. regulation and legislation. A review of the alcohol industry and special interest agendas to reduce alcohol abuse. *Brewers Digest* 65, 14-17.

Casswell, S. (2000). Science and policy advocacy. *The Globe,* Special edition, The Proceedings of the Global Alcohol Policy Advocacy Conference, 7-10.

The Century Council (n.d.). www.centurycouncil.org/index.cfm

Chaloupka, F.J. (1993). Effects of price on alcohol-related problems. *Alcohol, Health & Research World,* 17 (1), 46-53.

Cooke, E., Hastings, G., & Anderson, S. (2002). Social responsibility in the alcohol industry: actions speak louder than words. *The Globe,* Issue 2, 11-16.

Cook, P.J. (1981). The effect of liquor taxes on drinking, cirrhosis, and auto accidents. In M. H. Moore & D. R. Gerstein (Eds.), *Alcohol and public policy: Beyond the shadow of prohibition* (pp. 255-258). Washington, D.C.: National Academy Press.

Corrao, G., Bagnardi, A., Zambon, A.,& Arico, S. (1999).Exploring the dose-response relationship between alcohol consumption and the risk of several alcohol-related conditions: a meta-analysis. *Addiction,* 94(10), 1551-1573.

CSPI (1996) *Paying the Piper: The effect of industry funding on alcohol prevention priorities.* Report. Washington, DC: Center for Science in the Public Interest.

Distilled Spirits Council of the U.S (n.d.). Code of good practice of distilled spirits advertising and marketing.

Edwards, G. Anderson, P., Babor, T.F., Casswell, S., Ferrence, R., Giesbrecht, N., Godfrey, C., Holder, H.D., Lemmens, P., Makela, K., Midanik, L.T., Norstrom, T., Osterberg, E., Romelsjo, A., Room, R., Simpura, J., & Skog, O.-J. (1994). *Alcohol policy and the public good.* Oxford: Oxford University Press.

Federal Trade Commission (1999). *Self-Regulation in the alcohol industry - report.* FTC Reports on Industry Efforts to Avoid Promoting Alcohol to Underage Consumers. Washington, D.C.: Federal Trade Commission.

Foxcroft, D. R., Lister-Sharp, D., & Lowe, G. (1997). Alcohol misuse prevention for young people: a systematic review reveals methodological concerns and lack of reliable evidence of effectiveness. *Addiction* 92(5), 531-537.

Foxcroft, D. R., Ireland, D., Lister-Sharp, D. J., Lowe, G., & Breen, R. (2003). Long-term primary prevention for alcohol misuse in young people: A systematic review. *Addiction* 98(4), 397-411.

Giesbrecht, N. (2000). Roles of commercial interests in alcohol policies: recent developments in North

America. *Addiction,* 95 (suppl. 4), S581-S595.

Giesbrecht, N., & Mackenzie, B. (2000). Alcohol retailing by government liquor boards in Canada in the 1990s. In E. Österberg (Ed.), *Themes from Finland* (pp. 47-82). International Seminar on Alcohol Retail Monopolies: Exchange of Information and Experience, Ivalo, Finland, September 21-23, 1999. Helsinki: National Research and Development Centre for Welfare and Health.

Giesbrecht, N., & Greenfield, T. K. (in press). Preventing alcohol-related problems in the US through policy: Media campaigns, regulatory approaches and environmental interventions. *Journal of Primary Prevention.*

The Globe (2002). Self-regulation – for and against. Issue 4, 5-7.

TheGlobe (2003). Advocacy in action. Issue 1, 3-7.

Grant, M. & Litvak, J. (Eds.) (1998). *Drinking patterns and their consequences.* Washington: Taylor and Francis.

Godfrey, C. (1997) Can tax be used to minimize harm? A health economist's perspective. In M. Plant, E. Single & T. Stockwell (Eds), *Alcohol: Minimising the harm. What works?* (pp. 29-42). New York, N.Y.: Free Association Books Ltd.

Gogek, J. (2003). The booze lobby vs. America's youth. *The Washington Post*, July 15, 2003.

Grant, M. (1998). (Ed.) *Alcohol and emerging markets: Patterns, problems and responses.* ICAP Series on Alcohol in Society. Philadelphia, PA: Brunner/Mazel.

Grant, M. (2000). Letters to the Editor "Perils of partnerships": comments on an editorial. ICAP response. *Addiction*, 95(9), 1429-1430.

Greenfield, T.K., Giesbrecht, N., & Kavanagh, L. (1996). Drinking patterns among young adults in the US and Canada: the policy implications. Paper presented at the 10th International Alcohol Policy Conference, Toronto, Canada, May 4-6.

Greenfield, T. K., & Rogers, J.D. (1999). Who drinks most of the alcohol in the U.S.? The policy implications. *Journal of Studies on Alcohol*, 60(1), 78-89.

Greenfield, T.K., Giesbrecht, N., Johnson, S.P., Kaskutas, L.A., Kavanagh, L., Room, R., & MacKenzie, B. (1999). *U.S. Federal Alcohol control policy development: A manual.* Berkeley: Alcohol Research Group.

Grieshaber-Otto, J., & Schacter, N. (2002). The GATS: impacts of the international "services" treaty on health-based alcohol regulation. *Nordic Studies on Alcohol and Drugs,* 19 (English supplement), 50-68.

Grube, J. W. & Nygard, P. (2002). Adolescent drinking and alcohol policy. *Contemporary Drug Policy* xxxxxxxxxxxxx

Gunasekera, O. (2001) Profits or health. *The Globe,* New Series Issue 2, 20-21.

Hannum, H. (1997). Special Commentary: The Dublin principles of cooperation among the beverage alcohol industry, governments, scientific researchers, and the public health community. *Alcohol & Alcoholism*, 32(6), 641-648.

Hawks, D. (1992). Lying down with the lion: Co-operating with the alcohol industry? The 1991 Leonard Ball Oration. *Drug and Alcohol Review*, 11, 51-58.

Holder. H. D., & Edwards, G. (Eds.) (1995). *Alcohol and public policy: Evidence and issues.* Oxford:

Oxford University Press.

Holder, H.D., Giesbrecht, N., Horverak, Ø, Nordlund, S., Norström, T., Olsson, O., Österberg, E. & Skog, O.-J. (1995) Potential consequences from possible changes to Nordic retail alcohol monopolies resulting from European Union membership, *Addiction*, 90, 1603-1618.

Holder, H. (2003). Editorial. Population drinking and alcohol harm: What these Canadian analyses tell us. *Addiction* 98(7), 865-866.

Houghton, E. (1998). Comparative analysis of alcohol education programs sponsored by the beverage alcohol industry. *Journal of Alcohol and Drug Education*, 43(3), 15-33.

ILO (2003). *Drug and alcohol abuse – an important workplace issue.* Retrieved from http://www.ilo.org/public/english.

International Center for Alcohol Policies (n.d.- a). *Partners in progress.* Brochure. Washington: International Center for Alcohol Policies.

International Center for Alcohol Policies (n.d.-b). Policy Issues: Advertising self-regulation. Web address: http://www.icap.org/international/self_regulation.html

International Center for Alcohol Policies (n.d.-c). Policy Issues: Harm reducation and alcohol policies. Web address: http://www.icap.org/international/harm_reduction.html

International Center for Alcohol Policies (1997a). *The limits of binge drinking.* ICAP Reports 2, April 1997. Washington: International Center for Alcohol Policies.

International Center for Alcohol Policies (1997b). *Health warning labels.* ICAP Reports 3, September 1997. Washington: International Center for Alcohol Policies.

International Center for Alcohol Policies (2000). The Geneva Partnership on Alcohol - Towards a global charter. Web address: http://www.icap.org/about_icap/fc_english.html

International Center for Alcohol Policies (2001). *Self-regulation of beverage alcohol advertising.* ICAP Reports 9, January 2001. Washington: International Center for Alcohol Policies.

International Center for Alcohol Policies (2003). *Alcohol and the workplace.* ICAP Reports 13, August 2003. Washington: International Center for Alcohol Policies.

Jackson, M.C., Hastings, G., Wheeler, C., Eadie, D., & Mackintosh, A.M. (2000). Marketing alcohol to young people: implications for industry regulation and research policy. *Addiction,* 95 (Supplement 4), S597-S608.

Jernigan, D. (2000). Applying commodity chain analysis to changing modes of alcohol supply in a developing country, *Addiction,* 95 (Supplement 4), S465-S475.

Jernigan, D. (2001). Alcohol marketers find compassion in Bush's conservatism. *The Globe,* New Series Issue 1, 19-20.

Jernigan, D. H. (2003). Alcohol marketing and youth: Monitoring the effectiveness of the U.S. alcohol industry's self-regulation. *The Globe*, Issue 1, 8-11.

Leonard, K. (2001). Domestic violence and alcohol: What is know and what do we need to know to encourage environmental interventions? *Journal of Substance Use,* 6, 235-247.

Leverton, M., Buckingham, J., Naclerio, S., Alexander, B., Willersdorf, G., Montijn, S., Simpson, R.,

Jones, M., Macdonald, J. P., & Botha, A. (2000). Letters to the Editor "Perils of partnerships": comments on an editorial. Drinks industry response, *Addiction*, 95(9), 1430-1431.

Lieberman, L.R., & Orlandi, M.A. (1987). Alcohol advertising and adolescent drinking. Special Focus: The economics of alcohol abuse. *Alcohol, Health and Research World*, 12(1), 30-33, 43.

Mann. R., Macdonald, S., Stoduto, G., Bondy, S., Jonah, B., & Shaikh, A. (2001). The effects of introducing or lowering legal per se blood alcohol limits for driving: an international review. *Accident Analysis and Prevention,* 33, 569-583.

The Marin Institute (1999). *Federal Trade Commission's September 1999 Report on alcohol advertising.* Presentation to the Board of Directors, Marin Institute for the Prevention of Alcohol and Other Drug Problems, October 15, 1999

Max, G., & Willersdorf, G. (2001). The beverage alcohol industry and learning about drinking. In E. Houghton & A. M. Roche (Eds.), *Learning about drinking* (pp. 267-281). Philadelphia: Brunner-Routledge.

McCreanor, T., Casswell, S., & Hill, L. (2000). Editorial. ICAP and the perils of partnership. *Addiction*, 95(2), 179-185.

McKenzie, D. & Giesbrecht, N. (1981). Changing perceptions of the consequences of alcohol consumption in Ontario, 1950-1979. *Contemporary Drug Problems,* 10(2), 215-242.

Midanik, L. T., Tam, T. W., Greenfield, T. K., & Caetano, R. (1996). Risk functions for alcohol-related problems in a 1988 US national sample. *Addiction,* 91(10), 1427-1437.

Moore, M.H., & Gerstein, D.R. (Eds.) (1981). *Alcohol and public policy: Beyond the shadow of prohibition.* Washington, D.C.: National Academy Press.

Moser, J. (2000). Letters to the Editor "Perils of partnerships": comments on an editorial. Comment on ICAP. *Addiction*, 95(9), 1431-1432.

Mosher, J. (1999). Alcohol policy and the young adult: Establishing priorities, building partnerships, and overcoming barriers. *Addiction*, 94(3), 357-369.

Mosher, J.F. (2001). Partner or foe? The alcohol industry, youth alcohol problems, and alcohol policy strategies. Manuscript. Chicago, IL: American Medical Association.

Moskowitz, J.M. (1989). Primary prevention of alcohol problems: A critical review of the research literature. *Journal of Studies on Alcohol*, 50(1), 54-88.

Ogborne, A.E., & Giesbrecht, N. (1999). The development of alcohol control policies: What can be learned from case studies? Presented at the 25th Annual Alcohol Epidemiology Symposium, Kettil Bruun Society for Social and Epidemiological Research on Alcohol, Montreal, May 31-June 4, 1999.

Österberg, E. (1995). Do alcohol prices affect consumption and related problems? In H.D. Holder & G. Edwards (Eds.), *Alcohol and public policy: Evidence and issues* (pp. 145-163). Oxford: Oxford University Press.

The Portman Group (2002). *National Alcohol Harm Reduction Strategy* A response from the Portman Group to the Consultation Document from the Strategy Unit and Department of Health.

Ramstedt, M. (2003). Alcohol consumption and liver cirrhosis mortality with and without mention of alcohol – the case of Canada. *Addiction* 98, 1267-1276.

Room, R. (2000). Letter to the Editor: A new force--but for what and whom? The appropriation of networks and the importance of decision rules. *Addiction* 95(4), 627-629.

Room, R., Bondy, S. J., & Ferris, J. (1995). The risk of harm to oneself from drinking, Canada, 1989. *Addiction*, 90, 499-513.

Room, R., & Rossow, I. (2001). The share of violence attributable to drinking. *Journal of Substance Use,* 6, 218-228.

Rutherford, D. (2000). Social aspect groups. *The Globe,* Special edition, The Proceedings of the Global Alcohol Policy Advocacy Conference, 49-54.

Rutherford, D. (2002). The Amsterdam Group. *The Globe,* Issue 1, 8-11.

Saffer, H. (2002). Alcohol advertising and youth, *Journal of Studies on Alcohol*, Supplement 14, 173-181.

Single, E. Robson, L, Xie, X., & Rehm, J. (1998). The economic costs of alcohol, tobacco and illicit drugs in Canada, 1992. *Addiction*, 93(7), 991-1006.

Skog, O-J. (2003). Alcohol consumption and fatal accidents in Canada, 1950-1998. *Addiction* 98(7), 883-894.

Statistics Canada (1996-2002). *Control and sale of alcoholic beverages.* Ottawa: Statistics Canada.

Stockwell, T.R., Heale, P., Chikritzhs, T.N., Dietze, P., & Catalano, P. (2002). Letters: How much alcohol is drunk in Australia in excess of the new Australian alcohol guidelines? *The Medical Journal of Australia*, 21 January 2002, 1762, 91-92.

US Secretary of Health and Human Services (1997). *Ninth Special Report to the US Congress on Alcohol and Health.* Washington: U.S. Department of Health and Human Services.

Wallack, A. (1992). Editorial. The alcohol industry is not your friend? *British Journal of Addiction*, 87, 1109-1111.

WHO challenges the drink industry. (2001). *The Globe*, New Series Issue 1, 4-6.

World Health Organization (1999). *Global Status Report on Alcohol.* Geneva: World Health Organization.

AFFILIATION

Centre for Addiction and Mental Health,
33 Russell Street
Toronto, Ontario M5S 2S1 Canada
Phone: + 416 535-8501 ext. 6895; Fax: + 416 595-6899; email: norman_giesbrecht@camh.net

R. MÜLLER

SWISS ALCOHOL POLICY – "MODEL" OR "SONDERFALL"?

Key words: alcohol policy, history, globalization, neo-liberalism, self-responsibility, harm reduction

Abstract. Alcohol is not only an ordinary but the most easily available consumer commodity in Switzerland. The re-emergence of liberalism has led to the abolishment of many laws restricting alcohol availability. The globalization of the markets has significantly lowered the price of imported spirits and increased hard liquor consumption particularly among young people. In the minimally interventionist state the options for alcohol policy are restricted to information dissemination, educating the youth and to harm minimization without cutting down alcohol consumption. Alcohol policy should be judged by its impact in reducing alcohol problems. But the evidence is that those policy options that address economic and physical availability of alcoholic products are effective in reducing alcohol problems, whereas those policy options that address the responsibility of the individual and which privileged by neo-liberalism are largely ineffective. The Swiss Alcohol policy is neither a "model" nor a "Sonderfall" but simply a paradigm for the changing concern about the adverse consequences of drinking in times of neo-liberalism.

SWITZERLAND A "SONDERFALL"

The Swiss people have a special relationship to the term "Sonderfall" (particular case). And indeed, they only joined the United Nations in spring 2002, after long years of discussion. The Swiss think that Switzerland is the oldest democracy (which is not true), that they have the best cheese, the best chocolate and the best watches, and already small children are told that we are a rich nation, not because of the banking secret, but because the Swiss are so industrious. In one aspect, however, Switzerland may be considered as a "Sonderfall": namely its political system of plebiscite democracy, characterized by an extraordinarily stable democratic concordance or *amicable consent*. The instrument of popular initiative and, above all, the threat of the referendum by associations and interest groups necessitate constantly working out political compromises on all levels. Equally characteristic are the large number of honorary federal advisory committees and the presence of an almost unchanging all party government since 1959 (Klingemann 1989).

THE ORIGINS OF THE SWISS ALCOHOL POLICY

The Alcohol Legislation in Switzerland is a typical outcome of this culture of amicable consent: The basic legislation on the production, trade and consumption of alcoholic beverages in the Swiss Confederation was established at the end of the 19th century, under the pressure of strong abstinent and temperance movements and

R. Müller and H. Klingemann (eds.),
From Science to Action? 100 Years Later - Alcohol Policies Revisited, 185–192.

to face the flood of cheap potato and beet spirits. In 1887, the Swiss people voted to accept the first Federal Alcohol Legislation. Basically, all interest groups involved in the legislation process gained somehow: a State monopoly was installed, but for distilled spirits only; the interests of wine growers remained untouched. 90 percent of the net profit of Swiss Alcohol Board are attributed to the Federal Old Age and the Federal Disability Insurance. The cantons receive 10 Percent (alcohol tithe). This money is to be used for combating the causes and effects of alcoholism and drug abuse. For the fiscal year 2000/01 this amounted the considerable sum of 16 million US Dollars. An unusual feature of the Swiss alcohol laws is the positive promotion of alternative means of using raw materials of distillation: e.g. promoting the sale of fruit and potatoes for direct consumption. It is particularly noteworthy that the public health goals set up by the Alcohol Board are expressly anchored in the Federal Constitution (Cahannes, Müller 1981).

The law on alcohol has been amended several times since 1887. The principal modification was the enlargement of the Monopoly to include fruit and wine distillation (1932). But the acceptance of this modification had to be reached by concessions which resulted in vested rights for the peasantry. Home distillers who distill from their own orchard or vineyards or from gathered wild products are exempted from the law.

All attempts, however; to build up a Swiss alcohol policy which includes all alcoholic drinks were doomed to failure. Wine is still not taxed (except VAT) and as beer is concerned only very moderate tax is levied although these two products constitute about 80% of the total alcohol consumed in Switzerland today. In 1966, the electorate rejected by a large majority a national initiative demanding a more effective fight against alcoholism by taxing all alcoholic beverages according to their alcohol content. And recently a parliamentarian initiative to tax wine was rejected by the parliament. Two initiatives who advocated a total prohibition of publicity for alcoholic beverages and tobacco were rejected by the electorate and the cantons by large majorities.

It has to be added that not only the Confederation but also the 26 cantons enacted laws to control drinking. The Federal Constitution allows the cantons to restrict the freedom of trade granted to pubs and restaurants and also allow them to regulate the density of pubs and outlets according to the estimated demand.

In the last ten years, however, the Swiss alcohol policy changed profoundly. This change has to be seen against the background of the following tendencies:

- A new drift to self-responsibility ideologies
- The renaissance of the minimally interventionist state
- The liberalization of the Swiss alcohol policy in a globalized market
- Changing the paradigm: From lowering the mean consumption to reducing binge drinking

NEW DRIFT TO SELF-RESPONSIBILITY IDEOLOGIES

Let's have a brief look into history. The history of alcoholism is closely linked with that of madness. In neither the archaic community of prehistoric times nor the clerical society of the Middle Ages was the individual self-determined, but rather part of a God-ordained order. Neither madness nor alcoholism were therefore associated with self-responsibility. It was not until the burgeoning liberalism in the 18th-century with its concept of the independent individual that the precondition was created for blame to be assigned. Alcohol becomes the source of evil and anyone drinking excessively becomes a villain. "Drunkenness is a vice, not a disease" is the title of a widely circulated pamphlet in the USA in the 19th century. Socialist ideas in the 20th century give the individual a fundamentally new orientation. Everyone is rooted in their physical and sociopolitical environment and their own responsibility is limited accordingly. Alcoholism is increasingly defined as a disease and hence not associated with blame. At the same time the alcoholism of poverty is changing to the alcoholism of affluence.

With the revival of neo-liberal ideas at the end of the 20th century, a decisive change is again taking place: self-responsibility is the currency of the neo-liberal state. Everyone must bear responsibility for their behavior, and the costs resulting from their actions. The principle of joint liability for the costs of treatment is called into question. Self-responsibility ideologies are being revived and the disease status of addiction is increasingly being denied. Thus, in Switzerland, alcoholism only merits benefits from disability insurance funds if a mental illness or a physical or intellectual impairment is present.

The blind belief that market forces, the invisible hand can solve all problems and that the related primacy of the economy in all areas of life has also led to an economisation of the health care system and an immense pressure in terms of costs and reorganization on the whole rehabilitation system. Current as well as former addicts are also increasingly discriminated in the labour market; in this way discrimination reinforces dependency and perpetuates the course of addiction. Economic recession further strengthens the process of social discrimination and also encourages the attribution of guilt. This means that addicts are discriminated against twice, first in the world of work and secondly in insurance practice. Being employed is thus of crucial importance for the addict's recovery process. It is widely documented that the unemployed relapse more frequently, whereas employment increases the probability of the normal completion of therapy.

THE RENAISSANCE OF THE MINIMALLY INTERVENTIONIST STATE AND THE "NEW" ALCOHOL POLICY

The decline of the social welfare state, at the end of the 20th century, and the renaissance of the minimally interventionist state with its new drift towards self-responsibility ideologies, combined with the globalization of the markets and the abolition of trade barriers are also embodied in the Swiss policy on alcohol: alcohol has become a consumer good like any other. A large number of the laws which were passed as long ago as in the last century, limiting the availability of and access to alcoholic beverages as well as their marketing have also been abolished and, under the pressure of the WTO treaty, the taxes for imported spirits have been decreased substantially. In so doing the toxic and dependency-engendering properties as well as the socially destructive potential of ethanol are dismissed with the argument that individuals are responsible for themselves and, in any case, moderate alcohol consumption is healthy.

THE LIBERALISATION OF THE SWISS ALCOHOL POLICY

The liberalization of the Swiss policy on alcohol is embodied at both Federal and cantonal level.

1. The so-called «demand clause», which provided for a specific ratio of number of inhabitants to number of pubs before a license could be issued for a pub, has been abolished in all cantons but one.
2. The special training which a bar owner previously required has also been abolished in many cantons.
3. The liberalization of planning regulations allows bars to be opened everywhere. Practically anyone can open a bar anywhere. As a result the density of outlets selling alcohol in Switzerland has increased, despite the increasing competition.
4. The opening times for pubs have been liberalized in many cantons. In the Canton of Basel City, for example, the all-hours opening of bars has resulted in a significant increase in alcohol-related accidents.
5. The alcohol law, which governs the spirits market, has been liberalized. Regulations, for example, whereby spirits had to be sold separately from other alcoholic drinks in shops, have been revoked.
6. The lifting of the ban on advertising for alcoholic drinks in the electronic media is currently under discussion and will probably be abolished. The senate has already adopted a liberalization of the existing law, although there is no large scale domestic spirit and wine industry and only foreign producers will be able to afford expensive television spots.
7. The importation of wine has also been largely liberalized so that prices will fall in the medium term.
8. Probably the most important change in the area of alcohol policy is the introduction of the uniform tax rate for local and imported spirits of 1st July 1999. (The uniform taxation of local and imported spirits is a requirement that has resulted from Switzerland's signature of the WTO agreement). Although the Public Health Lobby has demanded a consumption-neutral uniform tax rate, the government, under pressure from parliament, has largely acquiesced to the demands of the spirits industry. The tax reform led to also to increased competition among importers, and therefore had an indirect effect on reducing former high profit margins of importers. As a consequence of the tax reform, the retail prices for imported spirits resulted in a 30-50% decrease. The prices of local products remained more or less constant, as the slight increase in tax on these products were compensated by a reduction in profit margins. The tax reform didn't change the prices for beer and wine. The consequences of the change in the price of spirits on purchasing behavior, consumption and public health has been investigated in a concomitant large-scale evaluation study. The findings demonstrate that younger people are more affected by price than older

persons and that price should be considered an effective policy to reduce alcohol misuse and alcohol-related problems, especially among the younger population (Kuo et al. 2003).

CHANGING THE PARADIGM: FROM LOWERING THE MEAN CONSUMPTION TO REDUCING BINGE DRINKING

Since the work of Lederman and since the edition of the famous purple book (Bruun et al. 1975), lowering the mean consumption was considered as kind of panacea to solve all emerging drinking problems. But research demonstrates that the total number of moderate drinkers report more problems than the total number of hazardous drinkers, binge drinkers report more problems than non-binge drinkers, and that there is a high proportion of binge drinkers which are moderate drinkers compared to hazardous drinkers.

These findings imply that prevention efforts should be targeted to lowering heavier drinking occasions rather than aiming these strategies towards decreasing overall consumption in a population. A focus on overall consumption can be misleading as it presupposes a "smoothing out" of drinking episodes that may ultimately disguise problematic patterns leading to greater probability of problems (Midanik 2001, p. 511).

The change of the paradigm from lowering mean consumption to dealing with binge drinking has to be seen against the background of a change in the societal value system which fosters binge drinking particularly among younger persons. We are moving towards a more hedonistic society where health no longer is a value for itself: Instant culture and instant pleasure are the devise; adventure and event orientation prevail; one has to be fit for fun, a new taste of morbidity emerges, fat is beautiful, abject art is in. It's against this background that the growing trend of binge drinking among youngsters has to be seen. This change in the value system is a real challenge for prevention.

The standpoint that patterns of drinking are the best predictor of whether an individual will experience positive or negative consequences of alcohol consumption is gratefully adopted by the drinks industry claiming that "policy makers should shift their focus to the elimination of negative drinking patterns and the promotion of beneficial pattern of drinking" (International Center for Alcohol policies). This standpoint fails as alcohol related harm in a society is determined by how alcohol is drunk, as well as by the volume of alcohol consumption.

It's not a mere coincidence that the Swiss drinks industry recognizes only recently some responsibility and tries to launch a campaign to stop binge drinking among youngsters. Whether a dialogue with the industry should be accepted or not is also discussed hotly in Switzerland. Indeed, dialogue does not necessarily mean seduction or bribery (El-Guebaly 2001), but beverage alcohol industry misrepresents constantly the base for effective policy to reduce alcohol problems.

ALCOHOL POLICY OPTIONS IN THE MINIMALLY INTERVENTIONIST STATE

The crucial question that faces proponents of alcohol and health policy when confronted with a state that increasingly confines its role to guaranteeing peace and security and avoids interfering in the choices of citizens is: "What are the remaining options for a health-oriented alcohol policy in the minimally interventionist state?" Three options specifically are compatible with the ideology of unconfined individualism:

1. protection of youth
2. informing citizens
3. harm reduction, without necessarily cutting down alcohol consumption.

Protection of youth

Even in the world view of John Stuart Mill, the state has the obligation to protect citizens from themselves if their independence of action is limited. "The young" in bourgeois society are not only a preservation area but also a protected area. To grant young people as it were the "benefits of prevention" is compatible even with archliberal ideas. It is against this background that the measures adopted by the Federal Alcohol Board should be seen, which had practically banned in 1997 the alcoholic mixed drinks (alcopops) from the market. The Swiss Alcohol Board, which has effective statutory powers, decided that Alco pops should be subjected to alcohol law and so taxed. This also had the following effects:

- they cannot be sold to anyone under the age of 18;
- advertising alcopops is restricted – there can be no advertisement at sporting events or on public buildings, nor may they portray people;
- a retail or wholesale permit is needed for the sale of alcopops: and
- a license is required for production.

The tax on imported alcopops made them so unattractively expensive that it was no longer worth bringing them into Switzerland. At the same time, the various restrictions mentioned have brought domestic production to a virtual standstill.

This practical ban, however, was annihilated by the tax cut in 1999. Imported products such as whisky, gin, vodka, or rum, which are especially popular with young people, became cheaper. In the following not only the consumption of distilled spirits rose sharply but also the import of a new generation of alcopops reemerged. In the years 2001 to 2002 the sales of alcopops drinks have been twenty folded and the consumption of premixed alcoholic drinks by youngsters became a major public issue for concern. Despite considerable efforts undertaken by the Federal Alcohol Board together with SIPA to reinforce the minimal purchasing age, a considerable part of alcopops are consumed by underaged people (Schmid 2003).

The commercial success to the two leading premixed alcoholic drinks (Smirnoff Ice and Bacardi Breezer) stems from extending the brand's core values from the adults spirit markets to give the younger drinkers seeking a more mature image. It also introduces the young drinkers to the spirit market in the hope that brand loyalty will ensure as consumers graduate from premix drinks (Jackson et al. 2000). The restrictions in advertisement were bypassed by marketing methods relying on subtle cultural codes rather than aggressive promotion. The introduction of production with particular appeal to underage consumers and increasing drinking in this age group has led the Swiss Alcohol Control Board to demand a special tax on alcopops referring to the experiences with taxation of premixed drinks in France. Not surprisingly, the drinks industry is fighting against such a taxation arguing that this would be in contradiction to the WTO treaties.

Informing citizens

In contrast to the experience with prevention, which shows that being informed about the consequences of an action is a necessary but by no means sufficient condition for a rational decision, market transparency and the awareness of the consequences of an action are sufficient preconditions for the self-responsible individual in the neo-liberal state to behave appropriately regarding health matters. Information therefore also features highly in the minimally interventionist state. Thus, for the first time in the history of the country, the Swiss government has made considerable funds available for information campaigns on the subject of alcohol. This campaign targets under the slogan "Handle with care" young binge drinkers in particular. The evaluation of the campaign, not surprisingly does hardly demonstrates any effect on drinking behavior.

"Responsible drinking can be learned just as responsible driving" is a key issue of the liberal state and adopted as well by the drinks industry. Which – not only in Switzerland but all over the world - supports such campaigns as well as educational programs not pointing out the dangers of drinking but focusing on a number of life skills such as communication skills and decision-making skills without applying these skills in situations which involve drinking. Overall, there is very little evidence that informational and educational campaigns have an impact in reducing the harm done by alcohol. This is not surprising since all these campaigns and educational efforts have to compete with pro-alcohol messages in social reality and with the universal availability of alcoholic drinks. The steady flow of images in the media representing alcohol consumption as a harmless and a sociability fostering activity is shaping the drinking behavior as a desirable act.

Harm reduction

Minimizing the harm is an attempt to present a pragmatic view of the effectiveness of key strategies designed to achieve a significant reduction in levels of alcohol problems *without necessarily cutting down the consumption.* Or as Buning (1993) states: "If a person is not willing to give up his or her drug use, we would assist them in reducing harm to himself or herself and others". Harm reduction strategies have proven to be effective in the drug field although the polemic about harm minimization is still ongoing. In the alcohol field the message in harm minimization approaches is simply: "avoid problems when you drink" (Plant et al. 1997, p. 7). This message fits perfectly the ideology of the minimal interventionist state and serves finally the interests of the drink industry. This fact, however, is not an argument for disregarding the harm minimizing approach. Unfortunately, there has been very little research to test harm reduction programs like designated driver campaigns and only little evidence is available about the effectiveness of server training programs. But any way, by abolishing laws, as for instance the mandatory training for bar and pub owners in most cantons in Switzerland, server training and responsible beverage service training are difficult to introduce and laws that require servers to refuse serving alcohol to intoxicated patrons are not easy to enforce.

At least one success of Swiss Alcohol policy in recent years has to be reported: After many years of discussion and against the harsh opposition of the drinks industry the Swiss parliament finally fixed a BAC limit of 0.5 per mille and adopted random breath testing by law in spring 2003. Enforcement and public awareness seem to be keys to the success of random breath testing. The future will demonstrate to what degree the cantons are willing to implement enforcement and sobriety checkpoints.

REFERENCES

Bruun, K., Edwards, G., Lumio, M., Mäkelä, K., Pan, L., Popham, R. E., et al. (1975). *Alcohol Control Policies in Public Health Perspective.* Helsinki: Finnish Foundation for Alcohol Studies.

Buning, E. (1993). *Presentation to workshop on "Harm Reduction and Health Promotion".* Fifth International Conference on Reduction of Alcohol-related Harm, Toronto.

Cahannes, M., Müller, R. (1981). Alcohol Control Policy in Switzerland: An overview of political compromise. In. Single et al. 1981 (Eds.), *Alcohol Society and the State.* Vol. 2. Toronto: Addiction Research Foundation.

El-Guebaly, N. (2001). A dialogue with the alcohol industry: prohibition or harm reduction. Letters to the editors. A*ddiction, 96*, 515-516.

Jackson, M. C., Hastings, G., Wheeler, C. Eadie D., MacKintosh A. M. (2000). Marketing alcohol to young people: implications for industrie regulation and research policy. *Addiction, 95 (Supplement 4),* 597-608.

Klingemann, H. (1989). *Supply and demand-oriented measures of alcohol policy in Switzerland – current trends and drawbacks.* Health Promotion, Vol. 4, No. 4, 305-315.

Kuo, M., Heeb, J.-L., Gmel, G., Rehm, J. (2003). Does Price matter? The effect of decreased price on spirits consumption in Switzerland. *Alcol Cli Exp Res,,* Vol 27, No 4, 720-725.

Midanik, L. T., Rogers, J. D., & Greenfield, T. K. (2001). Mode differences in reports of alcohol consumption and alcohol-related harm. In M. L. Cynamon, R. A. Kulka (Eds.), *Seventh Conference on Health Survey Research Methods* (DHHS Publication No. PHS 01-1013, pp. 129-133). Hyattsville, MD: National Center for Health Statistics, Centers for Disease Control and Prevention.

Plant, M., Single, E., Stockwell, T. (1997). *Alcohol – Minimization the harm.* London/NewYork: Free Association Books.

Schmid, H., Delgrande Jordan, M., Kuntsche, E. N., Kuendig, H. (2003). *Trends im Konsum psychoaktiver Substanzen von Schülerrinnen und Schülern in der Schweiz.* Lausanne: Schweizerische Fachstelle für Alkohol- und andere Drogenprobleme, Forschungsbericht 39.

GPSR Compliance

The European Union's (EU) General Product Safety Regulation (GPSR) is a set of rules that requires consumer products to be safe and our obligations to ensure this.

If you have any concerns about our products, you can contact us on ProductSafety@springernature.com

In case Publisher is established outside the EU, the EU authorized representative is:

Springer Nature Customer Service Center GmbH
Europaplatz 3
69115 Heidelberg, Germany

Batch number: 10823959

Printed by Printforce, the Netherlands